I dedicate this book to my wife Felicia and my kids, Erin and
Charles Jr. (CJ), for encouraging me to write this book even when
the hours were getting long. I also dedicate this book to all my colleagues who
encouraged me to put forth a unique take on teaching computer programming.

ACKNOWLEDGMENTS

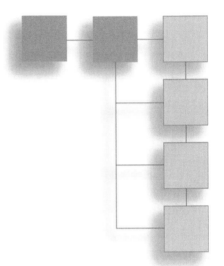

This type of project does not happen without the help of others. I would like to thank the following colleagues for their input as I developed ideas for this book: Andrea Lawrence, Alfred R. Watkins, and Iretta B. Kearse.

I would also like to thank the entire staff at Course Technology and Cengage Learning. In particular, I'd like to thank Mitzi Koontz for her project management, Karen Gill for her awesome editing, J.T. Hiquet for his insightful input from the teen perspective, and Keith Davenport for his technical comments and code testing.

ABOUT THE AUTHOR

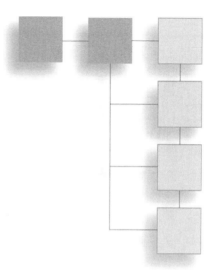

Charles R. Hardnett has developed C++ software for more than 20 years and has taught C++ programming courses to college and adult students for more than 15 years. After studying computer science at Prairie View A & M University and Georgia Institute of Technology, he developed professional and high-end research software in the areas of data communications, telecommunications, high-performance compilers for parallel computers, and compilers for embedded systems. He has taught computer science courses at Georgia Institute of Technology, Spelman College, and Gwinnett Technical College. Currently, he is teaching at Gwinnett Technical College, developing mobile applications for iPhone and Android phones, and managing his own nonprofit organization called SMART Academy (www.smartacademyonline.org).

Charles currently resides in a suburb of Atlanta, Georgia, with his wife and two children.

Contents

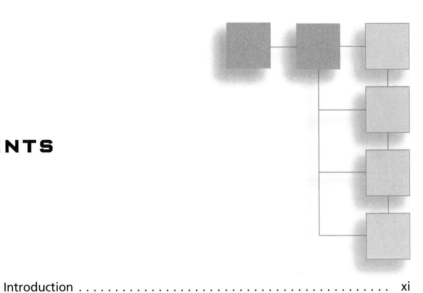

Introduction

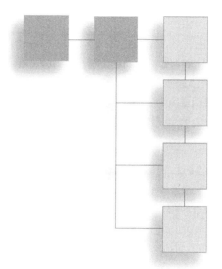

Hello, world! I like using this greeting for my books about computer programming. It's tradition in computer programming to introduce a programming language by writing a `Hello World` program. The program simply outputs the words `Hello World`. A website is devoted to storing the `Hello World` programs for programming languages, located at www.roesler-ac.de/wolfram/hello.htm.

There are many programming languages in the world; the aforementioned website boasts that it has more than 400 languages represented as `Hello World` programs, and that number is rising. An organization called ACM History of Programming Languages (HOPL) hosts conferences and produces journals for anyone interested in studying the history and genealogy of programming languages. This website, found at http://hopl.murdoch.edu.au/, has a list of more than 8,000 programming languages! Even more surprisingly, that astounding number of programming languages was developed in a relatively short amount of time. If you assume that the first programming languages were invented in the late 19th century, then on average about 50 languages are being created per year, or around 1 per week!

No matter how many programming languages there are, they all have a common purpose. There are many human languages, such as English, Spanish, Swahili, and Chinese, but their common purpose is communication between humans. In the same vein, programming languages are designed to enable communication between humans and computers. A programmer communicates an algorithmic solution to a problem to a computer so that the computer can solve the problem quickly and efficiently. The algorithm is a step-by-step process or sequence of actions. The actions are simple on their own, but the algorithms created can be as simple as adding numbers or as complicated as processing the graphics and animation of your favorite 3D video game. The ability to encode algorithms is the common attribute of all programming languages. Thus, mastering algorithmic thinking is a great asset to being a productive and efficient programmer.

In this book, you learn concepts related to algorithmic thinking and problem-solving. In addition, you learn the C++ language. C++ is a popular, general-purpose and object-oriented programming language that can be used in a variety of application domains. These domains may include personal, business, gaming, scientific, and multimedia applications. In addition, C++ is used for creating programs to execute on a number of computing platforms, including desktops, laptops, supercomputers, mobile devices, and gaming consoles.

Are you ready to learn how to program a computer? If so, you are in the right place. This book introduces you to the way a computer scientist or computer programmer thinks when creating software.

THE PHILOSOPHY OF THIS BOOK

The philosophy of this book was my main motivation for writing it. Most books about programming computers have titles such as *Learning to Program in X*, *Problem-Solving with X*, *Learn X in Y days*, or *Programming in X*, where X is the name of the programming language and Y is some small number of days (usually less than a month). Undoubtedly, you have seen these books before. These books usually have chapter headings like the following:

- "Introduction to Computers and Programming"

- "Data Types and Arithmetic Expressions"

- "Input and Output Statements"

- "Conditional Statements"

- "Looping Statements"

- "Functions"

- "Arrays"

- "Records"

- "Pointers"

- "Classes and Introduction to OOP"

Many successful books have been organized this way, which is fine for creating a reference book for the language. However, it is not necessarily the best organization for teaching how to develop software solutions using a particular language. This type of organization has a negative impact on many students and does not help them learn how to build software. This organization forces authors to introduce too many alternative concepts in a single chapter. For example, in the chapter about conditional statements, an author may decide to introduce `if-then`, `if-then-else`, `switch/case`, and arithmetic `if` statements. In addition, there might be some discussion about Boolean expressions and nesting of `if-then` and `if-then-else`. Those who write these types of chapters realize all the syntactical and semantic rules that must be explained and understood first. However, in most cases, readers are not very advanced at this stage of the book and are not likely to use all these concepts in any program they are writing unless the program is contrived to introduce the language feature. How much do beginners really learn from this exercise? How much confusion do they experience when trying to apply these different constructs to a software solution? The problem here is that the focus for the reader is now on the language, and not on solving problems with the language.

This book has a different paradigm that puts the focus on the problem-solving techniques and thought processes; the language features are secondary. In addition, this book introduces features at your level of complexity. For example, you will most likely use the `switch` statement in specific circumstances, such as for menu processing, which is best shown after learning loops. The problem also requires more complex software. Therefore, the complexity and sophistication of solutions for a class of problems should motivate or drive the introduction to language concepts. For example, instead of your seeing the `switch` statement in Chapter 5 and then in Chapter 6 or 7 being presented with a menu-driven program that is perfect for it (and requiring you to recall the `switch` statement and use it), this book introduces the `switch` statement as an alternative compact solution to the menu problem. At this time, you are engaged and interested in learning about the `switch` statement. In addition, you have a firm foundation of experience with the `if-then` statement to ease the understanding of the `switch` statement semantics. Finally, you are comfortable with the `if` statement at this time in the reading and can absorb the additional syntax without as much confusion.

Observations of students over the years have shown that when people are having trouble learning a programming language, the primary source of frustration is how to express the solution in algorithmic ways. Without the algorithmic solution, there is little to no hope of encoding a computer program that will be successful. Therefore, this book starts exploring algorithms and the core components of the C++ programming language. Then it presents introductory problem-solving techniques and moves to increasingly more advanced techniques, while starting with simpler problems to solve and moving to more complex problems that require the more advanced problem-solving techniques. This book does not cover every nuance of C++. It is not a C++ book; rather, it is a computer-programming book that uses C++ to implement the program.

This approach allows you to engage in meaningful programming experiences early in the book, which motivates you to continue.

How to Use This Book

This book introduces computer programming to teens using ideas and concepts that professionals use for programming every day. The book is suitable for any beginning programming course or CS1 course at the high school or collegiate level. It has been structured so that the C++ content of the book can be used to solve all the exercises at the end of each chapter. You should not use this book as a C++ reference book because it does not cover every aspect of the C++ language. If you would like to have a complete C++ reference as a companion to this book, look for *The C++ Programming Language* by Bjarne Stroustrup (C++ inventor) or *C++: The Complete Reference* by Herbert Schlidt.

Each chapter of this book presents a collection of ideas and concepts that are related to computer programming and C++. Each chapter has notes and sidebars to provide additional information about given topics. In addition, each chapter has complete pseudocode or C++ programs. You are encouraged to trace the pseudocode and compile and test the C++ programs for better understanding. At the end of each chapter are a handful of exercises to apply the knowledge of the chapter and previous chapters. The majority of the concepts that you need for solving an exercise are in that chapter; however, you need to keep previous chapters' concepts in mind as well.

You can find the solutions to all exercises, source code, and other learning materials online at www.courseptr.com/downloads.

How This Book Is Organized

Chapter 1, "Getting Started," contains background information on computers, programming languages, and computer systems.

Chapter 2, "The Nature of the Problems and Solutions," introduces algorithms, pseudocode, and flowcharts.

Chapter 3, "Introduction to the Core C++ Language," covers the most often used components of the C++ language that are directly translatable from pseudocode and flowcharts.

Chapter 4, "Numerical Problems," presents some of the issues related to solving numerical problems and the C++ library to support mathematics functions, formatted I/O, C++ user-defined functions, and for loops.

Chapter 5, "Divide and Conquer," introduces the divide-and-conquer problem-solving approach and how it is related to C++ iteration and recursive functions.

Chapter 6, "Small-Scale Problems," discusses two small-scale problems in the areas of games and social science along with complete C++ solutions. It also introduces the C++ library for character processing and C++ switch statements.

Chapter 7, "Top-Down Design," presents the top-down design methodology and its application for designing a Blackjack game.

Chapter 8, "Bottom-Up Design," covers the bottom-up design methodology and its application for designing a Blackjack game. This provides a contrast to the top-down approach shown in Chapter 7.

Chapter 9, "Medium-Scale Problems," discusses medium-scale problems that require more functions and more data processing using Blackjack and an expense report management program as the examples. In addition, it explains additional C++ concepts, including parallel arrays, multidimensional arrays, dynamic memory allocation, pass-by-reference parameter passing, file manipulation, and records.

Chapter 10, "Introduction to Object-Oriented Design," introduces the object-oriented design methodology. It revisits the Blackjack application as an object-oriented design for consistency across the design chapters.

Chapter 11, "Object-Oriented Programming in C++: Part I," discusses how object-oriented programming is supported in C++. It presents C++ classes in the context of creating user-defined types using two case-study examples: Cyber Bank and a Fractions data type.

Chapter 12, "Object-Oriented Programming in C++: Part II," presents other C++ object-oriented programming support, including pointers to objects, inheritance, and polymorphism. This chapter presents version 2 of Cyber Bank.

The Appendix, "Installing Development Software," gives step-by-step instructions for installing free C++ developer software on the Windows and Mac OS X platforms.

Who This Book Is For

This book has been written to appeal to those ranging in age from pre-teens to young adults who are interested in learning how to program, while also learning about one of the most used programming languages of all time.

This book is for instructors who are teaching introductory programming courses and their students. Students who would like to discover computer programming as a hobby will also find this book useful.

Companion Website Downloads

You may download the companion website files from www.courseptr.com/downloads. You will find source code, answers to exercise questions, and other learning materials for instructors and students. Please note that you will be redirected to the Cengage Learning site.

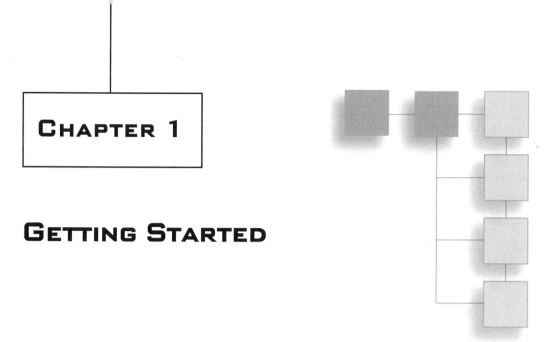

CHAPTER 1

GETTING STARTED

In This Chapter

- The Computer System: Hardware and Software
- What Is a Programming Language?
- The Elements of Programming Languages
- Software Development Process

Genius is 1 percent inspiration and 99 percent perspiration. As a result, genius is often a talented person who has simply done all of his homework.

—Thomas Edison

You are starting a wonderful journey in which you will learn to do some special things with computers. Besides the computers used in homes, there are unseen computers used in cars, appliances, roadways, farms, and more. Societies around the world have a general fascination with computers because of the wonderful things they can do to make life easier—and the way they can sometimes make life more difficult. All of these computer systems are made possible because of the cooperation between hardware and software. *Hardware* is defined as the tangible parts of a computer, such as the mouse, keyboard, processor, and monitor. *Software* is defined as the intangible parts, such as the application programs and operating system. For a fully functional and reliable computer system, the software and hardware must work as a team. This chapter explores how this happens and why it is important to you as a computer programmer.

In this book, you will learn the fundamentals of how software is written using the C++ language.

THE COMPUTER SYSTEM: HARDWARE AND SOFTWARE

The computer system is made up of components that could be sorted into two different categories, as shown in Table 1.1. You have probably seen a list like this in school or in another book. The components that are referred to as *hardware* are items you can touch. The components that are considered *software* are ones you can't physically touch.

Table 1.1 Examples of Hardware and Software

Hardware	Software
Keyboard	Operating system, such as Windows or Mac
System unit	Word processor
CPU[1]	Electronic spreadsheets
RAM[2]	Games
Hard drive	Web browsers
Mouse	Instant messengers
Camera	Photo organizers
Monitor	Movie editors
Printer	Multimedia players

1 CPU = central processing unit
2 RAM = random access memory

Hardware

You can divide the hardware of your computer system into five groups: input devices, output devices, storage devices, processing units, and memory devices. The memory and processing devices are always inside the system unit. The other devices may or may not be inside the system unit. Figure 1.1 shows how the devices inside and outside the system unit are logically organized. You should pay attention to what devices are inside the box and outside as well as the arrangement of the arrows. The arrows represent the direction of data moving from one place to another. For example, the arrows pointing from the input devices to the system unit show that data moves in only one direction, like a one-way street. For example, when you type something on the keyboard, the data is moved from the keyboard to the system unit. Do you see where a double-headed arrow is used? In this case, data is moved from storage devices into the system unit; this is called *reading data*. Data is also moved from the system unit to the storage devices; this is *writing* or *saving data*.

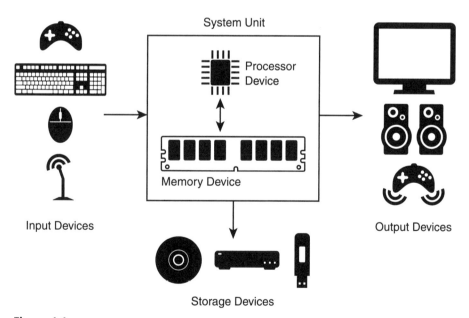

Figure 1.1
The relationships among the various devices of a computer system.

Boxes and Arrows

When you program a computer, you manipulate virtual objects. They are *virtual* objects because you cannot physically manipulate them. It is sometimes important to visualize how these objects relate to one another, which is where drawing pictures comes in handy. That's why you should get comfortable with reading diagrams with boxes, arrows, line segments, and circles. Also, pay attention to how the objects are connected. Are arrows used? Line segments? One-way arrows? Two-way arrows? These connections are the keys to how the objects are related; they can help you understand how your program manipulates its virtual objects.

Processing Device

The processing device has historically contained a single processor called the *central processing unit* (CPU). However, most of today's laptops and desktops are built with more than one *processing unit* (PU); therefore, there is no "central" PU. The purpose of these PUs is to perform the instructions from your software program. All professional programmers must know how the CPU operates so they can write efficient software and understand errors in their programs.

Acronym Overload

The acronyms used in technology are shorthand, just like you use in text messaging, and they were invented for the same reasons. In text messaging, you use acronyms like lol, bff, and omg so that you don't have to type all the letters and words each time you want to convey one of these common thoughts. In technology, we use acronyms such as CPU and PU so that we don't have to repeatedly spell out the words they stand for. Typically, these acronyms are pronounced by just saying the letters, such as *C-P-U*. However, some acronyms are pronounced as words. An example would be RAM, which is pronounced as *ram* and not *R-A-M*.

Unfortunately, the rules for pronouncing acronyms do not make a lot of sense, but you'll learn the correct pronunciations in due time. You can always consult the web when you are unsure about how to pronounce something. One of the sites that you can use is www.dictionary.com. If you look up an acronym on the site, it displays a speaker icon next to the acronym. Click the speaker icon, and a voice pronounces the acronym for you. (This actually works for any word!) Good luck.

Each PU in a computer system takes as input a single program instruction. The output is the result of that instruction. Got it? I am sure you could repeat that to someone, but you need to understand what it really means. Consider this example instruction:

$6 + 7$

This is an example of an addition instruction that would be input to the PU. The result for this instruction would be 13, and it would be the output from the PU. The software that is run every day is composed of millions of simple instructions like this one.

A PU is divided into two other components: the arithmetic logic unit (ALU) and the control unit (CU). These two units work together to process each instruction and generate its output. The ALU knows how to perform arithmetic operations such as addition, multiplication, subtraction, and division. It also knows how to perform logical operations such as equality, greater-than, and less-than. The CU manages the execution of instructions that the ALU performs. The CU processes instructions using four steps:

1. **Fetch instruction.** In this step, the CU fetches the next instruction of a program.

2. **Decode instruction.** In this step, the CU determines what type of instruction has been fetched, such as add or equality.

3. **Execute instruction.** In this step, the CU signals for the ALU to perform the instruction.

4. **Store result.** In this final step of the process, the CU stores the result of the instruction in memory (discussed next).

This four-step process is called an *instruction processing cycle* or *processor cycle*. You have seen reference to this cycle on television, on websites, and on the computer. For example, a computer manufacturer may boast that its computer has a 2.5 GHz (gigahertz) processor. The term *hertz* means cycles per second, and the prefix *giga* means approximately a billion, so this processor executes approximately 2.5 billion instruction cycles per second. In other words, it completes 2.5 billion four-step processing steps per second!

Some of the instructions that the CU processes control the peripheral devices, such as your mouse and keyboard. This is usually done by instructions storing data in particular parts of the computer's memory that are mapped to different peripheral devices. Devices also can notify the processor when they need to be data processed. For example, when you move your mouse, you expect the cursor on the screen to move. But what if the processor is already busy? The mouse device sends a signal called an *interrupt* that causes the processor to pause and process the request to move the mouse cursor. The CU is the processor component that handles these interrupt signals.

Power of Small Building Blocks

The instructions for a PU are a collection of simple arithmetic and logic operations. From these simple operations, software engineers have been successful in creating a range of complex software that is used every day. It's hard to imagine when you are using a word processor (like I am when writing this book) that everything that happens, from displaying the text you type to spell-checking to auto-saving, is done by some collection of arithmetic and logic operations. But it's absolutely true! Over the years, software engineers have learned to cleverly use these instructions to build the type of software that users rely on and enjoy using every day.

Here is a brief explanation of how this concept is applied to something like a word processor to display the letter that you type on the keyboard. You type the letter *t*, which is encoded as the number 84. The number 84 is represented in binary that sends an electrical signal from the keyboard to the main memory and processing unit. The *processing unit* is where the graphical unit interface (GUI) software determines the position where the letter is placed on the screen using the x,y coordinate system and using addition to x to provide space between the last character and the character *t* that was just typed. Then, using lots of arithmetic and the x,y coordinate system, it draws the image of a *t* at the computed position. Obviously, there are more details, but you can see that letters are actually just numbers (arithmetic representations), and the positions of objects on computer screens are just like positions in the x,y plane. By adding to x or subtracting from x, you can move right or left on the screen. Finally, drawing is a matter of coloring parts of the screen based on the (x,y) positions, like connecting dots, which is also a collection of additions and subtractions to x and y.

The PU works closely with the next hardware component, called the *main memory*.

Memory Devices

Several memory devices work with the processing unit. These are called *registers*, *cache* (pronounced *cash*), and *random access memory* (RAM). In this book, the RAM is the most important memory device. The RAM is where data and instructions are stored while the PU uses them. In the previous example where the instruction was

$6 + 7$

the data 6 and 7 are actually stored in RAM while the PU is performing the instruction. For this example, assume the 6 is stored in location 8 and the 7 in location 14. Check out Figure 1.2. The result of the instruction, the 13, is then stored in location 35 of the RAM at the completion of the instruction. You can see that if RAM is slow to access the 6 and 7, the instruction processing takes longer. Therefore, the time to access data in RAM directly impacts the speed of the PU processing the instruction.

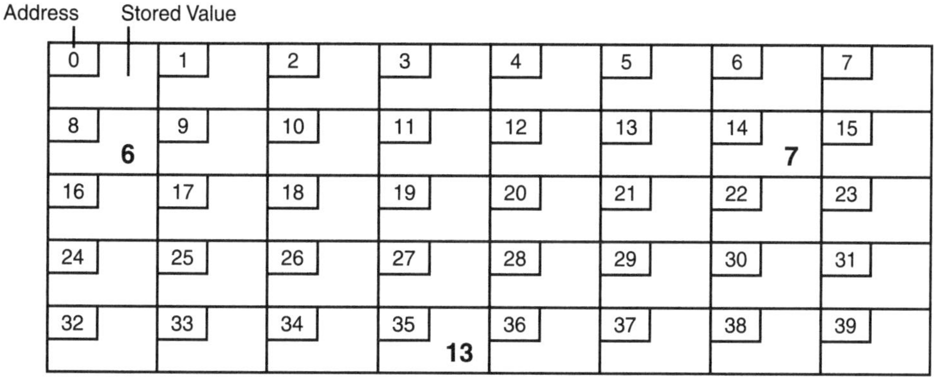

Figure 1.2
A diagram of RAM, where each location in memory has a unique address.

So why is it called *random access*? Well, it's because the PU can access data from any part of RAM at any time just by using the address of its location. Each data item, such as a number or letter, is stored at a location in RAM. And each location has a unique address associated with it, just like the lockers in your school. Furthermore, each locker has a number, and that number is how a locker is assigned to a student. When you need your books, you don't have to look in each locker one at a time to find your books. (This is called *sequential access*.) Instead, you just find the locker based on its number (or address) and then retrieve your books. This is called random access, and it allows fast access to the data being stored.

The RAM in your computer has some characteristics that you need to remember. These characteristics are summarized here:

- RAM is volatile, which means that it holds data only as long as the computer is on. When the computer is turned off, the data is lost from RAM.

- RAM is fast access, which means that the processor can retrieve and store data quickly.

- RAM is expensive and in short supply, which means that your computer will have a relatively small amount of memory for storing data compared to storage devices.

The RAM is an important part of your computer and is the most important device for your programs. For this reason, this book will refer to the memory diagram in Figure 1.2 at various points to remind you that you are using the memory device as you program.

Storage Devices

RAM is used for short-term storage of data and program instructions. For long-term data and program storage, the computer uses storage devices such as your hard drive, flash/thumb drive, CDs, and DVDs. These storage devices retain your data even after the computer is turned off or you stop using a program. Have you ever wondered why you are expected to save your files regularly? Well, remember that RAM is where your programs execute instructions and process data. When you are typing a term paper in your word processor, the word processing program is actively executing its instructions and processing your data (the term paper). At this time, you are using the RAM. When you save your term paper to a file (suppose it's called literature101.docx), the data (your term paper) is copied from RAM to the storage device you want to save it to (the hard drive or thumb drive). If you close the word processing program or turn off the computer at this time, the file can be loaded later so you can work on the paper again. If you don't save the data to the storage device, it's gone. This is an example of the volatility of RAM.

This example shows another difference between memory devices and storage devices. Storage devices use files and folders (directories) to organize your data, whereas memory devices just see data residing at different memory locations. Whenever you are working with a file, you are working with a storage device. At some point as a programmer, you will want your programs to use files for your data. This book will show you how to do this.

Storage devices also have characteristics that are related to the list presented for RAM:

- **Storage devices are nonvolatile.** This means your data remains intact for the long term even if you turn the computer off.

- **Storage devices have slow access.** This is true for two reasons. First, these devices are connected to the system unit through input/output wiring that is not located within the system unit. Second, their electronics are slower and less expensive (thumb drives), or they are mechanical (hard drives, DVD/CD drives), as shown in Figure 1.1.

- **Storage devices are cheap.** This means your computer is able to have significantly more storage space than RAM space. For example, a laptop today may have 4 gigabytes (GB) of memory space, while it has 500GB of storage! To top it off, that same storage may cost half as much.

Input Devices

Input devices are any hardware devices that are connected to your computer and accept input. The two most obvious input devices are the keyboard and mouse. However, computers have several other input devices, such as microphones and cameras. Special-needs users may require other input devices, such as tongue devices that allow them to interact with their computer using their tongue, or brain wave devices that read their brain waves to control their computer. Some input devices are used to play games, such as gamepads, steering wheels, and wands; others allow artists to draw on the computer just as they would on a piece of paper, using graphics tablets. Certain input devices are also output devices, such as touch screens used on many mobile devices.

The purpose of input devices is to provide an interface between the user and the computer. They allow the user to communicate ideas, wishes, and commands to the computer. One of the challenges for input devices is that users use analog means for communication.

Analog Versus Digital

Analog and *digital* refer to the way data is encoded as a signal. An analog signal represents continuous changes of a value over time. A digital signal represents changes of a value using discrete intervals of time. To illustrate this difference, consider two ways to watch a football game: watching it on TV or in person versus watching it through updates on a website. If you are watching the game on TV or in person, you see every movement by all the players and coaches. You see the quarterback drop back, you see him scramble, and you see him throw the ball. Then you see the flight of the ball and the receiver catching it. The receiver avoids one tackle but is taken down about 10 yards downfield after catching the ball. If you are watching live updates on the website, you see updates only every 5 seconds. So, the same play would be shown as 1st and 10 from the 20-yard line. Then 5 seconds later, the receiver catches the pass and runs 10 yards, for a total of 22 yards on the play. In the first case, you see the game continuously; in the second case, you get information every 5 seconds. The advantage of the second method is that it is predictable and reliable. You know that every 5 seconds there will be new data. This means you can predict when you will get new data and be prepared to process it. In the case of the live broadcast, you don't know when the new information will be sent. Therefore, you can easily miss some data because you are not expecting its arrival. You may also say to yourself, "Yes, but I lost information." That is true in this example. However, suppose you could get information every second or every 1/10 of a second. You would lose less information, yet it would still be predictable and reliable.

In sound and communications technology, the intervals are called *samples*, and a computer samples input thousands of times per second. A CD-quality sound recording requires 44,000 samples per second. This means that little information is lost, and the sound is predictable and reliable.

All input devices must have three parts. The first part is the receptor that provides some way to interact with it. It may be that you hold or touch the device, or you speak or make a sound for the device, or maybe you move your hands or fingers in certain ways. The second part is the controller that accepts your analog input motion and sound and converts it into a digital signal. The last part is the communication port that accepts the digital signal and transports it to the appropriate part of the computer system to allow a PU to process it.

Input devices have evolved over the years to support the needs of computer users and will continue to evolve as computers become more powerful and used for more exciting applications.

Starting as a programmer, your main input device will be the keyboard. However, as you grow as a programmer, you will find yourself programming for different types of input devices, such as gamepads, steering wheels, wands, and touch screens.

Output Devices

Output devices are electronic components connected to your computer that produce output. Output devices take digital information from the computer and present it to the user in an analog way. The most common output device is the monitor or display device. Other devices include speakers and rumble feedback (found in gamepads).

As a beginning programmer, you will primarily work with the display as your output device.

Software

The software is what this book is really all about. This book introduces you to the fundamentals of how software is designed and constructed using ideas that professional software developers use every day. Software is sometimes called a *program*, a *software application*, or just an *application*. So what really *is* software? It is a programmer's solution to a problem. Suppose you take a ride in a time machine before word processors such as Microsoft Word. People all over the world experienced problems related to using typewriters:

- They used lots of paper (excessive typing errors, making copies for review, and so on).

- Correcting typos was time consuming using Wite-Out and type correction tape.

- It was difficult to share writing with others (lots of photocopying).

- Formatting documents was time consuming.

These are just a few of the problems people had with typewriter use. Software designers dealt with this problem by creating software to run on desktop computers that allowed people to type and correct mistakes on the screen with no Wite-Out and no printing. People could share essays and reports by copying the files, sending them via email, or posting them on a website. Word processors provide features that allow people to format documents that at one time only the printing and publishing industry could access and required lots of man-hours to complete. Word processors have significantly reduced the time and frustration required to type documents—even those with complex formatting. In this example, the word processing software became the solution to several problems.

A programmer writes software using a programming language. In this book, the programming language will be C++.

WHAT IS A PROGRAMMING LANGUAGE?

A *programming language* is an artificial language that programmers use to communicate their solutions to a computer. Programming languages contain special words and symbols that are organized in a systematic way to create a program in much the same way that you take the English language and create sentences and paragraphs for your essays and reports.

Thousands of programming languages are available, and each has its own features, set of words and symbols, and rules for how programs can be constructed with the language. Some example programming languages include these:

- **Machine Code (binary code).** A language based on 0s and 1s. Today this language is used as the target language for compilers.

- **BASIC.** Beginners All-purpose Symbolic Instruction Code. A programming language for beginners to learn how to program. This language was developed in the 1960s.

- **Pascal.** The programming language developed in the 1960s for teaching high-level programming.

- **FORTRAN.** FORmula TRANslation. The first high-level compiled programming language. This language was created in 1950 and is focused on programming numerical and scientific computation software.

- **Java.** A modern object-oriented language invented in the 1990s by Sun Microsystems. This language gained popularity because its programs can be executed across many platforms, which makes it ideal for Internet/web applications.

- **C.** A high-level language developed by Bell Laboratories in the 1970s. This language became popular for building commercial software and systems software.

- **C++.** The most popular object-oriented programming language in software development. This language started in 1980 and was created by Bjarne Stroustrup at Bell Laboratories.

- **Visual Basic.** A language that Microsoft created for rapid prototyping for applications with GUIs.

Programming languages can be classified in many ways. One of these major classifications is *Low-Level Languages versus High-Level Languages*. Figure 1.3 shows examples of both categories. This classification refers to the amount of translation that is required to prepare the instructions for a processor to execute. Machine language is the lowest-level programming language. Its commands are sequences of 1s and 0s and do not require translation for a processor to execute them. Each line of this code is an individual instruction for the computer to process. The 1s and 0s are binary digits, which are known as *bits*. Every group of 8 bits is called a *byte*. In this binary code, each instruction is 16 bits or 2 bytes in length. The high-level language on the right side of Figure 1.3 performs the same thing as the machine code. One of the immediate observations is that the high-level programming example is easier for you to read and have a general understanding of what the program should do. Its main instructions are listed here:

```
a = 2;
y = 4;
z = a + y;
```

Low-Level Language	High-Level Language
0000000000000101	void main( ) {
0011000000000110	int a;
0001000000000111	int y;
1110000000000111	int z;
1111000000000000	
0000000000000010	a = 2;
0000000000000100	y = 4;
0000000000000000	
	z = a + y;
	}

Figure 1.3
Example of a low-level programming language and a high-level programming language.

These instructions suggest that a and y have the values 2 and 4, respectively. Those values are added together, and z will have the value of 6. The instructions for high-level languages are easier for humans to read and understand, but they are not for PUs to process. Therefore, it's important to translate programs from high level to low level. Fortunately, you don't have to do this by hand! Special programs called *compilers* and *interpreters* perform these translations. Compilers are the most efficient way to perform a translation; they result in translations that execute more quickly. Interpreters can be interactive and easier to use, but the translations are not as efficient. Compilers work by taking the entire program and translating it from beginning to end; then the PU can execute the entire translated program. In contrast, interpreters translate the instructions one at a time, as the PU requires them. An analogy might help here. Consider that you want to translate an essay from English to Spanish. The compiled technique would be for you to give the translator your essay; she would then translate your essay from English to Spanish. The interpreted technique would be where you would read your essay to the translator, and she would translate the essay sentence by sentence. The compiled technique would allow the translator to use the context of the essay to generate an appropriate and refined translation of your essay that the interpreted technique would not allow. The interpreted technique would allow you to interact with the translator, but it would not allow the translator to refine the translation because the entire essay is not known at one time.

C++ is a compiled high-level programming language. The programs that are written in C++ are generally executed efficiently.

THE ELEMENTS OF PROGRAMMING LANGUAGES

Programming languages are made up of components and rules. Every language has its own rules and components, just like French has a different set of letters and symbols than English does. French also has different rules about how words are put together to make a sentence than how sentences are composed in English. The elements of a programming language can be grouped into categories. The information in Table 1.2 summarizes the categories with descriptions and simple examples for the elements of a programming language.

Table 1.2 Programming Language Elements

Element Category	Description	Example
Keywords/reserved words	These are words that have a special meaning within the programming language. These words can't be given any other meaning in the programming language.	`if`, `then`, `else`, `for`, `while`, `case`, `repeat`
Operators	These are symbols in the language that have special meaning within the language. These symbols represent an action/command to be performed with data.	`+`, `-`, `/`, `*` (standard arithmetic operators) `!`, `==`, `=`, `.`, `?` (other operators)
Punctuation	These are symbols that have meaning in the language but do not represent actions to be performed.	`;` (means the end of an instruction) `,` (separates elements in a list) `"` (used as quotes)
Identifiers	These are names that programmers can create to label data or actions.	`count`, `maximum_value`, `first`, `last`, `mynum`, `mynum2`
Syntax	These are the rules that govern how language elements can be grouped to form legal instructions and legal programs.	`if (x < y) x = 5;` (this is proper) if x = 5 when (x < y); (this is improper)

The program in Listing 1.1 illustrates the elements of a programming language. This example is a legal C++ program, so any standard C++ compiler can compile and execute it. The objective here is not to try to understand what the program does or how it works. Rather, note how the elements of a programming language are organized to form a program.

Listing 1.1 A Sample C++ Program

```
1: #include <iostream>
2: using namespace std;
3:
4: int main(int argc, char** argv) {
5:     float GPA;
```

```
6:     cout << "Now enter your GPA: ";
7:     cin >> GPA;
8:
9:     if (GPA >= 3.0)
10:        cout << "You are a good student" << endl;
11:    else if (GPA >= 2.0 && GPA < 3.0)
12:        cout << "You need improvement, tutoring may help" << endl;
13:    else
14:        cout << "Seek tutoring, you may fail without changes" << endl;
15:
16:     return 0;
17: }
```

The keywords/reserved words in this example are on lines 2, 4, 5, 9, 11, 13, and 16. They are using, int, float, if, else, and return.

The operators in this example are on lines 6 and 7, 9 through 12, and 14; they are the <<, >>, >=, and < operators. Each of these operators is considered a binary operator because it has two operands. The >= operator on line 9 has the GPA identifier for data as one operand and the 3.0 value as the second.

The punctuation in this example is shown on lines 2, 4 through 7, 10, 12, 14, and 16. All of these lines have the semicolon at the end of the line. The semicolon in C++ has special significance; it signifies the end of a C++ statement. A C++ statement is like a sentence in English that ends with a period.

The identifiers on lines 2, 4 through 7, 9 through 12, and 14 include std, main, argc, argv, GPA, cout, cin, and endl. These names are created by either the programmer who wrote this program (GPA) or the programmers who built the standard libraries for C++ (cout).

The syntax rules of C++ specify how individual C++ statements are formed and how a complete C++ program is written. Relate the syntax rules to the rules of English grammar. For example, the English language has rules about constructing a sentence, such as subject + predicate, stipulating that a sentence should have a subject component followed by a predicate component. For example, "The dog ran home" is a sentence that follows this rule, where the subject is "The dog," and the predicate is "ran home." If you swap these to get the sentence "Ran home the dog." you have broken the rule, and the sentence is no longer proper in English. This same thing applies to programming languages, so (GPA >= 3.0) if is not a proper C++ statement. The statements of C++ can be arranged in a different order, just as you can arrange the sentences of a paragraph in a different order. Figure 1.4 shows examples where the first few sentences of Abraham Lincoln's Gettysburg Address are jumbled in English, and

Now we are engaged in a great civil war, testing whether that nation, or any nation so conceived and so dedicated, can long endure. Four score and seven years ago our fathers brought forth on this continent, a new nation, conceived in liberty, and dedicated to the proposition that all men are created equal. It is altogether fitting and proper that we should do this. We are met on a great battle-field of that war. We have come to dedicate a portion of that field, as a final resting place for those who here gave their lives that that nation might live.

```
if (GPA > = 3.0)

    cout << "You need improvement,
tutoring may help" << endl;
else if (GPA > = 2.0 && GPA < 3.0)

    cout << "Seek tutoring, you may fail
without changes" << endl;

else

    cout << "You are a good student" <<
endl;
```

Jumbled Gettysburg Address Excerpt

Jumbled C++ Program

Figure 1.4
Rearranging the sentences of English text or of a C++ program does not violate grammar rules.

the statements of the C++ program are jumbled. Each sentence is grammatically correct, and the paragraph is grammatically correct. However, the paragraph does not convey a coherent thought in its current form. In the C++ fragment, statements are rearranged from the order in Listing 1.1. The program would still be a grammatically correct C++ program, but it would not have the same meaning.

As you can see, programming languages are similar to natural languages such as English. Both types of languages have meaningful words, both have rules regarding how the words can be organized to form sentences and statements, and both allow you to reorganize sentences and statements. There are major differences between natural languages and programming languages, which you will explore in Chapter 2, "The Nature of the Problems and Solutions," but remembering the similarities helps you remove the intimidation of learning programming languages.

SOFTWARE DEVELOPMENT PROCESS

Learning to program like a pro requires an introduction to the process that is used for developing software. Whether you are developing software for a Fortune 500 company, for a small startup, for a class, or just for fun, you will use elements of the software development process. In this section, you will explore a professional software development process along with a beginner's software development process to use throughout this book.

The *software development process* is a set of stages followed by one programmer or a team of programmers to design, implement, and ship a software product. *Software engineering* is an entire discipline concerned with the study of team-based software development practices, models, methods, economics, and management. This section is intended to accomplish two goals. The first goal is to introduce a software development model that is used by teams of professional software engineers. The second goal is to provide you with a simpler software development process to use for this book and beyond.

A Professional's Software Development Process

Modern software engineering is complex and detailed. Some software projects require a team of 500–1,000 programmers or more. You can imagine how difficult it would be to coordinate 500–1,000 people in writing a novel! How do you break up the novel for writing? How do you maintain one voice throughout the novel? How do you maintain a consistent plot? How does someone start writing Chapter 10 when Chapters 1–9 have not been completed? These are the same types of questions that become real for software development every day. Computer scientists studied these problems and developed solutions.

You can develop software using several methods. An organization typically agrees on a process that works best for its industry and that is adopted by all teams within the organization. However, some circumstances dictate unique processes for software development projects for different application domains or that have a special set of requirements.

Figure 1.5 shows the spiral software development process. This process was introduced in 1988 and merged ideas from the waterfall and prototyping processes, used previously. The *spiral process* is an iterative or cyclical process that starts with a set of detailed requirements for the software that needs to be completed.

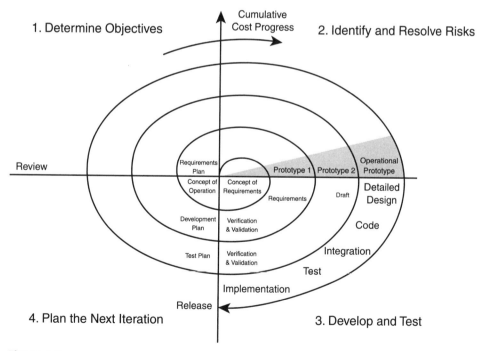

Figure 1.5
The software engineering spiral process. (http://en.wikipedia.org/wiki/Spiral_model)

Each cycle of the software development process has four basic steps:

1. **Determine objectives and requirements.** This is where software features and functionality are defined for the current cycle.

2. **Identify and resolve risks.** This is where alternative solutions to supplying features are explored and compared based on their costs and risks.

3. **Develop and test.** The features are programmed here, and each feature is tested for correctness and completion.

4. **Plan next iteration.** This is where the current cycle is evaluated and the next cycle is planned.

You can see that each cycle produces a prototype of the software with increasingly more features being added to the software. (This causes the spiral.) At the end of the process, that software is ready to enter the final implementation, test, and release phases.

The spiral process is ideal for large software projects, where teams of people are involved with each phase, and the software can be tested and verified as it is being developed. This process can also be agile; as requirements change, more prototypes can be created.

A Beginner's Software Development Process

Figure 1.6 shows the beginner's software development process that you can use as you proceed throughout this book and beyond. This process is easy to understand, and it will be explained in terms of what you will actually be doing when you are programming.

Following are the steps to complete the software development process:

1. Analyze the problem.

2. Design a solution to the problem.

3. Program the solution.

4. Test and debug the solution.

5. If your program works, you are done; otherwise, repeat steps 3 and 4 until the program works correctly.

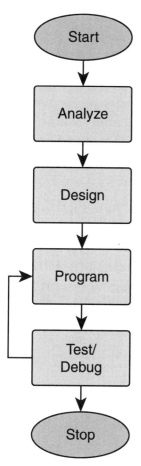

Figure 1.6
A beginner's software development process.

Analyze the Problem

The first step is to analyze the problem. This is where you read the problem carefully and try to understand every detail. You should be identifying the important information in the problem. You can list this information or draw a picture to help you sort it. Also, determine the parts of the problem needing more information that you may have to research. Finally, if you recognize characteristics of the problem that you have solved before, jot those down.

Design a Solution

This step is where you will create a solution to the problem, but you are not programming yet. First, you are developing a mental picture for how the solution would look if it were a computer program. Second, you are creating a plan for programming the solution.

Developing a mental picture is harder at first because you don't know the limitations of the programming that you have learned. Assume that there are no limitations; develop your mental picture from programs that you have used before. Also, sketch a picture of what you have imagined.

You can base the plan for programming the solution on several tools that require only a pencil and paper. You can use flowcharts, hierarchy diagrams, and pseudocode. Both *flowcharts* and *hierarchy diagrams* are pictorial representations of the software and its organization. *Pseudocode* is language that is based on programming language concepts and English. The language is not as strict as a programming language and allows the programmer—especially a beginner— to focus on the structure of the solution instead of on recall of the detailed rules of a programming language.

The analysis and design phases can be the most challenging parts of programming because they are a mixture of art, experience, and organized thinking. The next chapter lays the critical foundation for success with these phases. Throughout the book, more ideas and concepts will be introduced to help you.

Program the Solution

Programming the solution is where you will use your computer and write C++ code that follows the plan you developed in the previous phase. This can be an enjoyable phase of development. It's where you are typing your program into your computer so that you can build and test it. It's also where you start seeing your ideas come to life and become your software.

Caution

This phase can be frustrating for beginners who have not completed a thorough design that gives them a roadmap to write the solution. It causes beginners to resort to trial and error and guessing. Guessing and trial and error don't normally lead to success when used excessively due to a lack of adequate planning. The second cause of frustration at this phase is the lack of experience with programming or with C++. There will be many tips and words of advice to help alleviate this source of frustration.

Test and Debug the Solution

During this phase, either you have parts of your program ready to test or you may have the entire program ready for testing. *Testing* is where you execute the program and act as a user for your program. You will provide data to your program to make sure it behaves under different conditions. You should also try to break your program. Why? Well, if you can determine the types of data input that make your program crash, you can fix the program before other users start using it, assuming it works. Think of how annoying it is to you when you use software that crashes each time you try to use a certain feature. You can track down these types of errors or bugs during this phase.

Debugging a program is where the programmer is trying to locate the source of the bug and then fixing the program so that the bug doesn't appear. Bugs are typically caused by logical errors and typos that the programmer makes. You should always assume that a bug is caused by a mistake you have made. One mistake that many beginners make is assuming that they did "everything right," and the computer is at fault. Many times this is an okay assumption for someone who is using a computer; a user clicks on a button, and the program crashes or does the wrong thing. In these cases, the fault lies with the programmer who wrote the software, not the user. However, when you are the programmer and you are testing your software, then by the same logic the fault lies with you. You're the programmer now!

Throughout the text, there will be tips to help you deal with bugs better, technically and emotionally.

Determine If It Works

Of course, "it" is your program at this point in the process. If this is your first time getting to this step for a program, then it probably won't work right away. Be prepared for this, and realize that even professional programmers don't write programs perfectly the first time (even if they're simple programs). Be ready to make changes to your program and test it again. Keep in mind that sometimes you have to go back to the design because the flaw in your program leads you to earlier assumption or fault in your logic.

SUMMARY

This chapter started with an overview of the computer system, including hardware and software. This gave you a foundation of how computers will process your programs and what types of resources you have available as a programmer. The next topic involved programming languages. Programming languages are the artificial languages that programmers use for creating software. You saw that several programming languages are available, and they have a variety of characteristics and uses. You also learned the basic elements of a programming language, using C++ as an example. After that, you were introduced to software development processes. A professional process was presented as a goal to the types of processes you may have to use as a professional. Finally, a beginner's process was presented to help organize your approach to writing programs.

EXERCISES

The following questions test your knowledge of the material from this chapter. You can find the answers to these questions on the book's companion website at www.courseptr.com/downloads.

1. Describe the difference between main memory and secondary storage. Which storage device is used while you are typing a paper in a word processor? Which storage device is used when you save the paper?

2. What are the two internal parts of a PU?

3. What is the difference between high-level and low-level programming languages? Give an example of two high-level languages.

4. What are the five steps to the software development process?

5. Why do you have to test your programs?

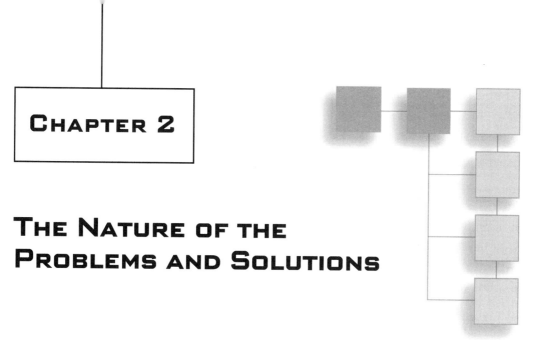

CHAPTER 2

THE NATURE OF THE
PROBLEMS AND SOLUTIONS

In This Chapter

- Problems, Problems, and More Problems
- The Algorithm
- Creating Solutions

> First, solve the problem. Then, write the code.
>
> —John Johnson

Computer science often talks about problems and constructs solutions to problems. In this chapter, you learn more about these problems and their acceptable solutions. How do you begin to create these solutions?

Computer scientists have been solving problems for a short period of time when you consider how long mathematics and other sciences have been around. There is evidence showing that people have been solving mathematical problems for thousands of years. Quantifying time and counting date back more than 20,000 years, and the Pythagorean Theorem dates back to 2500 B.C. The idea of computing dates back to 2400 B.C.; however, automatic general-purpose computing devices date back to only the 1600s. One such device is called the Pascaline, invented by Blaise Pascal. This may seem like a long time, but compared to other sciences such as mathematics, biology, chemistry, and physics, this is an extremely short period.

You are going to learn about some of the key ideas of this young and vibrant science in this chapter by learning how to specify problems and their solutions.

PROBLEMS, PROBLEMS, AND MORE PROBLEMS

A *problem* in computer science is the statement of specifications that requires a solution by an algorithm. These problems are similar to word problems that you may find in your math class. Here are some sample word problems found in math classes:

1. Felicia would be one-half as old as Nathan if Felicia were four years older. Nathan is eight less than three times as old as Felicia. How old is Nathan?

2. Seventy-four more than 5 times a number is 114. What is the number?

3. Jason drove to Mike's house at 62mph. Mike's house is 80 miles away. Jason arrived at Mike's house at 3:22 p.m. What time did Jason leave?

You can solve all these word problems using algebra. You create an equation that represents the information in the problem, solve the equation, and that becomes your solution. Here are solutions for those word problems:

1. In problem 1, the equation $N = 3F - 8$ represents Nathan's age in relation to Felicia's age. An equation for Felicia can also be formed as $F = 1/2N - 4$. With substitution of N in the second equation, you have $N = 3 (1/2N - 4) - 8$. Now distribute the 3 to get $N = 3/2N - 12 - 8$, and then $N = 3/2N - 20$. Finally, the equation becomes $-1/2N = -20$ which is just $1/2N = 20$ and $N = 40$. So by either equation, $F = 16$.

2. In problem 2, the equation $5X + 74 = 114$ is formed from the problem description. By following the rules of algebra and solving for X, you obtain the answer $X = 8$.

3. In problem 3, you have to use the formula distance = rate × time. By solving for time, the formula is rearranged to be time = distance / rate = 80 miles / 62mph. The time then is 1.29 hours. You have to convert

hours to minutes using the equation minutes $= 60 \times$ hours $= 60 \times$ 1.29 $= 77.4$ minutes. If you round down to 77 minutes (which is 1 hour and 17 minutes) and subtract that from 3:22 p.m., you obtain a time of 2:05 p.m.

These problems are concrete. In other words, they have known values to use in making the solution as opposed to abstract problems that don't use particular values. An example of an abstract problem follows. It's called the Traveling Salesman Problem, or TSP for short:

> Given a collection of cities and the cost of travel between each pair of them, the TSP is to find the cheapest way of visiting all the cities and returning to your starting point. (Courtesy of www.tsp.gatech.edu/)

This problem does not specify particular distances or costs between cities. It doesn't even state what cities are involved! Problems such as this are the types that computer scientists are faced with every day. They're abstract. Other examples of abstract problems would be these:

1. Create a program to compute the area of a circle when given its diameter.

2. Suppose there is a room of people, and you want to collect data about the number of brothers and sisters each person has. Analyze the data to determine the average number of siblings a person may have.

3. Suppose you have a list of 50,000,000 names. You want to develop a way to determine if a person's name is on the list.

Now back to concrete problems that have known values. These problems require a point solution, which is designed to solve a single problem. The solution does not take into account any considerations other than those presented in the problem. If one of these problems is changed, you must create a new solution. For example, suppose problem 3 is altered to be the following:

> Jason drove to Mike's house at 80kph. Mike's house is 80 miles away. Jason arrived at Mike's house at 4:32 p.m. What time did Jason leave?

In this case, solving the problem would require converting 80kph to mph. Then you'd need to calculate the time based on 4:32 p.m. instead of 3:22 p.m.

On the other hand, an abstract problem requires an abstract or general solution. The solution created will be able to solve several solutions when concrete information is given. For example, in the TSP problem, the solution would provide an answer for the problem when a user provides the name of the cities and the distances to find a solution for. Or in the case of finding a name in a list, the solution would be able to accept any number of names in a list and determine if any given name is in the list. So each time you use the abstract solution, it provides an answer using the information provided.

This is a powerful concept because it means that once you solve the problem, it can provide solutions to users for eternity or at least as long as there is a computing device that is available to execute your solution.

This chapter keeps talking about these abstract or general solutions, but what does one of these solutions look like, and how do you create one? In the next section, you are introduced to the basic concept that governs all of computer science: the algorithm.

THE ALGORITHM

The algorithm is the foundation for everything in computer science. An *algorithm* is a procedural solution to a problem that is composed of individual steps, where some of the steps may be repeated, and when the steps are completed a result is produced. The algorithm is used in every area of computer science. It is used to make robots move on Mars, assemble cars, and assist with operations. Algorithms are at the heart of how your web browser is able to display web pages and provide buttons and menus for you to use. They are what make it possible for antilock brakes in your car to work by reacting to your foot on the brake pedal and regulating the automatic pumping of your brakes to maintain control of the vehicle. Many algorithms are used in your favorite video games to add realism, make your characters move, and react to your cat-like movements! All of this and more is a result of the algorithm concept.

So where did algorithms come from? Their origins date back to the ninth century. A Persian mathematician named Muhammad ibn Mūsā al-Khwārizmī wrote a book titled *On the Calculation with Hindu Numerals*, which discussed the Indian number system. This title was translated into Latin as *Algoritmi de numero Indorum*, and from that title the term *algorithm* was formed. al-Khwārizmī's book explains the process of using the Hindu number system and the processes and steps required to perform calculations in that number system. One such process might be how to multiply. This process can be applied to problems like 5 × 10, 678 × 1045, or even 1,050,500 × 6,781,210. Regardless of the size of the numbers or the numbers themselves, the same process or algorithm is used.

Computer scientists have formalized the idea of an algorithm so that it can be used to build computing systems, both hardware and software. All the hardware components, including the central processing unit (CPU), memory devices, and storage devices, operate based on algorithms. For example, the CPU has an algorithm for processing each instruction, and the arithmetic logic unit (ALU) is composed of several algorithms for performing each arithmetic and logic operation. Software is written using a computer programming language. These programming languages are developed to implement algorithms. Therefore, all software programs are essentially composed of several algorithms.

Algorithms can be expressed in various formats that are independent of a programming language or hardware device. The two traditional ways to express an algorithm are using pseudocode and flowcharts. Pseudocode is an English-like language that expresses an algorithm. Flowcharts are diagrams that use particular symbols and arrows to represent an algorithm. The next section introduces you to the algorithm representations as well as some basic computer algorithms.

Representing Algorithms: Pseudocode

Pseudocode is one way to represent an algorithm when you are designing a solution to a problem. It is universal for programmers because it does not depend on the details or features of a particular programming language. It provides a way to discuss the efficiency and correctness of the algorithm without having to commit to a programming language. This book discusses algorithms and solutions to problems as you are learning the C++ language.

There is no standard pseudocode, but all pseudocode is designed to allow programmers to develop algorithmic solutions using a natural language. Pseudocode looks like English, but it has some rules you should follow when writing it. The pseudocode for this book is based on a small collection of statements.

Pseudocode Statements

Each pseudocode statement can be placed in one of three categories:

- Sequential statements
- Conditional statements
- Repetitive/looping statements

Sequential statements are executed in order, one after the other. You don't have to make decisions. For example, consider the following recipe:

1. Preheat the oven to 350 degrees.
2. Combine the cake mix, milk, and eggs in a bowl.
3. Beat the mixture for 3 minutes on medium speed.
4. Pour the batter into a cake pan.
5. Bake the cake in the oven for 45 minutes.

This recipe is composed of sequential statements. You are to follow each statement one after the other with no deviation. You don't perform a later step until you've completed the previous ones. This is the essence of a sequential statement. Pseudocode has sequential statements also. These statements usually perform input, output, and arithmetic assignment operations. The input statements in your pseudocode are based on the Input command. The Input command is how the algorithm gets data it needs to perform its computation. For example, if the algorithm is computing the average grade for an exam given to a class, the algorithm needs to get all the test scores. This is the job of the Input command. An input statement starts with the Input command and is followed by the variables that represent values provided by the user of the algorithm. Here are examples of input statements:

```
Input student name, student numeric grade
Input length and width
Input stock prices price1, price2, price3, price4, price5
```

Notice that all these statements start with the command Input, and then there are names of the values the algorithm expects to be separated by commas or a conjunction word like "and."

The next type of sequential statement is the output statement. Output statements display information for the user. For example, the algorithm may need to display a prompt to ask the user to input the test grades; and at the end, it needs to display the average. An output statement is used for these tasks. An output statement begins with the Output command that is followed by what should be displayed. Here are some examples of output statements:

```
Output "Enter Name: "

Output final grade

Output "The area is ", TheArea, " and the circumference is ",
TheCircumference
```

All these examples start with the Output command that is followed by what to display. Output statements can display quoted information or nonquoted information. Quoted information such as "Enter Name: " is called a string literal in computer science. The quotes suggest that the algorithm will display the information verbatim. However, nonquoted values such as final grade, TheArea, and TheCircumference are variables that represent values. In these cases, the output statement outputs the values that are represented and not the names of the variables. Therefore, in all the cases an actual number is seen as the output of the algorithm. The commas that are used in the last example are there to separate quoted values from nonquoted ones.

The final sequential statement is the arithmetic assignment statement. This statement saves the result of a computation inside a variable. It is one of the most heavily used statements in algorithms. The arithmetic assignment statement uses the equal sign, =, just like in math classes. On the left side of the equal sign is the variable, and on the right side is the expression that performs the computation.

```
PriceAverage = (price1 + price2 + price3 + price4 + price5) / 5

TheArea = PI * Radius2

TheSlope = (Y2 - Y1) / (X2 - X1)
```

Note

Pi is a known constant in mathematics that is computed by the ratio C/D, where C is the circumference of the circle and D is the diameter of the circle. An estimate for pi is 3.14159265. This is an estimate because pi is irrational; it has never been computed, nor has it been shown to be a repeated decimal. Many people simply use 3.14 for formulas that require the use of pi. Programmers use a convention in pseudocode and programming where constant values are written in all capital letters. For example, pi in an algorithm or program will be written as PI.

These statements represent arithmetic assignment statements. The right side of the statement is the arithmetic expression using standard mathematical notation. The left side is where the result of the computation is held for further processing.

Conditional statements are decision-making statements that alter the flow of execution in the algorithm. Unlike sequential statements, conditional statements may execute differently, depending on the conditions that control their execution. Consider the following recipe:

> Cut each carrot crosswise in half. In a 3-quart saucepan, over medium heat, heat carrots to boiling. Cover and simmer for about 20 minutes or until tender crisp. Add butter, brown sugar, and lemon juice. Cook until sugar is completely dissolved.

This recipe has two instances of conditional statements. The first one refers to simmering for 20 minutes or until the carrots have become tender crisp. This means that the simmering process may take 20 minutes, give or take a few minutes. The second example is where you are to cook the final mixture until the sugar is dissolved. Both of these examples could be rewritten as follows:

- If carrots are tender crisp and they have been simmering for close to 20 minutes, then stop simmering; otherwise, keep simmering.
- If sugar is dissolved, then stop cooking; otherwise, continue to cook.

Now you can see that there are options in both cases to either continue the cooking process or stop it. These are not sequential statements because there are two possible actions based on an observed condition. In the pseudocode, there will be two types of conditional statements: the if-then statement and the if-then-else statement. The condition for all if statements must evaluate as a true/false condition such as these:

```
Age > 0
Count <= N and Found = false
Num > Largest
```

The preceding examples evaluate to true or false. For example, if the variable Age is 16, then Age > 0 is true, and if the variable Age is −1 then Age > 0 is false. Another example is to suppose that N is 100, Count is 45, and Found is false; and then Count <= N and Found = false will be true. Why will it be true? First, you evaluate Count <= N, which will be true. Second, you evaluate Found = false, which will be true also. Because both conditions are true and joined by and, the entire statement is true.

These true/false expressions are then used within the if statements to determine how execution takes place. Here are some simple examples of the if-then statement:

1. If Age < 0 Then

       Output "Age must be a positive number"

  Endif

2. If Count <= N and Found = false Then

       increment Count

  Endif

3. If Num > Largest Then

       Largest = Num

  Endif

These examples illustrate how you can use the if-then statement to control whether other instructions are executed. The output statement in 1 is executed only if Age is less than 0. In statement 2, the increment Count statement is executed only if both conditions are true. Finally, the Largest = Num assignment is executed only if Num is greater than Largest. These are the types of decisions that an algorithm may make.

So what happens if the condition is false? With an if-then statement, if the statement is false, the next statement that follows the if-then is executed. For example, consider the following:

1. If Age < 0 Then

2.   Output "Age must be a positive number. Try again."

3.   Input Age

4. Endif

5. Output "The entered age ", Age

This code shows that statements 2 and 3 are executed if Age is a negative value. However, if Age is positive, only statement 5 is executed. Notice that statement 5 is also executed after statements 2 and 3 are executed if Age is negative when statement 1 is executed. So what if you want something special to be done when the condition is true and something else done when the condition is false? This is where the if-then-else statement is used. The else part executes when the condition is false. The following are examples of the if-then-else statement:

1. If Number < 0 Then

         Output "Number is negative"

    Else

         Output "Number is 0 or positive"

    Endif

2. If Found = True Then

         Output "The name was found"

    Else

         Output "The name was not found"

    Endif

```
3. If Count > 0 Then

        Average = Sum / Count

    Else

        Output "Count is not a positive value"

    Endif
```

The `if-then-else` examples show that the `else` part of the statement does not have a condition like the `if-then` portion does. The condition for the `else` is implicitly the opposite of the `if-then` condition. You can combine these `if-then` and `if-then-else` statements in various ways:

```
1. If Number < 0 Then

        Output "Number is negative"

    Else If Number = 0 Then

        Output "Number is 0"

    Else

        Output "Number is positive"

    Endif

2. If Choice = True Then

        If Found = True Then

            Output "The name was found"

        Else

            Output "The name was not found"

        Endif

    Endif
```

The first example is where the first `else` has a condition, and the last `else` actually goes with the second `if`; it is the opposite of a number not equal to 0. This is called a cascading `if-then-else` statement. The second example is an example of nesting `if` statements. In this case, an `if-then-else` is nested within an `if-then` statement. There is no limit to the degree of nesting, and you can have if-then statements nested within if-then-else statements. This allows flexibility in creating algorithms to solve problems.

Repetitive/looping statements are statements that enable an algorithm to repeat steps until a certain condition is met or a count is reached. This is the last category of statements needed to specify algorithms. Here's another excerpt from a recipe:

- With the mixer running at the lowest speed, add the eggs, one at a time, making sure each egg is fully incorporated before adding the next.
- Whisk egg with molasses, salt, pepper, celery salt, mustard, Worcestershire sauce, 1/4 cup of the evaporated milk, and 1/2 the glaze mixture until combined.

These statements convey a repeated activity. For example, the statement, "Whisk egg with molasses, salt...until combined" implies that you have to repeatedly whisk the mixture until an objective is achieved. In this case, the objective is met when you observe the mixture is completely combined. This is where looping statements come in handy. In the pseudocode, there will be while-do and repeat-while statements that provide the repetition and looping capability to the algorithms. Both the while-do and the repeat-while statements rely on conditional expressions. As long as the conditional expression is true, the loop continues, but when it's false, the loop ends. Consider the following examples of both loops:

1. While Number < MAX Do

    Output "Enter Score: "

    Input Score

    Sum = Sum + Score

  EndWhile

2. Repeat

    Output "Enter grocery item: "

    Input storeItem

    Count = Count + 1

  While Count < Num

The first example is of a `while-do` loop. It continues to execute the three statements inside until the `max` number of scores is entered. The second example is a `repeat-while` loop that reads in grocery items from the user. The `while-do` is considered a *pretest loop* because it tests the condition before executing any of the statements in its body. The `repeat-while` loop is a post-test loop that executes once; then it tests the condition. Each time a loop executes, it's called an *iteration*.

Note

In both of these loops are statements like $X = X + Y$. In the first example, X is `Sum`, and Y is 1. In the second example, the X is `Count`, and the Y is 1. These statements perform the operation of "update X by adding Y to X." These statements are called *accumulator* statements. They are common inside of loops and should be remembered and become second nature to you.

This concludes the types of statements that can be found in algorithms. You have already seen the idea of having variables to store data like numbers and words. However, it is common for computers to need to work on a collection of data. For example, you may need to put a list of names in order or add a bunch of numbers together. In either case, it is useful to have a way of representing a collection of data.

In pseudocode, a collection of data is referred to as a *list*. The list has an integer index for each item in the list. Therefore, you can refer to $LIST_1$, $LIST_2$, $LIST_3$, to $LIST_N$ when you need to access an element of the list. For example, consider that you have a list called Grades that has 30 grades in it, and you want to count the number of grades greater than or equal to 90. The following algorithm illustrates a solution and shows how a list can be used:

```
1.  Index = 0
2.  While Index <= 30 Do
3.      If Grades_Index >= 90 Then
4.          Count = Count + 1
5.      Endif
6.      Index = Index + 1
7.  EndWhile
8.  Output "The total number of A's are ", Count
```

In the algorithm fragment, there is a loop using lines 2–7. Line 1 initializes `loop control variable`, `Index`. Line 2 is the start of the loop that contains the condition for stopping the loop. Line 7 is the end of the loop. The condition in line 2 ensures that the loop will continue to execute as long as Index is less than or equal to 30. When Index becomes 31, the loop will stop execution and execute the first statement after the loop. In this case, this is line 8, which outputs the result of the number of As. How does it count the number of As? Line 3 is the answer. Line 3 contains an if-then statement that determines whether the current grade is greater than or equal to 90 and adds 1 to the Count variable. Because the grades are in a list, each grade is referenced as Grades$_{Index}$. This example shows a looping statement controlling access to a loop, but it also shows how you can put sequential, conditional, and looping statements together to form a complete idea.

Pseudocode Examples

You have seen parts of pseudocode, and here you put it all together to form some simple algorithms to show you how a full algorithm would look. The first algorithm determines if an object weighs more than a ton based on its mass, and the second algorithm shows interest earned on a bank balance by month for a year.

Algorithm 2.1 starts by asking the user for the mass of an object on lines 1 and 2. The input is a number that represents the number of kilograms for the object. Line 3 of the algorithm converts the kilograms to pounds using the formula Force = Mass * Acceleration, where the force is the weight, and the acceleration is the gravitational constant of 9.8 m/s^2. Lines 4–7 are where the if statement determines which output is displayed.

Algorithm 2.1 Mass and Weight

```
1.  Output "Enter the object's mass (in kilograms): "
2.  Input mass
3.  Object weight = mass * 9.8
4.  If Object weight > 2000 Then
5.      Output "The object weighs at least a ton"
6.  Else
7.      Output "The object weighs less than a ton"
8.  Stop
```

Algorithm 2.2 displays the updated balance if interest is applied each month for a year. The output for 5% interest with a balance starting at $500.00 would be as follows:

```
Balance after month 1 is 502.08
Balance after month 2 is 504.18
Balance after month 3 is 506.28
Balance after month 4 is 508.39
Balance after month 5 is 510.50
Balance after month 6 is 512.63
Balance after month 7 is 514.77
Balance after month 8 is 516.91
Balance after month 9 is 519.07
Balance after month 10 is 521.23
Balance after month 11 is 523.40
Balance after month 12 is 525.58
```

Algorithm 2.2   Updating Interest and Balance

```
1.   Output "Enter an annual interest rate: "
2.   Input IntRate
3.   Output "Enter a starting balance: "
4.   Input Balance
5.   Month = 1
6.   While Month <= 12 Do
7.       Interest = Balance * IntRate/12
8.       Balance = Balance + Interest
9.       Output "Balance after month ", Month, " is ",Balance
10.      Increment Month
11. EndWhile
12. Stop
```

This algorithm prompts the user for the interest rate and balance. In this example, the user inputs an annual interest rate of 5% and a starting balance of $500.00. Line 5 initializes the loop counter to 1 to count the months up to 12 months. Line 7 computes one month of interest based on the current balance. The IntRate/12 in line 7 converts the annual rate to a monthly rate. Line 8 computes the new balance based on the current balance and the interest computed in line 7. Line 9 outputs the results for one month. Line 10 increments the Month variables to the next month by adding 1. Then the loop continues back to step 6. If Month is less than or equal to 12, the loop executes steps 7–10 again with the new balance. You should follow this algorithm and use a calculator to make sure you can compute the same balances.

As you can see, pseudocode is a written communication tool that professional programmers and software developers use to convey ideas to one another before creating programs. A pseudocode algorithm acts as a guide to explain how a program is supposed to work. You will see more pseudocode throughout this book as you learn to solve problems and write programs. Now it is time to look at another way of describing an algorithm. In the next section, you are exposed to a graphical way of representing algorithms called a *flowchart*.

Representing Algorithms: Flowcharts

A flowchart is a graphical way of representing an algorithm. Flowcharts have been around for decades and have been used in various ways beyond computer science. For example, you can use a flowchart to explain procedures for hospital emergency room staff by providing them with direction on the steps to take and the questions to ask themselves as they take these steps. You can also use flowcharts to map the flow of ideas or topics in a large complex document. Finally, flowcharts are routinely used in fast food restaurant training manuals for explaining how to prepare food, take orders, and clean. The flowcharts make the training process easier. Figure 2.1 is a sample flowchart of what you can do if you have a desk or table lamp that is not working.

Flowcharts: The Symbols

Flowcharts are composed of different shapes and arrows. The flowchart in Figure 2.1 shows the use of rectangles for sequential steps and diamonds for decisions. Figure 2.2 shows the most common set of flowcharting symbols used for creating algorithms. Each symbol has a specified meaning.

The meaning of the symbols correlates with pseudocode statements. Therefore, any pseudocoded algorithm can be represented by a flowchart and vice versa. This relationship is explored in Table 2.1.

Pseudocode uses Input and Output commands, as shown in the first row of Table 2.1; in a flowchart, you use the parallelogram for these statements. Any other sequential statements are found in the rectangle process blocks. The

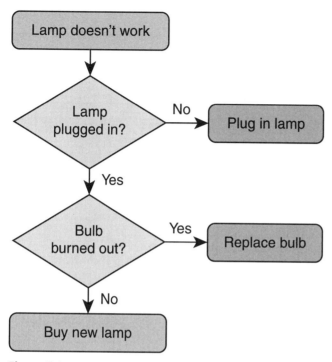

Figure 2.1
A sample flowchart that can determine why a lamp does not work. Courtesy of Wikipedia.

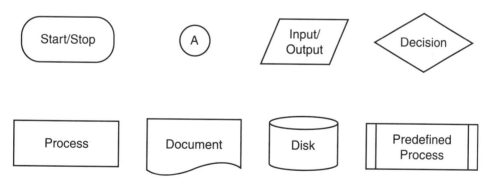

Figure 2.2
The standard flowchart symbols used in this book.

conditional and looping statements in pseudocode are done using decision statements. The key insight here is that conditional statements are statements with a yes or no decision. Each decision executes a different set of statements. A

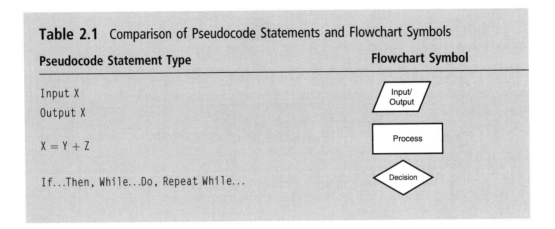

Table 2.1 Comparison of Pseudocode Statements and Flowchart Symbols

Pseudocode Statement Type	Flowchart Symbol
Input X Output X	Input/Output
X = Y + Z	Process
If...Then, While...Do, Repeat While...	Decision

looping statement also requests that a decision be made. After a loop iteration is completed, the loop decides whether another iteration is performed or whether the loop should end. To understand this better, check out a few examples based on the pseudocode examples from earlier. The first example is of a conditional statement.

Figure 2.3 shows how the diamond symbol can model the decision of an if-then-else statement. The diamond always has two arrows leaving it. One arrow is used if the statement is true, and the other if the statement is false. Both decision paths lead to the statement immediately following the Endif. In this case, that statement is Sum = 0.

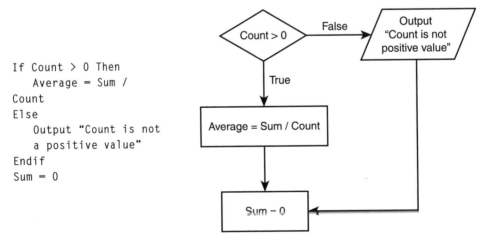

```
If Count > 0 Then
    Average = Sum /
Count
Else
    Output "Count is not
    a positive value"
Endif
Sum = 0
```

Figure 2.3
Example of a conditional statement.

The second example is of a repetitive or looping statement.

Figure 2.4 shows how loops are made using flowcharts. The last statement in the loop always has an edge that goes back to the condition node. If the condition is false, the loop exits and executes the statement following the loop; in this case that statement is Sum = 0.

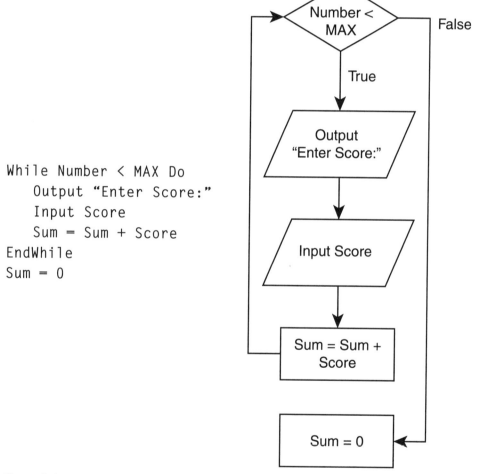

```
While Number < MAX Do
    Output "Enter Score:"
    Input Score
    Sum = Sum + Score
EndWhile
Sum = 0
```

Figure 2.4
Example of a looping statement.

Flowcharts are a great complement to describing algorithms in pseudocode. Now you will revisit the pseudocode examples seen in the previous section, but this time they are illustrated as flowcharts.

Flowchart Examples

Flowcharts can represent entire algorithms just like pseudocode. It is sometimes more useful to have a visual representation of an algorithm than just a pseudocode representation. In Figure 2.5, you see the flowchart for the first example algorithm that you saw in pseudocode. This flowchart takes the mass of an object as input and determines if its weight is greater than or less than a ton. In Figure 2.6, you see the flowchart of the second example, where the balance of an interest-bearing account is displayed over a 12-month period.

The flowcharts allow you to see more clearly the potential paths of execution of statements that are created by the if statement and while loops. Figure 2.5 has two paths of execution to display the proper results. Figure 2.6 also has two paths of execution: executing the body of the loop or exiting the loop. One edge goes back to the decision diamond. This edge is an unconditional edge, just like the edges between sequential statements. It is the only time you see an edge that goes in the reverse direction.

CREATING SOLUTIONS

One of the most difficult parts of being a programmer is developing a solution to a problem in an algorithmic form. There is a process you can follow, but the process is not enough. You will learn from experience that developing algorithms is partially science (the process) and partially art (creativity). Therefore, this section provides guidelines for creating algorithmic solutions to problems and insights to help you develop solutions to problems.

Preparing to Create Solutions

I have compiled five preliminary principles to help you get your mind ready for working with algorithms. The first principle to writing an algorithm is to make sure you clearly understand the problem. If you do not clearly understand the problem you are attempting to solve, you will not be able to solve it. Therefore, it

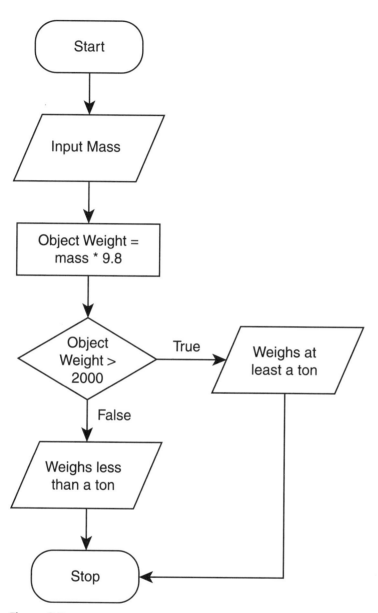

Figure 2.5
Algorithm to determine if object weighs more or less than a ton.

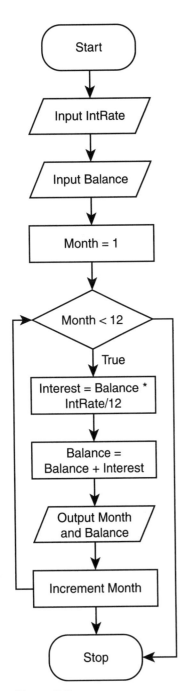

Figure 2.6
Algorithm to display the changing balance of an interest-bearing account over 12 months.

is important that you get accustomed to examining the details of a problem that is presented to you by carefully reading and rereading as necessary.

The second principle is that many algorithms can solve the same problem. You should view your quest for a solution as a search for one of the many solutions to the problem, and not the search for the one and only solution. Many beginners frustrate themselves by trying to find *the* solution, when really they should be looking for *a* solution. You can verify algorithms for correctness, so once you have a solution to the problem, you can trace the algorithm and verify its correctness.

The third principle is not to be afraid of being wrong. Many students seem to be mentally paralyzed from starting to write the algorithm because they do not want to be wrong. But you're going to make mistakes when writing algorithms or doing anything at all, even as a professional. It's part of being human. In fact, you will make more mistakes and revisions as the solutions become more complex. You have likely used software that had errors in it. These errors are the result of algorithmic errors and implementation errors. In this business, you have to welcome your errors and learn from them.

The fourth principle is to devote adequate time to writing and verifying your algorithm. In professional software development environments, the majority of the time spent is with developing algorithms as a part of the design steps. For example, I have been a part of many software development projects and have heard other developers talk about their experiences. It is not uncommon for a developer to spend ¾ of a year designing software (that is, developing the algorithms) and the other ¼ of the year writing and testing the software. The algorithm design is the intellectually intensive part of the process. Do not rush the process.

The fifth principle is to test your algorithm thoroughly before writing the program. You can have a classmate trace your algorithm or have someone else read the algorithm to you as you trace the steps. You should not only test with data that you expect, but test for data that is unexpected. Try to break your algorithm.

If you take these five principles to heart before starting the process of developing algorithms, you will increase your efficiency when writing them, and you will enjoy the process more.

How to Develop an Algorithm

As mentioned, developing an algorithm is a combination of science/engineering and artistry.

Step 1: Analyze the Problem

The first step is to analyze the problem. This requires you to read the problem carefully and then make some observations about it. Suppose you have the following problem:

> Write an algorithm that gets a sequence of numbers, computes the average of those numbers, and prints out the average. The last number in the sequence will be a –1 that signifies the end of the input.

You should visualize your algorithms as a Black-Box, as shown in Figure 2.7. A Black-Box Visualization is a common tool that demonstrates abstractions in software design. An abstraction hides the details of the way something is constructed, but it provides enough information to understand its purpose. The term *Black-Box* conveys the idea that you cannot see inside your algorithm, just like an abstraction hides details. This visualization for an algorithm is used at the start of algorithm development to help you focus on the analysis questions instead of trying to determine how the solution will work. Figure 2.7 shows arrows going into the box that are the input data objects such as numbers, names, and database records. The box also has arrows leaving the other side that would be the resulting output, such as a table, chart, or list of important information. The box is the processing. This is where the input data is converted or transformed into the information in the output. The algorithm you develop is

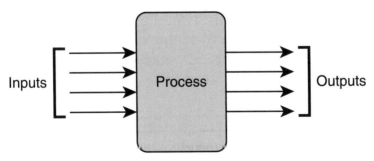

Figure 2.7
A Black-Box Visualization for an algorithm.

the box in the middle. Therefore, the analysis starts by answering these questions about the problem:

- What would be considered the input data (entering the box in the figure)?

- What would be considered the output information (exiting the box in the figure)?

- What are the formulas/processes you have to create to solve this solution by hand?

- Are there any special conditions?

Determining the inputs and outputs is usually the easiest part of developing the algorithm; determining the process and special conditions is more difficult.

What is the input data? You answer this question by looking at the problem and thinking about what information the algorithm needs from the user. Input data is data that is well known and needed to solve the problem. For example, if you needed pi = 3.14159, you could consider it a known constant and a part of the input needed by the algorithm. In the computing the average algorithm, you have the input of the numbers needed for the average; the −1 is a special input value that signals the end of the input.

What is the output data? This question requires you to visualize the output of the algorithm. The format of the output is unimportant. You only need to consider what information will be in the output. In the computing the average algorithm, you have only the average value as the output.

What are the formulas/processes needed to solve this problem? This question requires you to use pencil and paper and think about how to transform the inputs to outputs. You can do this using a sample set of data inputs and trying to determine how you might generate the proper outputs. For example, consider having to figure out an algorithm to find the largest number in a list:

First, you write down a set of numbers in no particular order: 10, 5, 77, 15, 25. Then you look at the list, and you might say that you will just pick the first number in the list to be the largest and then compare it to all the other numbers until you find a number that is larger. So you start with the 10, and you compare it to the 5 and then the 77. You notice that 77 is the largest, and then you compare 77 to 15. The largest is still 77, and then you compare 77 to 25. After this comparison, 77 is still the largest. You determine that 77 must be the largest in the list because once it became the largest value, there were no other values in the list that were larger than it. If there were a larger value in the list before 77, that value would have been the largest, and when compared to 77, it would have remained the largest. If there were a value after 77 that was greater, it would have become the largest value when it was compared to 77. If you are not convinced, you should try this idea with any collection of numbers listed in no particular order.

That example found a process that you have to use as the solution. Now consider an example that may require something different, such as a formula. In this example, the problem requires you to determine how fast you have to drive to drive a certain distance in a given time.

In this case, you can do some research online if you don't remember the distance = rate * time formula. Once you have this formula, you realize that you have the distance and time as input. This means you can use algebra and rearrange the formula to be rate = distance / time. Suppose the user gives a distance of 300 miles and 4.5 hours; after substitution, you have 300 miles / 4.5 hours, which equals 66.666mph.

After working out the problem by hand, you have a better feel for the steps needed to solve the problem; therefore, you are better prepared for writing the algorithm that needs to mimic those steps.

In the case of computing the average algorithm, you could start with a list of numbers, such as 10, 25, 15, 30, and 28. The process involves summing and counting the numbers to get a sum total of $10 + 25 + 15 + 30 + 28 = 108$ and counting to get a total of 5. Then you divide the sum total by the count total to get the average: $108 / 5 = 21.6$.

Are there special conditions? The special conditions may appear in the algorithm when certain input data is given or a condition exists that is not a part of the main processing. For example, in the case of computing the miles per hour, you may want to say that the speed must be between 45mph and 70mph because speeds slower or faster than this range may result in a ticket. In the case of computing the average, you should consider what happens if only a –1 is given in the input, so there are no values to sum, and you can't divide by 0.

Now the analysis is complete, and the next step is to write the algorithm.

Step 2: Write the Algorithm

You can write the algorithm in pseudocode or as a flowchart. This section shows how computing the average can be written as pseudocode, and creating a flowchart can be an exercise for you.

To perform step 2, you need to write the basic steps from the "by-hand" solution that you found in the analysis step. You might develop something like the following:

1. Get the numbers one at a time.

2. Add each number to the total, and count the numbers.

3. After the number –1 is given, compute the average (total/count).

4. Output the average.

Notice that this version of the steps follows a familiar pattern: input, processing, output. This is the pattern that your algorithms typically have. First you get the input, then you process the input data, and finally you produce the output. It's a simple pattern that can help you get started when you are stuck.

Now you have steps, but they are not in pseudocode. To get to pseudocode, you should start looking for hints in your algorithm that lead to creating loop or conditional statement(s). For example, in this draft are phrases like *one at a time*, *add each number*, and *count the numbers* that illustrate performing an action repetitively. This means that you need a loop, so you might have the following:

1. Start the loop.
   a. Get a number.
   b. Add the number to the total.
   c. Increment the counter.
   d. End the loop if the number is –1.

2. Compute the average with the total and the counter (if the counter is not 0).

3. Output the average.

The algorithm looks more like pseudocode, but it's not quite there. The loop needs to be either a `repeat until` or a `while` loop; there needs to be some set of instructions to perform the arithmetic. Suppose you decide to use the `while` loop, as shown in Algorithm 2.3:

Algorithm 2.3   Computing Average

```
get number
count = 1
while number not equal -1 do
    add number to total
    increment count
    get number
end while
if count > 1
    average = total/count
Output "The average is ", average
```

Notice that you have add number to total instead of total = total + number. This is the flexibility of using pseudocode. Also notice that the special case has been incorporated as an `if` statement. Your goal is to write the algorithm as close to pseudocode as possible to make it easier to translate to your programming language. Another solution to this problem could look like this:

```
count = 0
number = 0
total = 0
repeat
    add number to total
    increment count
    get number
while number is not equal to -1
if count > 1
    average = total/count
Output "The average is ", average
```

This shows you that there are at least two algorithms that solve this problem. See if you can come up with another way to write the algorithm. When you have completed writing an algorithm, the next step is to verify its correctness.

Step 3: Verify the Algorithm

The next step in the process is to verify the correctness of the algorithm. The verification requires you to pretend that you are the computer and follow the steps of your algorithm explicitly while keeping track of how the variables are changing. The fundamental tool for this process is called *table tracing*.

A *table trace* involves creating a table that contains a column for each variable in the algorithm. Then you track the values of the variables in the rows of the table. The last row in each column always provides the current value of each variable.

Table 2.2 shows a table for the compute average algorithm with headings corresponding to the variables in the algorithm. Now it's time to start processing the algorithm. The input from the example contained these numbers: 10, 25, 15, 30, and 28. After following the first two steps of the algorithm, the trace table would be filled in as shown in Table 2.3.

Table 2.2 Headings for the Trace Table

Number	Count	Total	Average

Table 2.3 Trace Table Before Loop Starts

Number	Count	Total	Average
10	1		

Then you check the condition of the `while` loop: number not equal to −1. This condition is `true`, so the body of the loop is executed to obtain the trace shown in Table 2.4.

Table 2.4 Updated Trace Table After First Iteration

Number	Count	Total	Average
10	1	10	
25	2		

Then you check the condition of the loop again: number not equal to –1. The condition is still `true`, and so the body of the loop is executed again. This will happen for each of the inputs to create the trace shown in Table 2.5.

Table 2.5 Trace Table After Processing All Input

Number	Count	Total	Average
10	1	10	
25	2	35	
15	3	40	
30	4	70	
28	5	108	21.6
–1			

The loop ends when the –1 is entered. The total and count are not changed. Then the `if` statement is executed where the `count > 1` condition is `true`, so the average is computed. To fully understand the `if` statement, you assume a –1 is entered first; the count is 1 because the `while` loop body is not executed to change it.

Now the algorithm has been verified with a table trace. You may want to try several table traces with your algorithms to make you more confident about the correctness of the algorithm. After you complete the verification, it's time to write your program based on your algorithm. That's the subject of the next chapter.

SUMMARY

This chapter started by giving you a glimpse of what a problem is like in computer science and how a computer problem is different from a mathematical word problem. Mathematical word problems require point solutions, where the solution solves only that problem. Computer science problems require you to develop a general solution that can be written as an algorithm to solve a more general version of the problem.

Then you were introduced to algorithms and how computer scientists specify them. Two formats are primarily chosen for specifying algorithms: pseudocode and flowcharts. The pseudocode format is based on writing specific steps in English using a small set of commands. The flowchart format is a geometric format that uses predefined shapes connected by arrows to represent the algorithms.

Finally, you were given some guidelines for creating an algorithm from scratch. This involves analyzing the problem, writing the algorithm, and verifying the algorithm. This process is a combination of science and art. The science is the process that was shared with you in this chapter whereby you can follow the steps to create an algorithm. The art is in how you decide to solve the problem based on the analysis and research that you do in determining the solution. Keep in mind that the same problem might have several solutions.

The next chapter introduces you to the core C++ language for this book. It shows you how to take pseudocode and flowcharts and write equivalent C++ programs using a small subset of the C++ language.

EXERCISES

The following questions test your knowledge of the material from this chapter. You can find the answers to these questions on the book's companion website at www.courseptr.com/downloads.

1. What is the difference between an abstract problem and a concrete problem?

2. What is an algorithm?

3. What are the two methods for representing an algorithm?

4. What are the three categories of statements in pseudocode? Give an example for each category.

5. What flowchart symbols correspond to the pseudocode statements?

6. Write pseudocode or flowcharts for the following problems:
   a. Write an algorithm that computes the area of a circle.
   b. Write an algorithm that takes the prices of three items and computes the subtotal and total with 8% tax.
   c. Write an algorithm that finds the maximum of three input values.
   d. Write an algorithm that can find the maximum of N values.
   e. Write an algorithm that finds the sum and product of N values.

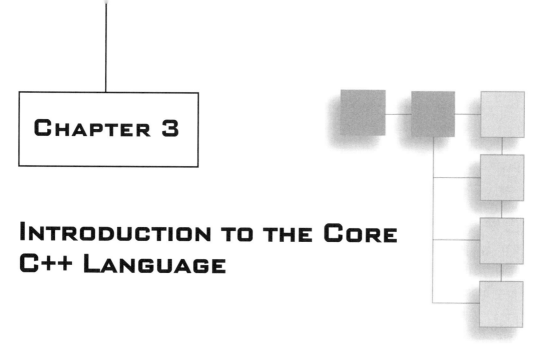

CHAPTER 3

INTRODUCTION TO THE CORE C++ LANGUAGE

In This Chapter

- C++ Program Template
- Your First C++ Program
- How Your Programs Execute
- The Core C++ Language

If you don't think carefully, you might believe that programming is just typing statements in a programming language.

—W. Cunningham

The core C++ language is the portion of the C++ language that directly correlates with the pseudocode, flowcharts, and hierarchy diagrams that were presented in Chapters 1, "Getting Started," and 2, "The Nature of the Problems and Solutions." The C++ language is a large language with numerous features. However, to get your feet wet, this chapter covers the portion that can be translated directly from design mechanisms that you have learned thus far. The other components of C++ provide further flexibility and richness for expressing your ideas in elegant and succinct ways. You will be introduced to the remainder of the C++ language at key points throughout this book.

The core C++ language includes the three classes of statements presented in the previous chapter: sequential, conditional, and iterative (looping). It also includes data in C++. Let the adventure begin.

C++ PROGRAM TEMPLATE

All programming languages have a structure that is used for building them, and C++ is no different. The basic C++ program structure is shown in Listing 3.1. The brackets ([]) indicate optional parts of the structure.

Listing 3.1 Template Structure for a C++ Program

```
[header comments]
[include directives]
[using directives]
[function prototypes]
[class declarations]
[global constant declarations]

int main( ) {
     [main function body      return 0;
}

[function definitions]
```

Here's what the parts actually mean:

- **Header comments.** *Comments* in a program are embedded documentation about how the program works. They make it easier for other programmers to follow what the program is achieving. The header comments are presented at the beginning of every program file. Their purpose is to summarize the contents of the file; they usually contain a minimum of the author(s) name(s), date of creation, a summary of what the file contains, and the name of the file.

- **#include directives.** The #include directives inform C++ that you want to use features that are not standard in every C++ program. These special features are stored in *libraries*. The libraries you're familiar with have books that you can borrow for a finite time and share with other readers so you don't have to buy your own copy of every book you want to read. C++ libraries are there for the same reason. They contain useful features that programs need; instead of each program having to create its own or maintain the common features, the C++ library does this for you. A book library may be arranged by fiction, nonfiction, children's books, new releases, and periodicals. Language libraries may be grouped as input/output, math, network, and graphics. The #include directive allows you to specify which group you want to include and customize your program with the features you need. You will learn about some of these libraries in this book.

- **using directives.** The using directives allow you to further customize the features your program employs. A library may have its features divided into *namespaces*. If you go back to the library analogy, these namespaces act as shelves. When you get to the nonfiction section of the library, the books are arranged on the shelf by topic. The namespaces act as the topics for the library. Therefore, you can further customize what parts of the library are directly accessible by your program.

- **Function prototypes.** Functions represent the idea of subtasks within your C++ program. Functions have names that you create for your program. You have to properly introduce these names to C++ so that it knows the function exists before it starts being used.

- **Function definitions.** The function definitions are where you encode the algorithm in C++ that performs the job of the subtasks. These definitions correlate with the function prototypes.

- **class declarations.** C++ has the ability to do object-oriented programming as well as task-oriented programming. The class declarations are used for the object-oriented programming model. These declarations will not be needed until the latter part of this book.

- **Global constant declarations.** *Constants* are values used in your program that you shouldn't change. For example, you have a program that needs to use the value of pi (3.14159). You would create a constant called pi and place that declaration in this position. This allows every subtask to use the pi constant.

- **The main function.** This is the starting point for every C++ program. If you remember, the hierarchy diagram has a top-level box. The main function implements that box. Because this is not in the brackets, it is required for every C++ program. C++ also requires the return 0 at the end of the main function body. Its purpose is to provide a successful termination signal to your operating system when the program completes. If you do not have this, your operating system may think your program terminated with an error.

- **The main function body.** This is where you encode the algorithm for the top box of your hierarchy diagram. This algorithm largely determines how and when your subtasks are executed. The first statement in the main function body is the first statement your program executes, and the return 0 is the last statement your program executes.

Every C++ program, no matter how simple or complex, has this same structure. This makes reading C++ programs predictable, just like reading books, reports, or essays where there is an agreed-upon format for writing the documents.

YOUR FIRST C++ PROGRAM

Now that you have been introduced to the structure of a C++ program, it's time to see your first C++ program. You need to have your programming environment set up to test this program. If you have not done this, look at the Appendix, "Installing Development Software," for details, and then come back to this point.

The convention in every programming book or manual is to introduce the language with a Hello World program. It's given its name because all it does is output the phrase "Hello World!" So to be a part of tradition, you will also see the C++ Hello World program.

The program shown in Listing 3.2 is the Hello World program written in C++.

Listing 3.2 The Hello World C++ Program

```
#include <iostream>   // Includes the input/output library

using namespace std; // Makes std features available
```

```
// The main function of the program
// It outputs the greeting to the screen
int main () {
    cout << "Hello World! I am a C++ Program." << endl;
    return 0;
}
```

When the program is executed, the output becomes this:

```
Hello World! I am a C++ Program
```

A Special Note for Visual C++ Users

If you are using Visual C++ or Visual C++ Express, when you run your programs, a window briefly shows up on the screen and then disappears. To fix this, you need to add the statement `system ("pause")` before the `return 0` so that your program looks like this at the end:

```
system("pause");
return 0;
```

The `system("pause")` statement holds the terminal window open so that you can see the output. Your output will be slightly different; it will look like the following:

```
Hello World! I am a C++ Program
Press any key to continue...
```

The phrase `Press any key to continue...` is the result of putting the `system("pause")` statement in your program. Once you press any key on the keyboard, your terminal window disappears.

The `#include` directive includes the input and output features. In this program, this encompasses the `cout`, `<<`, `>>`, and `endl` components. Notice also that there are statements written in English with either `//` (pronounced *double slash*) in front of them or `/*` (pronounced *slash star*) and `*/` (pronounced *star slash*). These are called *comments*. Comments are considered documentation in a C++ program; they allow the programmer to provide notes and explanations about the C++ code that has been written. You should develop the habit of documenting your programs using comments. There will be more on this later. For now, you need to know that there are two types of comment syntax:

- **Inline comments.** These are comments that are typically only one or two lines of text. In this case the comment begins with the `//` (double slash) symbol. The comment ends at the end of the line where the `//` symbol exists regardless of where the slashes are placed.

- **Block comments.** These are comments that are going to be multiple lines of text. In this case the comments have a beginning symbol, the /* (slash star) and an ending symbol, the */ (star slash).

In the beginning code of Listing 3.2, there is an example of a header comment. Note that the extra asterisks (*) are there for decoration to provide a border. This is a common practice by programmers. There are also examples of inline comments. There will be more on programming style and commenting throughout the book as notes and sidebars. Please be sure to look for them and learn from them.

How Your Programs Execute

You are probably wondering how the instructions you have in the Hello World program are able to produce the results on the screen. This section gives a brief explanation of what is happening. If you recall from Chapter 1, there are high-level programming languages and low-level programming languages. The C++ language is a high-level programming language. With the aid of software, your programs are automatically translated to a low-level binary equivalent program. The binary program is then executed by the processors that were discussed in Chapter 1.

In the Appendix, after installing your development software, you are shown how to build the program. You click a Build/Play button in the IDE that causes the program to be translated and executed in the terminal/console window. The software that executes when you click the Build/Play button is called a *compiler*. A compiler is a complex software tool that translates your C++ source code into binary. Figure 3.1 shows a diagram of the steps taken by the compiler to generate your binary program that executes for you.

The *source code* is what you call any program code that a programmer writes. In your case, the source code is written in C++. You always have your source program in a file with a .cpp or .cc filename extension. This is the convention, just as Word files end with .doc or .docx. Here are the phases:

1. **Pre-Process.** This is the part of the compiler that processes the #include directives and the comments. It takes the comments out of your program and uses the #include directives to find the source code files for the libraries that you need to have prepended to your file. That's right; your source code is slightly changed by this step by adding code from the libraries you specified and by removing your comments.

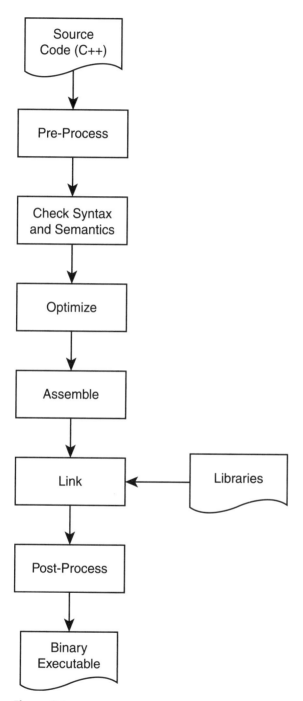

Figure 3.1
A diagram of the process carried out by the compiler software.

2. **Check syntax and semantics.** This step is where the compiler determines whether you have typed the source code properly according to the rules of C++. This is just like when you write a research paper or essay in your word processor and then perform a spell-check and grammar check. After that check, you know that your document conforms to the rules of English. In C++, this phase may find errors in the way you entered the instructions; you get error messages that help you determine how to fix the problem. This is similar to the way the grammar checker identifies grammar errors in your document and then encourages you to fix them.

3. **Optimize.** This step tries to find ways to make your program execute faster or more efficiently. This is where a large amount of intelligence is programmed into the compiler.

4. **Assemble.** This step is where your program is converted to an intermediate binary representation in a hidden file. Now it's ready for the next phase.

5. **Link.** The link step combines the binary version of the program you wrote with the binary versions of the libraries that you included with the #include directives. After linking, a new hidden file is created that contains your binary program and the libraries.

6. **Post-Process.** This phase is where the executable binary is created. It is the result of the binary program that you wrote and linked plus some special operating system–specific code.

```
10110011100110101
11110011000111100
00110100100111101
00111011100111111
00110110101111101
```

Once the compiler completes its work and you have a binary file, the instructions that you typed in as C++ are converted to a binary format that can be visualized in the previous code. Each line of the binary file represents an instruction from your program. The processors take each instruction, its circuitry determines how to execute the instruction, the ALU performs the operation, and then it goes to the next instruction. This process is continued until all the instructions of your program are executed; then the program terminates. This process of executing all the instructions in your program is called *running* or *executing* the program.

THE CORE C++ LANGUAGE

Now you have seen the structure of a C++ program and understand how your computer translates and executes your program. Here is where you are introduced to the core C++ language so that you can start writing your own C++ programs. The structure of this section is to use the pseudocode concepts from Chapter 2 and show how they are translated to equivalent C++ statements and structures. Therefore, at the completion of this section, you can translate well-formed pseudocode into equivalent and working C++ programs. Pretty cool, huh?

C++ Punctuation

There are special symbols in C++ that are the punctuation for the language. In English you have the period, comma, semicolon, and other symbols that designate the end of a sentence, the end of a clause, or a list of information, among other things. C++ also has punctuation symbols. A punctuation symbol in C++ may be one or more characters. The core symbols are shown in Table 3.1.

Table 3.1 The Core C++ Punctuation Symbols

Symbol	Name	Meaning
//	Double slash	Beginning of an inline comment
/*	Slash star	Beginning of a block comment
*/	Star slash	End of a block comment
#	Pound sign	Beginning of preprocessor directive; that is, #include
< >	Open/close brackets	Delimit filename in #include
( )	Open/close parentheses	Enclose conditional and arithmetic expressions, parameter lists for functions, and control structures
{ }	Open/close braces	Create a statement block
" "	Open/close quotation marks	Enclose a string of characters
;	Semicolon	End of a programming statement
,	Comma	Separate elements in a list

Representing Data

In Chapter 2, you learned how to write algorithms using pseudocode and flowcharts. In many of the pseudcode statements and flowchart blocks, you had variables to represent values like distances, the number of grades, or a person's age. In this section, you learn how to represent your variables in C++.

Finding the Variable Names

These variables are found in the various statements of your pseudocode. Here are some statements:

```
set sum to num1 + num2 + num3
while (count < N)...
output average
input name
```

In these instructions, the variables are sum, num1, num2, and num3. In the while instruction, the variables are count and N; in the input and output instructions, the variables are average and name, respectively. By searching your algorithms, you can identify your variables, which are the names that you want to translate into C++. There are certain names that the programming language reserves; you cannot use these as variable names. These names are called *keywords* and are listed in Table 3.2.

Table 3.2 C++ Keywords

auto	const	Double	float	int	short	struct	unsigned
break	continue	Else	for	long	signed	switch	void
case	default	Enum	goto	register	sizeof	typedef	volatile
char	do	Extern	if	return	static	union	while
asm	dynamic_ cast	namespace	reinterpret_ cast	try	bool	explicit	new
catch	false	operator	static_cast	typeid	class	friend	private
const_ cast	inline	Public	template	typename	delete	mutable	protected
and	bitand	Compl	this	using	throw	virtual	true
wchar_t	and_eq	Bitor	not	not_eq	or_eq	xor_eq	or
xor							

In C++ terminology, the names of your variables are *identifiers*. Identifier names are names that you choose just like you did with your algorithm, but there are rules in C++ for creating the names:

- The identifier name must begin with a letter (lowercase or uppercase).
- The identifier name may contain any number or letters, numbers, or underscores (_).
- The identifier name cannot be a keyword (as in Table 3.2).
- The identifier names are not case sensitive.

In Table 3.3 are examples of legal and illegal identifier names. Once you have used the rules to create the names of your identifiers, you need to think about what types of values these variables will represent. Will they be integers, real numbers, names, or some other type of value?

Table 3.3 Legal and Illegal Identifier Names Based on C++ Identifier Naming Rules

Legal Identifier	Illegal Identifier
Count	2ndRound
last_name	_home
myNumber	$balance
Level_4	big-num

Declaring the Variable Names

Declaring a variable means that you are alerting C++ that you want to store data. You have to specify the identifier name and the data type:

```
<data-type> <identifier-name>;
```

The `<identifier-name>` is what you determined in the previous subsection. The `<data-type>` is what you will determine now. Your answer to the question about what kinds of values your variables will represent determines what C++ data type you associate with your identifier name. C++ gives a set of data type names to you:

- `int`. This type is for variables that represent positive and negative whole numbers.

- **unsigned in.** This type is for variables that only represent positive whole numbers.

- **double.** This type is for variables that represent positive and negative real numbers.

- **char.** This type is for variables that represent a single alphanumeric or symbol character, such as any character found on your keyboard.

- **string.** This type is for variables that represent a collection of characters, such as a person's name and home address. This type requires an #include directive.

- **bool.** This type is for variables that represent true or false values. The values for Boolean variables are either true or false, or the values can be the integers 1 or 0, respectively.

Variables: Names and Types?

Recall that values in your programs are stored in random access memory (RAM). Each location in RAM has a unique memory address. The programmer creates variable names to take the place of having to remember memory addresses. For example, if you stored your age in RAM, would it be easier to remember that your age is at location 5027 or that you named the variable myage? Of course, it's easier to remember the variable name instead of the memory location. The types that are used in C++ have two purposes: to check the semantics of your program and to determine how much memory to give to the value. There is a phase where the compiler checks the syntax and the semantics of your program. The types help with semantic checking. This is where the compiler determines whether you are using a variable properly. For example, you may accidently type an expression like this:

year + name

In this case, you don't actually want to add a year, which is an integer, to a name, which is a string. The compiler can identify these errors and alert you of them.

The other reason for types is for RAM management. The compiler needs to know how much RAM to reserve for your data values. If you specify a variable to be a char, it only needs 1 byte of RAM, but if you specify it to be an int, you need at least 4 bytes of RAM.

You choose the type from the list that is best associated with your type of values. For example, if you need to store the amount of your allowance, you want a real number to be stored, so choose double. If you want to store your age, you want an integer, so you would choose int. And if you want to store your first name, string is the best choice. The program in Listing 3.3 shows declarations for these variables and a few others.

Listing 3.3 Program That Shows C++ Variable Declarations and Their Output

```
/**************************************************************
 **
 ** program03_02.cpp - C++ Declarations
 ** This program demonstrates how to declare variables in C++
 **
 ** (c) 2011 Charles R. Hardnett
 **************************************************************/
#include <iostream>
#include <string>

using namespace std;

int main() {
    int     age;         // Your age
    string  firstname;   // Your first name
    double  allowance;   // Your allowance
    char    gender;      // Your gender
    bool    happy;       // Your current mood status

    // Store values in each variable
    age = 16;
    firstname = "Erin";
    allowance = 25.25;
    gender = 'F';
    happy = true;

    // Output the stored values onto the screen
    cout << firstname << endl;
    cout << age << endl;
    cout << allowance << endl;
    cout << gender << endl;
    cout << happy << endl;

    return 0;
}
```

Output:

```
Erin
16
25.25
F
1
```

If you look at the program closely, you notice that there is a new #include directive:

```
#include <string>
```

This directive is required for you to use the string type. It tells the C++ compiler that you need to have access to the string type in your program. The string type is not considered part of the standard C++ language, but it is a member of the standard C++ library. Therefore, you always need to use an #include directive to access the string type.

Note
_____

> Programs frequently use strings. Therefore, make it a habit to always have this directive in your programs so that you do not forget it.

_____

Now you know how to examine your algorithms, translate your variable names to C++ names, and declare your variables in your C++ programs. The next section looks at sequential statements.

Sequential Statements in C++

In your pseudocode, there was a group of statements called *sequential statements* because of their execution in consecutive order. These statements were set, input, and output. C++ has statements that are equivalent, and guess what? You have already seen some of them. In this section, you learn how to translate pseudocode sequential statements into C++ sequential statements. The first of these sequential statements is the assignment statement.

Assignment Statements: Translating Arithmetic Set Operations

The set statements in pseudocode store the value of an arithmetic expression in a variable. Examples include these:

```
set area to PI * R²
set length to 56
set area to LW
set answer to "Georgia"
```

These set statements in your algorithms are translated into C++ assignment statements. In an *assignment statement*, a value is assigned or stored in a variable. The syntax of the assignment statement in C++ is similar to the set statement in pseudocode; here's the general format for the assignment statement:

```
<identifier-name> = <arithmetic expression>;
```

The <identifier-name> corresponds to your variable, and the <arithmetic expression> is the computation that is evaluated whose result is stored in the variable. Using the previous examples, here are the C++ equivalent statements:

```
area = 3.14159 * (R*R);
length = 56;
area = L * W;
answer = "Georgia";
```

From these examples, you can see that a semicolon completes each line, and an asterisk (*) character represents multiplication. C++ is not able to handle "LW" as the multiplication of L times W. Why is that? The answer is relatively simple. In C++, the LW would be considered an identifier, so there needs to be a clear way to express multiplication in C++.

The examples in Table 3.4 are relatively straightforward. However, a couple operations require further explanation: division (/) and modulus (%). The division operation behaves differently based on the types of the operands presented as the numerator and the denominator.

- If both the numerator and the denominator are integer type values, the result is an integer value.
- If either the numerator or the denominator is a floating-point type value, the result is a float.

The rules for division are displayed in the program shown in Listing 3.4. The result of dividing the two integers 16 and 5 gives the result of 3 instead 3.2. To get the result 3.2, either the numerator or the denominator must be a floating-point data type.

Table 3.4 Results of Expressions Using the Fundamental Mathematics Operations

Symbol	Operation	Example	Value of val
+	Addition	val = 12 + 6;	18
-	Subtraction	val = 12 - 6;	6
*	Multiplication	val = 12 * 6;	72
/	Division	val = 12 / 6;	2
%	Modulus	val = 12 % 6;	0

The modulus operator determines the remainder from division. The symbol is the percent sign (%). The value of 10 % 2 is the remainder of dividing 10 by 2, which in this case is 0. However, the value of 10 % 4 produces a remainder of 2. The modulus operator requires that both the numerator and the denominator are integer data types. Several examples of the modulus operator are shown in the listing. Notice that if the numerator is less than the denominator, the result is the same as the numerator.

Listing 3.4 Nuances of Working with the Division and Modulus Operators

```
/****************************************************************
**
** program03_03.cpp - C++ Division and Modulus
** This program demonstrates how the types of numerators and
** denominators affect the outcome of division and modulus.
**
** (c) 2011 Charles R. Hardnett
*****************************************************************/
#include <iostream>

using namespace std;

int main () {
    int     numerator;          // An integer numerator
    int     denominator;        // An integer denominator
    double  numeratorFloat;     // A floating-point numerator
    double  denominatorFloat;   // A floating-point denominator
    int     resultInt;          // An integer result
```

```cpp
double   resultFloat;           // A floating-point result
// Store values in each variable
numerator = 16;
denominator = 5;

numeratorFloat = 16.0;
denominatorFloat = 5.0;

// Dividing an integer by an integer
resultInt = numerator / denominator;
cout << resultInt << endl;

// Dividing a floating point by another floating point
resultFloat = numeratorFloat / denominatorFloat;
cout << resultFloat << endl;

// Dividing with mixed types
resultFloat = numerator/denominatorFloat;
cout << resultFloat << endl;

resultFloat = numeratorFloat/denominator;
cout << resultFloat << endl;

// Using modulus to get the remainder
resultInt = 0 % denominator;
cout << resultInt << endl;
resultInt = 1 % denominator;
cout << resultInt << endl;
resultInt = 2 % denominator;
cout << resultInt << endl;
resultInt = 5 % denominator;
cout << resultInt << endl;
resultInt = 6 % denominator;
cout << resultInt << endl;
resultInt = 7 % denominator;
cout << resultInt << endl;


return 0;
}
```

Output:

```
3
3.2
3.2
3.2
0
1
2
0
1
2
```

Note

The modulus operator may seem like a useless operator. However, it is actually a powerful operator for games. Consider a game that involves rolling dice. The dice have exactly six sides; therefore, only values 1 through 6 can be generated. You would like for your game program to randomly roll the dice. In C++, there is a way to generate a random number, but this number will be between 0 and approximately 4,000,000,000! And you want numbers between 1 and 6 to represent the sides of the dice. The modulus operator is the tool to use; consider the following assignment statement:

```
side = (myrand % 6) + 1;
```

Assume that myrand in the assignment statement is a random number generated by C++; the myrand % 6 will produce values from 0 to 5 (the only possible remainders when dividing by 6). You want values from 1 to 6, so by adding 1 to the result, you can change the range from 0 to 5 to be 1 to 6. This gives you the range of values to model the rolling of dice in a game.

Is there precedence of operators? Associativity? The answer to both questions is yes. But you do not have to learn new rules; the rules for both are the same as they are for mathematics from highest to lowest:

( )   Left-to-right associativity

* / %   Left-to-right associativity

+ -   Left-to-right associativity

Remember that associativity is applied when you have two or more operations that are at the same level; then in all three cases, you process them from left to right. Consider the following example (num1 = 25, num2 = 10, and num3 = 3):

```
value = num1 * 4 / 2;
```

The expression evaluates from left to right because both the * and / operators are at the same level of precedence. Thus, value is set to the result of the expression, which is 50. That was an example of the associativity rule. Now look at an example for the precedence rule (num1 = 25, num2 = 10, and num3 = 3):

```
value = num1 + (num3 - num2) * 2;
```

In this statement, the quantity (num3 - num2) is evaluated first because it is in parentheses. This is followed by multiplying by 2 because of the precedence between multiplication and addition. The last operation performed is the addition. The result of this expression is 25 + (3 − 10) * 2 = 25 + (−7) * 2 = 25 − 14 = 11.

Assignment Statements: Translating Nonarithmetic Set Operations

You can use the string data type in assignment statements. It has its own set of operations that can be performed to manipulate string data. You can combine strings to create new strings, extract substrings from a string, replace or remove parts of a string, and insert a substring into a string.

Combining strings is called *concatenation*. It's done using the + operator that is used for addition of numbers, but with strings it performs concatenation:

```
firstName = "Charles";
lastName = "Hardnett";
FullName = firstName + " " + lastName;
FullNameRev = lastName + ", " + firstName;
```

The sequence of statements here contains assignment statements that concatenate strings. The results of the last two statements are the strings "Charles Hardnett" and "Hardnett, Charles", respectively.

A substring is simply a portion of a larger string. You can obtain a substring from a C++ string by using the substr method. The substr method has the format:

```
substr(start, length)
```

The start is the position of the character where the substring starts, and length is the number of characters in the substring. You must remember that the first character of a string is always at position 0. The substr method does not remove the substring; it just extracts a copy. Consider the following examples:

```
firstFour = firstName.substr(0, 4);
username = firstFour + lastName.substr(0, 4);
```

This code creates a username using the `substr` method. The first assignment statement extracts a copy of the first four characters of the string `firstName`. The second assignment extracts the first four characters of `lastName`. These two parts are combined to get the value of `username` that in this case would be `"CharHard"`.

The `substr` method does not alter the string, but you can use the `erase` method to remove parts of a string. The `erase` method uses a format similar to `substr`:

```
erase(start, length)
```

The `start` is the position of the character where the erasing should start, and `length` is the number of characters that should be erased. Consider the following assignments:

```
fullName = "Christopher James Lowe";
fullName.erase(12, 6);
```

The `erase` method will change `fullName` to the string `"Christopher Lowe"`. The 12 is the position of the `J` in the string. The 6 includes the characters in `"James"` and the trailing space, to leave only one space between the first and last name.

You can replace a portion of a string with a new string by using the `replace` method. The replace method has a format that builds on the format of the `erase` method:

```
replace(start, length, repstr)
```

The `start` is the position of the character where the replacing should start, and `length` is the number of characters that should be replaced. The `repstr` is the string that is replacing the removed characters. The `repstr` can be longer or shorter than the length of the removed characters. Here is an example:

```
fullName = "Christopher James Lowe";
middleName = "Michael";
fullName.replace(12, 5, middleName);
```

The `replace` method will alter `fullName` to have a new middle name. The five characters of `"James"` are replaced with `"Michael"` to get the new string `"Christopher Michael Lowe"`.

You have seen that there are operations for numeric data types as well as the string data type. All these operations can be used in assignment operations. The next section discusses input and output sequential statements.

Translating Input and Output Pseudocode Statements into C++

The other two types of sequential operations used in pseudocode were input and output operations. These operations provided interactive ability for your algorithms. You could receive input data from the user, and you could output data to the user. Recall that your input statements used the command Get or Input, and the output statements used either the Print or Output command. Some examples of input and output pseudocode statements follow:

```
Get the value of X and Y
Print the value Average
Get firstName
Print "The average is " Average
```

In C++, input and output are accomplished by the use of a library. The name of the library is called *I/O stream*. The I/O stream library contains two main objects to assist with input and output. There is one object that represents the keyboard in your C++ programs, and it's named cin. A second object represents the terminal window or screen, and it's named cout. You can translate the preceding pseudocode statements in the following way:

```
cin >> X >> Y;
cout << Average;
cin >> firstName;
cout << "The average is " << Average;
```

The input streams use an operator called *extraction*. The extraction operator is formed using two greater-than symbols with no space (>>). The output streams use the *insertion* operator. This operator is formed by two less-than symbols with no space (<<). These operators are flexible and can be daisy-chained together to either input multiple values or output multiple values as shown earlier. Listing 3.5 shows examples of using cin and cout.

Listing 3.5 Program to Illustrate Use of cin for Input

```
/****************************************************************
**
** program03_04.cpp - C++ Input
** This program demonstrates the use of cin for input into a
** program.
**
** (c) 2011 Charles R. Hardnett
*****************************************************************/
#include <iostream>

using namespace std;

int main () {
    int num1, num2, num3; // Declaring three integers

    // Read input in 3 separate instructions
    cout << "Enter 3 integers: ";
    cin >> num1;
    cin >> num2;
    cin >> num3;

    // Output a comma-separated list
    cout << num1 << ", " << num2 << ", " << num3 << endl;

    // Read input in one instruction
    cout << "Enter 3 more integers: ";
    cin >> num1 >> num2 >> num3;

    // Output a comma-separated list
    cout << num1 << ", " << num2 << ", " << num3 << endl;

    return 0;
}
```

Output:

```
Enter 3 integers: 5 10 15 [Enter]
5, 10, 15
Enter 3 more integers: 2 4 6 [Enter]
2, 4, 6
```

Style: Commenting Your Code

You have seen a few examples of C++ programs to this point. You should have noticed that each program starts with a long comment that gives the name of the program file, a description of the program, and an author and copyright. This is called a *program header comment*. You should have a header comment in every program file you create. Header comments help people read source code that is printed out or distributed on websites because the comment tells them which file they are reading and what its purpose is. Header comments are also helpful if you'd like to know who authored the code so you can contact them or give them credit. Copyrights are always important in header comments because your programs are your intellectual property. A copyright controls the way others use your code. You should develop your own header comment style and determine what other kinds of information you would like to put in your header comments.

Input Statements Input statements do not produce output on the screen. When the processor reaches an input statement, it waits. The user must input the values and then press the Return/Enter key. Once the Return/Enter key is pressed, the values typed on the screen are stored in the variable(s). The program in Listing 3.6 shows the use of *prompting*. Prompting is where you use an output statement to tell the user what the program expects. Without the prompting statement, nothing would be displayed on the screen except a flashing prompt. Examining the output, you see that the user types in 5, 10, and 15 separated by spaces and then presses the Return/Enter key.

In addition, the program in Listing 3.6 demonstrates the flexibility of the C++ input statements. As you can see, three values are inputted in both parts of the program. In the first part, the program reads the three input values on separate lines. In the second part, the program reads all three input values on a single line.

Listing 3.6 Program to Illustrate Use of cin for Input

```
/******************************************************************
 **
 ** program03_05.cpp - C++ output
 ** This program shows how output statements can be used for basic
 ** formatting.
 **
 ** (c) 2011 Charles R. Hardnett
 ******************************************************************/
#include <iostream>
```

```
using namespace std;

int main () {
    // Uses two couts to output onto one line
    cout << "Programming Like A Pro: ";
    cout << "For Teens";
    cout << endl;          // Moves to next line

    // Outputs onto two separate lines
    cout << "Programming Like A Pro: " << endl;
    cout << "For Teens";
    cout << endl;          // Moves to next line

    // Also outputs onto two separate lines
    cout << "Programming Like A Pro: " << endl << "For Teens";
    cout << endl;          // Moves to next line

    return 0;

}
```

Output:

```
Programming Like A Pro: For Teens
Programming Like A Pro:
For Teens
Programming Like A Pro:
For Teens
```

Output Statements Output statements produce output on the screen. You have seen several output statements to this point, so here is an explanation of what you have seen and some nuances. The output statements in C++ use the cout object with the insertion operator (<<). There is a special object named endl (end line) that moves the cursor to the start of the next line on the output screen. In Listing 3.6, the program uses two output statements to output the string "Programming Like A Pro: For Teens" on one line on the screen even though there are two output statements. In C++, the output stream is a continuous stream to output data. If you do not explicitly tell C++ to go to the next line, it assumes that all the data should be on one line. The endl object moves the cursor to the next line. It can be used in an output statement alone, at the end of the statement, or in the middle (shown in the last example in Listing 3.6).

This completes the core sequential operations. Keep in mind, there are more details and variations for these statements. However, the goal was to introduce you to the core C++ that would directly translate from the pseudocode. Now it's off to decision-making statements.

Decision-Making Statements in C++

The decision-making statements in your algorithms were related to if-then-else statements. These were statements where the computer could make a decision based on an expression evaluating to true or false. In this subsection, you learn to translate your pseudocode decision-making statements into equivalent C++ statements.

Here are some examples of if-then-else statements in pseudocode:

```
If Balance < 1000 Then
    Set the value of LastBalance to LastBalance - Withdrawal
End If

If Hours > 40 Then
    Set OverTime = Hours - 40
    Set Regular = 40
Else (Hours < 40)
    Set OverTime = 0
    Set Regular = Hours
End If
```

These statements are translated to C++ using the C++ if-then and if-then-else statements. The general syntax for these two statements is as follows:

```
if (<boolean expression>) {
    <statements>
}
```

and

```
if (<boolean expression>) {
    <statements>
} else {
    <statements>
}
```

The syntax of C++ decision-making statements is similar to their pseudocode counterparts. Because C++ is case sensitive, the keywords if and else must be lowercase. In addition, the parentheses are mandatory. The following are the translations of the pseudocode to C++:

```
if (Balance < 1000) {
    LastBalance = LastBalance - Withdrawal;
}

if (Hours > 40) {
    OverTime = Hours - 40;
    Regular = 40;
} else {
    OverTime = 0;
    Regular = Hours;
}
```

As you can see, the translation is almost one-to-one. Note that it was necessary to translate the set statements also. Now you have C++ equivalent if statements and if-else statements.

The Boolean expressions of the if and if-else statements are composed of relational operators and compound operators. All of these operations result in a true or false value. The relational operators are comparison operations and are shown in Table 3.5.

Table 3.5 C++ Relational Operators and Examples

Symbol	Operation	Example	Result
>	Greater-than	10 > 6	true
<	Less-than	10 < 6	false
>=	Greater-than or equal-to	10 >= 6	true
<=	Less-than or equal-to	10 <= 6	false
==	Equal-to	10 == 6	false
!=	Not equal-to	10 != 6	true
!	Not	!true	false
		!false	true
		!(10 == 6)	true

The Boolean expressions in the previous examples are simple versions of Boolean expressions. These expressions evaluate as either true or false. The last row of the table contains an inverse operation that inverses the result of any Boolean expression. If the expression is true, the result is false and vice versa.

Note

The single equal sign does not mean "equal to." Instead, the single equal sign always means "is assigned to." When you pronounce assignment statements to yourself and out loud, you should say "is assigned." For example, X = 5; is pronounced *X is assigned 5*. The double equal sign (==) means "equal to." Thus X == 5; is pronounced *X equals 5*. You should commit this to memory to alleviate frustrating debugging sessions later.

The second type of operator is known as *compound*. These operators are &&, which represents the logical AND operation, and ||, which represents the logical OR operation. Table 3.6 shows the truth table for these operations. The true and false in the table would be the results from the expressions on the left or right of the operator.

Table 3.6 Truth Tables for the && and || Operators in C++ Boolean Expressions

and (&&)		or (||)	
Expression	**Value**	**Expression**	**Value**
true && true	true	true || true	true
true && false	false	true || false	true
false && true	false	false || true	true
false && false	false	false || false	false

Using the truth tables in Table 3.6, consider the following example:

```
(index < N) && (found != true)
```

Suppose index = 6, N = 100, and found = false; the expression evaluates to true because (index < N) is true and (found != true) is true. If you look at the first row of the && side of the truth table, you see that true && true results in a true expression. The parentheses promote precedence of the operations. The following is the order of precedence for Boolean operators from highest to lowest:

( )	Left-to-right associativity
<, >, <=, >=, !=, ==	Left-to-right associativity
&&, ||	Left-to-right associativity

Boolean expressions can be arbitrarily complex and tailored to your needs. Do not hesitate to use more than one or two conditions if necessary. In the next section, you learn to translate loops.

Looping Statements in C++

You are making progress through the core C++ language. You started with learning how to declare C++ variables for the variables in your pseudocode. Then you learned how to translate sequential statements, where set statements become assignment statements, input statements become cin statements, and output statements become cout statements. In the previous section, you learned to create C++ if and if-else statements from equivalent pseudocode statements. Now the final category of statements, iterative or looping statements, will be addressed.

Looping statements in pseudocode begin with the word while, and they have a condition that is similar to the Boolean conditions examined under if statements. The following are some pseudocode loops:

```
While (found not equal true) and (count >= 0) Do
        Get the value of val
        If val equal to target Then
        Set found to true
        End If
        decrement count by 1
End While


Set num to 0
While num <= 10 Do
        Print num²
        Increment num by 1
End While
```

C++ has several looping structures; however, for simplicity, the core C++ language defined here contains only one looping structure, called the while loop. The template for C++ while loops looks like this:

```
while (<boolean expression>) {
    <statements>
}
```

As you can see, the header of the while loop looks similar to the if statement. Sometimes this is a source of confusion for beginning programmers. The difference between the while loop and the if statement is that the <statements> in the while loop are repeated as long as the <boolean expression> is true. The if statement executes its statements only once when its <boolean expression> is true.

Note

The "if loop" is a common statement made by beginning programming students. This is primarily because the if statement and while statement look similar. One way to remember the difference is to think about what it means in English. If you say to your friend, "If you see the ball, hit it!," you want your friend to hit the ball the next time he sees it. If you say, "When you see the ball, hit it!," you want your friend to consistently look for the ball and hit it every time. The second statement implies doing something over and over, but the first statement does not. I hope this helps; there will be no talk of "if loops."

If you use the template for the C++ while loop, you can translate the pseudocode loops into C++ loops as follows:

```
while ( (found != true) && (count >= 0)) {
    cin >> val;
    if (val == target) {
    found = true;
    }
    count = count - 1;
}

num = 0
while (num <= 10) {
    cout << pow(num, 2.0) << endl;
    num = num + 1;
}
```

The C++ versions use brackets ({}) instead of Do and End While. As you can see, the Boolean expressions use the same format as those with the if statement.

Note

It is common to have counters in the loop to keep track of the number of iterations that have passed and to know which iteration is executing. C++ provides a shortcut for incrementing and decrementing counters. Two special operators, ++ and -, perform an increment by 1 and a decrement by 1, respectively. Here is how they are used:

```
count-- // Same result as count = count - 1
num++; // Same result as num = num + 1
```

Translating an Entire Algorithm to C++

This section shows how to build a program using the translation techniques in this chapter. Assume you have created the pseudocode in Listing 3.7 that reads in numeric grades from the user and outputs pass or fail based on the grade being greater-than or equal to 60 or less-than 60, respectively. The user is allowed to enter grades until he enters a negative value. At the completion, the code outputs the number of passing and the number of failing grades.

Listing 3.7 Pseudocode to Determine the Number of Pass and Fail Grades

```
Set passes to 0
Set fails to 0
Print "Please enter a numeric grade (> 0): "
Get value of grade
while grade >= 0 Do
      If grade >= 60 Then
      print "pass"
      increment passes
       Else
      print "fail"
      increment fails
       End If

      Print "Please enter a numeric grade (> 0): "
      Get value of grade
End While
Print "You passed ", passes, " classes and failed ",fails," classes."
```

The first step is to create a template C++ program. The template for this program shown in Listing 3.8 is a great start. You should use this template to start all your C++ programs while you are learning the language. You can follow along by typing the code in this section as you read. This is a good way to get more practice typing C++ and getting to know your C++ development environment.

Listing 3.8 A Starting C++ Template

```
/***************************************************************
 **
 ** program03_06.cpp - Pass or Fail
 ** A program that reads in grades and determines if the grade is
 ** pass or fail. When a negative grade is entered, the input
 ** is stopped and the program outputs the number of pass and
 ** fail classes.
 **
 ** (c) 2011 Charles R. Hardnett
 ***************************************************************/
#include <iostream>
#include <string>

using namespace std;

int main () {

    return 0;
}
```

The next step is to translate the pseudocode, starting with the variable declarations, assignment operations, and input/output operations before reaching the loop:

```
/***************************************************************
 **
 ** program03_06.cpp - Pass or Fail
 ** A program that reads in grades and determines if the grade is
 ** pass or fail. When a negative grade is entered, the input
 ** is stopped and the program outputs the number of pass and
 ** fail classes.
 **
```

```
    ** (c) 2011 Charles R. Hardnett
    *************************************************************/

#include <iostream>

using namespace std;

int main () {
    int passes;   // The number of passed classes
    int fails;       // The number of failed classes
    double grade;    // Current grade to be analyzed

    // Initialize number of passes and fails
    passes = 0;
    fails = 0;

    // Prompt for the first grade
    cout << ?Please enter a numeric grade (> 0): ?;
    cin >> grade;
    return 0;
}
```

Note

As you translate your pseudocode, it's wise to compile/build your program periodically. I like building after I have completed a major part of the program, which may be 10–20 lines of code. As a beginner, this periodic compiling helps you handle syntax and semantic errors before they build upon each other. It's much easier to correct 10 lines of C++ than 100 lines of C++.

If you look at the section for creating variables, you will recall that you first had to examine the pseudocode to find the variables in the program. Based on the fact that the passes and fails variables will be counts, those should be integers. Grades, on the other hand, can be numbers like 92, 83, 85.5, and 90.1. Therefore, you need to use a data type for real numbers. Finally, you can translate the set, print, and get instructions from the pseudocode into assignment statements and C++ input/output statements.

The while statement and if statement need to be translated to create the final program shown in Listing 3.9. The Boolean expressions for the while loop and if-else statement are translated directly from the pseudocode. By taking advantage of the previous note, you can use passes++ instead of using pass = pass + 1. Now you can test the program.

Listing 3.9 Final Program After Full Translation

```
/****************************************************************
**
** program03_06.cpp - Pass or Fail
** A program that reads in grades and determines if the grade is
** pass or fail. When a negative grade is entered, the input
** is stopped and the program outputs the number of pass and
** fail classes.
**
** (c) 2011 Charles R. Hardnett
****************************************************************/

#include <iostream>

using namespace std;

int main () {
    int passes;      // The number of passed classes
    int fails;       // The number of failed classes
    double grade;    // Current grade to be analyzed

    // Initialize number of passes and fails
    passes = 0;
    fails = 0;

    // Prompt for the first grade
    cout << "Please enter a numeric grade (< 0): ";
    cin >> grade;

    // Process grades when a value > 0 is entered
    while (grade >= 0) {

        // Determine if the grade is pass or fail
        if (grade >= 60) {
            cout << "pass" << endl;
            passes++;
```

```
    } else {
        cout << "fail" << endl;
        fails++;
    }
    // Prompt for the next grade
    cout << "Please enter a numeric grade (> 0): ";
    cin >> grade;
}

cout << "You passed " << passes << " courses and you failed "
    << fails << " courses." << endl;
return 0;
}
```

Output:

```
Please enter a numeric grade (< 0): 90 [Enter]
pass
Please enter a numeric grade (> 0): 82.5 [Enter]
pass
Please enter a numeric grade (> 0): 55 [Enter]
fail
Please enter a numeric grade (> 0): 59 [Enter]
fail
Please enter a numeric grade (> 0): 60 [Enter]
pass
Please enter a numeric grade (> 0): -9 [Enter]
You passed 3 courses and you failed 2 courses.
```

Style: Indentation and More Commenting

Throughout this chapter, you probably noticed that there are 3–4 spaces of indentation of statements within the main() function. Programmers use indentation to show that statements belong within a function like main() or a control structure like if, if-else, or while statements. For example, if you look at Listing 3.9, you will see that the statements located within the while loop are indented at the same level, and those statements within the if-else statement are further indented. The customary indentation is 3–4 spaces. The indentation makes your program easier to read and understand. It also makes it look professional.

Commenting is used within the body of the programs to describe why statements are in the program. The first rule is to write at least one comment for each phase of your program: input, process, and output. The second rule is to write a comment for each control structure. For example, in Listing 3.10, there is a comment for the while loop and for the if-else statement. Notice that the comments explain the purpose of the statement in solving the problem. You should always comment your code and comment it as you are writing it. Comments will help you recall what the program was doing and how it was accomplishing its tasks. They also aid other programmers in understanding your logic.

If you followed along and built the code for yourself, congratulations! Next, you will learn about implementing lists of data in C++. This is necessary because in some of the pseudocode algorithms, the solution requires a list of data.

Lists in C++

Computers are designed to solve large problems efficiently. But large problems require large amounts of organized data. A fundamental way to organize data is to use a list. In Chapter 2, you looked at algorithms that required the data to be processed as a list. In C++, arrays can manage basic lists. An *array* is a list of homogeneous data types that has a position for each data item in the list. The homogeneity means that an array must be an array of integers, an array of strings, or an array of doubles. You cannot have an array that has a mixture of data types.

Figure 3.2 shows an array that has 12 elements. In C++, the first element of the array is at position 0, and the last element is at position 11. In general, arrays of size N have their first element at position 0 and their last element at position $N - 1$. An array is declared like a variable, but with an associated size. The template for an array declaration follows:

```
<data-type> <identifier-name> [size];
```

Therefore, you can have the following array declarations:

```
double Grades[30];      // An array of 30 doubles representing grades
int months[12];         // An array of 12 integers for the 12 months of the year
string webpages[100];   // An array of 100 webpage URLs for bookmarks
```

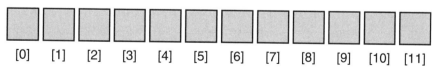

[0]   [1]   [2]   [3]   [4]   [5]   [6]   [7]   [8]   [9]   [10] [11]

Figure 3.2
An array with 12 elements.

The preceding examples show how to declare arrays. The size that is chosen for the array is a maximum size. You can have an array of 30 grades but have only 10 grades in the array. However, you cannot change the size of the array after the declaration. Therefore, you should choose a size that is greater than what you can foresee needing for the program.

The algorithm in Listing 3.10 finds the largest value in a list of integers. This algorithm was devised in Chapter 2, and its strategy is to start at the beginning of the list. It assumes the first item in the list is the current largest number in the list. It then compares the current largest number with each number in the list and updates the current largest if it finds a larger value.

Listing 3.10 Algorithm for Finding the Largest Value in a List of Integers

```
Get N
Get List₀, List₁, ..., Listₙ₋₁.
Set largest to List₀
Set position to 0
Set index to 1
While (index ≤ N) do
    if List_index > largest then
        Set largest to List_index
        Set location to index
    Increment index
End While
Print largest and position
```

To convert this pseudocode to C++, you would follow the same general translation rules. However, statements that involve the List elements for input and output such as the following are problematic:

```
Get List₀, List₁, ..., Listₙ₋₁.
Print List₀, List₁, ..., Listₙ₋₁.
```

These statements require writing a C++ input/output statement that can contain an arbitrary number of variables, depending on what N happens to be. This is not possible in C++; therefore, you must use a C++ loop. Following is an example loop for getting N values of the array List:

```
index = 0;
while (index < N) {
```

```
cout << "Enter a number: ";
cin >> List[index];     // Accesses the position at index in the array
index++;   // Increment the index value
}
```

The previous loop illustrates some fundamental ideas related to processing arrays. First, processing an entire array requires an integer variable to represent the positions in the array. In this example, index is the name of that variable. Second, you need a loop to process the array because you need to visit each element of the array. In this example, the while loop does not allow index to become greater than N, and the index++ statement increments the index to move to the next position in the array.

You can take the idea for handling the input of the array and translate the remainder of the algorithm to obtain the solution shown in Listing 3.11.

Listing 3.11 Program That Finds the Largest Value in an Array

```
/*******************************************************************
 **
 ** program03_07.cpp - Find the Largest
 ** This program implements the find the largest algorithm. It
 ** reads a list of numbers from the user and displays the largest
 ** value and its position.
 **
 ** (c) 2011 Charles R. Hardnett
 ******************************************************************/
#include <iostream>

using namespace std;

int main () {
    int index;        // Index for the array
    int List[100];    // The array of integers (maximum of 100 ints)
    int position;     // The position of the largest value
    int largest;      // The largest value in the list
    int N;            // The number of values to process


    // Get the value of N
    cout << "Please enter the quantify of numbers you need to process: ";
```

```
cin >> N;

index = 0;
while (index < N) {
    cout << "Enter a number: ";
    cin >> List[index];
    index++;
}

// Assume the largest value is the first value in the array
position = 0;
largest = List[0];

index = 1; // Start at the next number in the array

while (index < N) {
    if (List[index] > largest) {
        // Found a larger value than the current largest
        largest = List[index];
        position = index;
    }
    index++;
}

// Output the largest value and its position in the array
cout << "largest = " << largest << endl;
cout << "position = " << position << endl;

return 0;}
```

Output:

```
Please enter the quantity of numbers you need to process: 5
Enter a number: 10
Enter a number: 5
Enter a number: 25
Enter a number: 15
Enter a number: 50
largest = 50
position = 4
```

SUMMARY

This chapter introduced to you the core C++ language, which directly correlates with the pseudocode and flowcharts presented in Chapter 2. The chapter began with an overview of C++ and its program structure. Then you learned how the C++ compiler translates C++ programs into binary and how the computer executes that binary code. Then you were introduced to the core C++ language based on the pseudocode and how to translate sequential statements, decision statements, and looping statements from pseudocode to C++. Finally, you saw how a list of data could be represented using an array in C++.

EXERCISES

The following questions test your knowledge of the material from this chapter. You can find the answers to these questions on the book's companion website at www.courseptr.com/downloads.

1. Write a complete C++ program to read the user's first name, last name, age, and gender (m/f), and then echo these things to the screen.

2. Write a complete C++ program to read in a number. If the number is less than 5, write it to the screen, but if it's greater than 5, write out the number doubled.

3. Write a complete C++ program that asks the user to enter a number, and then use a loop to output all the numbers from 0 to that number.

4. Write a complete C++ program that receives input numbers from the user until the user enters a –1. The algorithm outputs the largest value of the numbers entered.

5. Write a complete C++ program that computes the area of a circle. The program should have a function called `circleArea(float radius)` that uses the `radius` parameter to compute the area of the circle and returns the area as a float to the main program.

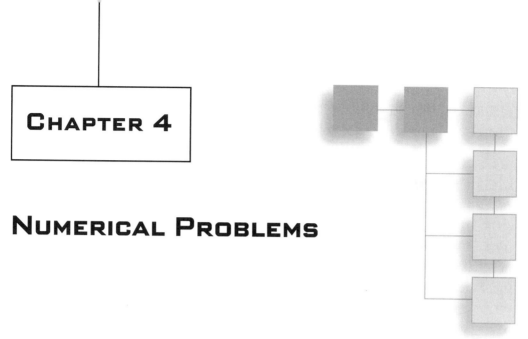

CHAPTER 4

NUMERICAL PROBLEMS

In This Chapter

- Compound Interest
- C++ Feature: Formatted Output
- Computing the Square Root
- C++ Feature: Functions
- C++ Feature: The Math Library
- C++ Feature: Counting Loops

Inside every large program, there is a small program trying to get out.

—Tony Hoare

Numerical problems are those that require some mathematical formulation to solve. These problems may come from finance, statistics, science, and many other subjects. Typically, there is a mathematical formula or concept you must understand prior to solving the problem, and then it is your job to convert the mathematics into an algorithm that can be written in C++. When working with numerical problems in a programming language, you must address various concerns. One of these concerns is preventing illegal mathematical operations such as division by zero. A second concern is reporting your results with the proper precision. Finally, you may have to compensate for round-off error.

In this chapter, you are introduced to a collection of mathematical problems and solutions. In the process, you learn about some features of C++ that are handy when writing programs for solving numerical problems.

COMPOUND INTEREST

Compound interest is a fundamental financial calculation that affects the world every day. It can be used for your benefit or for your detriment. *Compound interest* involves your balance increasing by the interest each month to form a new balance. Therefore, if you have some money in the account, at the end of the month the banking institution uses the balance to compute the interest earned, which is some fraction of the balance. This interest earned is then added to the balance, which increases every month as long as you do not withdraw money. You can think of the interest as the amount the bank pays you each month to allow it to use your money. With a credit card, the roles are reversed, but compound interest is still used. When you make purchases on a credit card, you have a balance that you owe on the card. Each month the bank adds interest to the current balance; the interest is a fraction of the balance. If you never make payments to reduce the balance, the interest continues to be added to your balance. In this case, the bank is charging you interest for the convenience of using its money through a credit card purchase. So what are the implications?

Your balance will grow at a fast rate if the interest rate is high and a slow rate if the interest rate is low. A high interest rate could be 10% or greater, and a low interest rate would be less than 10%. If you are investing money, then higher interest rates mean that you will accumulate wealth at a faster pace than lower interest rates; this is where compound interest is beneficial to you. If you are using a credit card or taking out a loan, higher interest rates require larger payments to pay off the card or loan because the balance increases each month due to the interest. Therefore, in a loan or credit scenario, interest can work against you, but in a savings scenario, interest can work for you. In both scenarios, compound interest is the tool that increases the balance.

Compound Interest Mathematics

Now consider a specific scenario so that you can understand how compound interest is computed mathematically. Suppose you have made $500.00 worth of purchases on a credit card with an annual finance charge of 12%. This means that each month 1% interest is added to your balance because there are 12 months, and 12% / 12 months = 1% per month. After 1 month you will owe 1% more than the $500.00 balance, which is $500.00 * 0.01 = $5. This means that the interest you were charged in the first month for the $500.00 is $5.

Now your balance will be $505.00 after the first month. If this continues, you will see the following growth in your balance with each successive month:

Month 2: 505.00 * 1% = 510.05

Month 3: 510.05 * 1% = 515.15

Month 4: 515.15 * 1% = 520.30

Month 5: 520.30 * 1% = 525.51

Month 6: 525.51 * 1% = 530.76

In the first month the increase is $5.00, the increase in the second month is $5.05, and by the sixth month the total increase is more than $30. If you do not make payments on the balance you owe, your debt grows. Would the balance go up or down if you pay $3 per month? $4 per month? $6 per month?

You have to pay more than 1% of the balance. This is because 1% is added each month. If you pay less than 1% of the balance, the interest becomes more than your payment, and your balance continues to grow by the difference. The only answer to the previous paragraph's question that will decrease your balance is to pay $6 per month. Of course, you want to pay more than that to pay off your debt as quickly as possible.

The good news about compound interest is that if this were an investment, your money would increase by about $30 in less than 6 months without your depositing money beyond the $500.00 initial investment.

The Algorithm: Compound Interest

In developing the compound interest algorithm, you need to identify the main formula and how the formula is going to be applied. You can derive the formula from the example. Based on the example, you can see that the same formula is used in each period. That formula involves an old balance (OB) and a new balance (NB). You can put these together to get the formula NB = OB * percentage + OB. This formula is repeated for each period. In fact, it is common to use a subscript for each period to make it easier to follow:

$$Balance_2 = Balance_1 * percentage + Balance_1$$

$$Balance_3 = Balance_2 * percentage + Balance_2$$

$$Balance_4 = Balance_3 * percentage + Balance_3$$

Here you can see that old balance is just the balance computed in the previous period. Subscripts are useful when the same variable is being reused as part of a sequence. In addition, whenever you use subscripts, it is a hint that a loop can be used. In Chapter 3, "Introduction to the Core C++ Language," you learned about the `while` loop. Using the `while` loop, you end up with the following loop for your algorithm:

```
Set period = 1
While Period <= Last Period Do
    Balance = Balance * percentage + Balance
    Period = Period + 1
End While
```

This loop assumes that you set the initial balance and percentage rate before the loop starts. With this algorithm, you are ready to write a C++ program that performs the algorithm.

The C++ Program: Compound Interest

The C++ program is based on the compound interest algorithm, with additions to make the program more interesting. The program will to the following:

- Output a table with headings: Period, Interest, and Balance.
- Ask the user for input values for initial balance, annual interest rate, and number of periods.

The input from the user is based on the core C++ input/output; however, the table requires the introduction of some new features. This program has the following example output, given a starting balance of $500.00, an annual interest rate of 12%, and five periods:

```
Period  Interest($)  Balance($)
    1          5.00      505.00
    2          5.05      510.05
    3          5.10      515.15
    4          5.15      520.30
    5          5.20      525.51
```

First compare this output to your example to see that it matches, and notice that the output is in formatted columns. This is done using the C++ I/O Manipulator library. The program that produces this output is shown in Listing 4.1.

Listing 4.1 Compound Interest in C++

```cpp
1: #include <iostream>
2: #include <iomanip>    // Input/output manipulation objects
3:
4: using namespace std;
5:
6: int main () {
7:    int periods;           // The number of interest-bearing periods
8:    double rate;           // The annual interest percentage rate
9:    double interest = 0.;  // The interest in the current period
10:   double balance;        //  The current account balance
11:   int currPeriod;        //  The counter to keep track of periods
12:
13:   cout << "Please enter the number of periods: ";
14:   cin >> periods;
15:
16:   cout << "Please enter the annual interest rate: ";
17:   cin >> rate;
18:
19:   cout << "Please enter the starting balance: ";
20:   cin >> balance;
21:
22:   currPeriod = 1; // Initialize the periods
23:
24:   // Two decimal places of precision
25:   cout << setprecision(2) >> fixed;
26:
27:   // Set up the table header
```

```
28:   cout ≪ setw(8) ≪ "Period" ≪ setw(13) ≪ "Interest($)";
29:   cout ≪ setw(12) ≪ "Balance($)" ≪ endl;
30:
31:   // This loop computes the interest and balance for each period
32:   while (currPeriod <= periods) {
33:      interest = balance * rate/12.0;
34:      balance  = balance + interest;
35:
36:      cout ≪ setw(8) ≪ currPeriod ≪ setw(13) ≪ interest;
37:      cout ≪ setw(12) ≪ balance ≪ endl;
38:
39:      currPeriod++;
40:   }
41:
42:   return 0;
43: }
```

The code in Listing 4.1 implements the compound interest algorithm that was developed in the earlier section. Line 2 uses the #include directive to include the iomanip library that produces the columns and will be discussed in the next section. Lines 7–11 declare the variables that are needed in this program. The data types are chosen based on the type of data the variable represents; the variables that represent money are doubles to allow for the two decimal places for cents. The variables related to periods are integers because periods are whole numbers, such as 1, 2, 3, 4, and 5.

Lines 13–22 perform the user interaction to obtain the input from the user as well as to initialize the starting period to 1. (See line 17.) The remainder of the algorithm is found in lines 32–40. The condition for the while loop is in line 32, and the formula for computing the new balance is found in lines 33–34. It is broken into two lines to support the output into columns. Now you'll learn about formatted output in C++.

Style: Properly Using Spacing

Languages like C++ allow you to use whitespace such as tabs, spaces, and blank lines to format your programs. Programmers typically use blank lines to separate elements of the code to make it easier to read. For example, in Listing 4.1, the blank line on line 12 separates the variable declarations from the code. The blank lines on lines 15, 18, and 21 make the output prompts and input statements easier to read. You can develop your own style in spacing. You should start by always separating the phases of your program: input, process, and output. Then you should consider putting spaces between lines of code that are not logically performing the same function. For example, because the prompt and input statements work together, there is no space between them; however, the different prompts and inputs could be considered logically different, so the blank line is useful. Finally, consider readability; if your program looks cluttered or is difficult to read, adding blank likes may open things up and improve readability.

C++ FEATURE: FORMATTED OUTPUT

The columns you see in the compound interest output are a result of using formatted output. Formatted output is accomplished in C++ by using the I/O Manipulator library, or iomanip, as it is commonly called. To access this library, you need to include it using the following #include directive:

```
#include <iomanip>
```

This #include directive should be placed at the top of your file with the other #include directives, as shown in Listing 4.1, line 2. This gives you access to a collection of stream manipulators that allow you to format the output stream. Consider line 25:

```
cout << setprecision(2) << fixed;
```

This line uses two manipulators: setprecision(x) and fixed. The setprecision(x) manipulator sets the number of significant digits to use in the output. In this example, it is set to two digits. Your output is going to contain monetary values, so you need just two decimal places for the cents to be displayed. The fixed manipulator puts the output in fixed-point mode, as opposed to scientific notation, which would represent 505.00 as 5.05×10^2. Floating-point output manipulators are summarized in Table 4.1.

The manipulators stay in effect until another manipulator is used in the program that changes the state. So if you use setprecision(2) at some point in the program, all subsequent output of floating-point values shows two significant digits. You can change it by issuing another setprecision(x) later in the program.

The compound interest program has additional manipulators. There is another category of manipulators that affects the output of all data types; these are called *general output manipulators*. A summary of general output manipulators is found in Table 4.2. To see how some of these are used, look at lines 23–24 and 31–32. You see setw(8), setw(13), and setw(12) being used to create the

Table 4.1 Floating-Point Output Manipulators in C++

Name	Description
setprecision(x)	Sets the number of significant digits to display. This affects every output through the remainder of the program. The default precision is 6.
fixed	Sets the output to have a fixed decimal point instead of scientific notation. This affects every output through the remainder of the program.
scientific	Sets the output for floating-point numbers to be in scientific notation. This affects every output through the remainder of the program.
showpoint	Sets the output to always display a decimal point when the value has zeros after the decimal point. This affects every output through the remainder of the program.
showpos	Sets the output to show a plus sign for positive values. This affects every output through the remainder of the program.

Table 4.2 General Output Formatting Manipulators in C++

Name	Description
Setw(x)	Sets the minimum field width to x characters. This applies only to the next outputted item in the stream.
endl	Outputs an end-of-line on the screen so the next output starts on the next line. Immediately applied.
left	Left-justifies the output within a field, and must follow a setw. This applies to the next outputted item in the stream.
right	Right-justifies the output within a field, and must follow a setw. This is the default behavior. It applies to the next outputted item in the stream.
setfill(ch)	Sets the fill character for a field where the data does not fill the field. The default fill character is the space. This affects every output through the remainder of the program.

columns in the table. Adding 2 to the number of characters in the heading determines these values. For example, the string literal period has a length of six characters; therefore, the width of the column is set to 8 = 6 + 2. The other column widths are chosen similarly. Keep in mind that you can also determine your column widths by the size of the data in the columns and not the headings. Do you see the other manipulator that is used? If you said the endl, you're correct! The endl is used on lines 25 and 32 because these lines output the last column and are the end of a row in the table. If you were to put endl on lines 24 and 31, you would split each row of your table and not have the desired format.

The lesson to learn here is that `endl` is not at the end of every output statement. It is not an end-of-statement command; it is a manipulator that changes the format.

If you have typed in the compound interest program, this is a perfect opportunity to experiment with the manipulators that have been discussed in this section. You can use the `left` and `right` manipulators to adjust the justification of the columns. You can use `setfill(ch)` to fill the spaces in the columns with other characters. Remember: experimenting with the language is the best way to learn the language.

The Flexibility of Output Manipulators

Output manipulators are flexible. You can apply them in various ways to create the effect that you want to see. They do not affect the computation, and using them in different orders does not cause compiler or run-time errors. For example, all of the following produce something:

```
cout << varx << endl << vary << endl << varz;
cout << setw(5) << left << varx << setw(5) << vary << endl << endl << setw(5)
    << total;
cout << setprecision(2) << setprecision (3) << showpos << varx << endl;
```

These examples show that you can use `endl` in the middle of an output statement, you can use several `endl` manipulators consecutively, you can mix manipulators, or you can use manipulators that semantically override one another, where only the last `setprecision` affects `varx`. Feel free to explore the manipulators, and have fun with them!

COMPUTING THE SQUARE ROOT

You can compute square roots using several algorithms. You will learn how square roots are computed using the Newton-Raphson method. You will also see some features of the C++ language that are useful with some numerical problems, including the C++ math library and the idea of convergence.

Background: Newton-Raphson

The Newton-Raphson method is a popular algorithm that comes from an area of math and computer science called *numerical analysis*. This algorithm is named after two mathematicians: Isaac Newton and Joseph Raphson. You have most likely heard of Isaac Newton as the mathematician who formulated the understanding of gravity and the laws of motion. Newton wrote his version of this algorithm in 1671 in French as part of other writings, but the English version was not translated and published until 1736 by John Colson. Joseph Raphson published his version of the method in 1690. Both were independent versions of similar methods written in different languages, but Raphson wrote the simpler version, and it is the version that is used in textbooks and this book.

The Newton-Raphson algorithm uses a fundamental law of calculus, but don't worry, you are not expected to know calculus to understand this algorithm. This method is generally used to find the solutions to polynomials. A polynomial is a formula that looks like these examples:

$ax^2 + bx + c$ is the general format

$x^2 + 3x - 4$

$2x^2 + 5x + 2$

The first example is the general format for a polynomial where the a, b, and c would be numbers or coefficients. Polynomials have values for x that make the polynomial evaluate to 0. Because these polynomials have an x^2, there are two values for x that cause the polynomials to evaluate to 0. These values for x are called the *roots of the polynomial*. Roots are found by factoring the polynomial. Here is how factoring is applied to the preceding polynomials:

$x^2 + 3x - 4 = (x - 1)(x + 4)$ and the roots are $x = 1$ and $x = -4$

$2x^2 + 5x + 2 = (2x + 1)(x + 4)$ and has the roots $x = -1/2$ and $x = -4$

In these examples, you have two factors for each polynomial. The values for x are obtained by determining how each factor can become a 0. For example, the factor $(x + 4)$ is 0 if $x = -4$. You can substitute the other values for x into the other factors to see that a 0 is produced for each. Now this idea can be applied to finding square roots.

To find the sqrt(N), you need to solve the following polynomial: $0 = x^2 - N$. The roots for this polynomial are $x = 3$ and $x = -3$, because if you substitute these values for x, the polynomial will be 0. Now because the square root has to be a nonnegative number, the square root is 3. Therefore, if an algorithm can solve these special polynomials, it can be used to find the square root of any number.

You can apply the Newton-Raphson method to this special polynomial. You end up with this equation:

$$x_{new} = x - (x^2 - N) / (2x)$$

The transformation of polynomial is based on calculus, but understanding this transformation is not required to understand how it is used. This equation computes a new x based on an old x. Each time a new value of x is computed, the values get closer to the sqrt(N). In the next section, you will see an example of how this is used in an algorithm.

Algorithm: Computing the Square Root

The formula from the previous section is used as part of an iterative algorithm that converges on the square root. *Convergence* occurs when a formula or algorithm is applied repeatedly until the same answer or nearly the same answer is produced. As an example, apply Newton-Raphson to finding the square root of 512. Because you don't know the square root, the algorithm requires that you make a guess to get started. The initial guess in this example is that the square root is 10, so the first value for substitution is x = 10:

$$x_{new} = 10 - (10^2 - 512) / (2 \times 10) = 30.6 \text{ (this becomes the next x)}$$
$$x_{new} = 30.6 - (30.6^2 - 512) / (2 \times 30.6) = 23.7$$
$$x_{new} = 23.7 - (23.7^2 - 512) / (2 \times 23.7) = 22.7$$
$$x_{new} = 22.7 - (22.7^2 - 512) / (2 \times 22.7) = 22.6$$
$$x_{new} = 22.6 - (22.6^2 - 512) / (2 \times 22.6) = 22.6$$

This example shows how the same formula is applied several times, where the X_{new} value is used as the x value in the next application. Each application of the formula produces a result that seems to converge onto a single value. In this case, the convergence is 22.6. The same value is produced in steps 4 and 5, so the algorithm is said to have "converged." In some cases it may take more or fewer steps to find convergence. The following is a pseudocode algorithm to do the same computation automatically:

```
Current = 10
theNumber = 512
```

```
Repeat
    Previous = Current
    Current = Previous - (Previous^2 - theNumber)/(Previous*2)
    Difference = |Previous - Current|
While Difference is not close to 0
Print "The square root is ", Current
```

This algorithm applies the same formula within the loop. The current value represents the current approximation of the square root. Initially, the current value of 10 is a best guess of the square root. The previous value is the previous guess of the square root. The difference is how the algorithm determines how close the current approximation is to the last approximation. If the two approximations are the same, the difference will be 0 (just like in the example where step 5 and step 4 have 22.6). When the two values are close to 0, the loop exits and the current value is the square root.

The next section shows the C++ program that is derived from the preceding algorithm.

The C++ Program: Computing the Square Root

This C++ program finds square roots by using the Newton-Raphson method. This program demonstrates the following numerical programming principles:

- Handling of numeric convergence
- Using functions in a program
- Using the C++ math library

Listing 4.2 is a C++ program to implement the algorithm.

Listing 4.2 Computing Square Root in C++

```
1: #include <iostream>    // The C++ I/O library
2: #include <cmath>       // The C++ math library
3: #include <iomanip>     // The C++ I/O Manipulator library
4:
5:
6:  using namespace std;
7:
8:  // Function prototypes
```

```
9:   double fx(double x, double square);
10: double fxPrime(double x);
11:
12:
13: int main()
14: {
15:
16:     double current;        // Current sqrt approximation
17:     double previous;       // Previous sqrt approximation
18:     double theNumber;      // Number to get root of
19:     double thePrecision;   // Precision error
20:
21:
22:     // Get input from the user
23:     cout << "Enter number to find square root for: ";
24:     cin >> theNumber;
25:
26:
27:     // Make an initial guess
28:     if (theNumber < 100)
29:         current = 2;
30:     else
31:         current = 10;
32:
33:
34:     // This loop computes approximate sqrts and compares
35:     // approximations of consecutive iterations until
36:     // the difference is less than 0.001
37:     do {
38:         previous = current;
39:
40:         // Compute next approximation
41:         current = previous - fx(previous, theNumber)/fxPrime(previous);
42:
43:         // Output approximations to show convergence
44:         cout << setprecision(3) << fixed << current << endl;
45:
46:         // Determine how close the approximations are
47:         thePrecision = current - previous;
48:
```

```
49:
50:      } while (abs(thePrecision) > 0.001);
51:
52:      cout << "The Square Root is " << fixed;
53:      cout << setprecision(3) << current << endl;
54:
55:      return 0;
56: }
57:
58:
59: // This function computes the F(x) = x^2 - square numerator in the
60: // Newton-Raphson, where square is the number you are getting the
61: // square root of.
62: double fx(double x, double square) {
63:      return pow(x, 2.0) - square;
64: }
65:
66:
67: // This function computes the F'(x) = 2*x denominator of the
68: // Newton-Raphson method.
69: double fxPrime(double x) {
70:      return 2*x;
71: }
```

This C++ program implements the algorithm for finding the square root using the Newton-Raphson method. One of the key elements of this program is that it must determine if two successive iterations are generating approximate square root values that are equivalent or near equivalent. This is done on lines 41–47. On line 41, the new approximation is computed using the previous approximation; the new value is set to current. In line 47, the difference between the previous and current approximations is computed. If the difference is 0, the two approximations are identical, and the algorithm converges to an answer that is the square root. However, in C++, these approximations are floating-point values with several decimal places of precision. For example, it's possible to have previous = 22.612312 and current = 22.612214. If you subtract these two values, you get 0.000098, which is not 0, but it is close to 0. As the programmer, you have to determine what difference is the threshold for considering the two values the same. In the program in Listing 4.2, the threshold is 0.001, so any difference between `current` and `previous` that is less than 0.001 is considered 0. This is shown in line 50, where the absolute value of the difference (to remove negatives) is compared to 0.001. This is a standard way of handling convergence. You can increase the precision by adding more leading zeros or decrease the precision by removing leading zeros.

Another concept used here is the use of functions. It is common to use functions in programs to make them easier to read and to maintain. Functions are natural in numerical programs where formulas are usually expressed as mathematical functions `F(x)`, `G(x, y)`, and `H(y)`. For example, you have the following:

$$F(x) = 3x + 2$$

The name of this function is `F`, and `x` is called the *argument* to the function. The `3x + 2` is called the *definition* of the function. This `F(x)` function can compute `F(2)`, `F(10)`, and `F(15)` by substituting for x. If you do this, you find that F(2) = 3(2) + 2 = 8, F(10) = 3(10) + 2 = 32, and F(15) = 3(15) + 2 = 45 + 2 = 47.

In the square root program in Listing 4.2, functions were used for the numerator and denominator for the formula in line 41. The numerator is `fx(x, square)`, which computes the x^2 square that is found in the definition of the Newton-Raphson formula. The denominator uses the function `fxPrime(x)`, which computes 2 * x, which is also from the Newton-Raphson formula. These functions are actually defined in the program on lines 62–71. The next section discusses the details for defining your own functions. Other functions are used in this program: `pow(x, y)` and `fabs(x)`. These functions compute x^y and $|x|$, respectively. They are not defined in the program but are found in the math library. This library is also discussed later in this chapter.

C++ FEATURE: FUNCTIONS

Functions are a mechanism in C++ where you can assign a name to a block of statements to be reused. A function is also considered an abstraction for an algorithm. You can use the function without knowing the details of the algorithm that performs the function. You can use the `pow()` function at line 56 to raise a value to a particular exponent; however, it's not necessary to know how the algorithm operates to achieve this task.

Functions as Tasks

Functions are sometimes called the tasks of a program. When you are developing a program, you identify the tasks that the algorithm needs. A task should become a function if it requires more than a handful of statements, may be used more than once by the program, or can be viewed as an independent entity. Consider the following tasks:

1. Update the number of registered voters.

2. Read inventory data from a file.

3. Compute the average rainfall for the year.

4. Print the score.

5. Make sure the input value is between 1 and 10.

All of these are tasks, but they are not all functions. The first task can be done with a statement that increments a variable; this is not a function. The second task is a function because it requires opening and testing the file and then the instructions to read the data properly. The third task is a function, because computing the average requires accumulating a sum and performing division. The fourth task is not a function; a variable for the score can be outputted with a single statement. The final task is not a function; this is usually part of a function that reads input values.

As you gain experience and read along in this book, you will get better at identifying which tasks are functions and which are just parts of other functions.

Functions in Pseudocode

Functions are determined during the analysis and design phase of writing programs. Therefore, you need to write functions in your pseudocode. The format for a function in pseudocode is as follows:

```
Function <Name of Function>(<Parameters>)
    <Body of the Function>
End Function
```

The <Name of Function> in the first line is the name to use when you need the function in other parts of your algorithm. The <Parameters> are the data you must give to the function so that it can perform its operation. The `<Body of the Function>` is the algorithm that the function uses to perform its task:

```
Function SumRange(start, end)
    sum = 0
    While start <= end Do
    sum = sum + start
    incrememt sum
    End While
    Return sum
End Function
```

This function returns the value of the sum of values in the range start – end. The name of the function is `SumRange`. The parameters are `start` and `end`, which represent the beginning and end of the range of values. The body of the function is the statements that compute the actual sum. The return statement at the end of the body tells you what value the function returns to the part of the algorithm that is using it.

Once you have defined the function, you can use it in other parts of your algorithm. You may use a function as many times as you want:

```
mySum = SumRange(1, 100)
Output mysum
Input value1 and value2
anotherSum = SumRange(value1, value2)
Output anotherSum
```

There are two examples of a *function call*. In a function call, an algorithm uses or calls on a function to perform tasks. The algorithm here has called on `SumRange` twice. The first time it was to sum the values from 1 to 100. The second call sums the range that the user specified through the input statements. The same algorithm is used both times but produces different results. As you can see, using functions can also save space because you are able to reuse the algorithm without having to rewrite it each time you use it.

This is just one example of a function you could write; you will see more functions throughout the remaining chapters of this book. Now you need to learn how to write a function in C++.

Functions in C++

Functions in C++ serve the same purpose and motivation as the functions in your pseudocode. In C++, you have programmer-defined functions and library functions. *Library functions* are predefined functions that you do not have to create because another programmer wrote them for you to use. You will see the math library in the next section. *Programmer-defined functions* are those that you write for your program.

Creating a C++ function means that you need to create two parts:

- **A function prototype.** The declaration of a function is its name, parameters, and type of return value.

- **A function definition.** The definition of the function is the algorithm that the function executes to complete the task.

The function prototype is how you declare that the function exists in your program. It's similar to declaring a variable to your program. It must be done before the function is used, and it's placed outside and before the `main()` function. Sample prototypes are shown in Listing 4.2, lines 9 and 10. A C++ function prototype has the following syntax:

```
<return type> <function name>(<parameter types>);
```

The `<return type>` is any data type such as `int`, `float`, and `string`. It is the type of value that the function can return. The `<function name>` is the name of the function that the program uses. And the `<parameter types>` are comma-separated types for the parameters. The following are sample prototypes:

```
int SumRange(int, int);
int FindMax(int, int, int);
void DisplayResults(float, int);
```

These prototypes have different types of parameters and varying quantities of parameters. Some functions won't have a value to return. An example may be a function that outputs information. These functions should have a return type of `void`. The `void` type is an empty type that refers to no data.

The definition of a function is a combination of function header, which resembles the prototype, and function body, which holds the statements for the function. The syntax for a function definition is listed here:

```
<return type> <function name>(<parameter names and types>) {
    <local variable declarations>
    <body>
}
```

The `<return type>`, `<function name>`, and `<parameter names and types>` are the function headers. The curly braces and the `<body>` are the function body. The `<local variable declarations>` are variables that are declared within the function. These variables are visible only within the body or scope of the function. This means it is okay to use names that you have used in other functions, including `main()`, because the variables represent different storage locations in memory. The `<parameter names and types>` is a comma-separated list of types and parameter names. These parameters or arguments are called *formal parameters* or *arguments* because they are part of the definition of the function. The list of parameters resembles a list of variable declarations. Here are a few function headers based on the earlier prototypes:

```
int SumRange(int start, int end) {...}
int FindMax(int num1, int num2, int num3) {...}
void DisplayResults(float tax, int month) {...}
```

The parameters in the headers need names inside the function to create the algorithm inside. Consider the definition in Listing 4.3.

Listing 4.3 The SumRange() Function

```
int SumRange(int start, int end) {
    int sum = 0;
    while (start <= end) {
    sum = sum + start;
    ++sum;
    }
    return sum;
}
```

Listing 4.3 shows the definition of the `SumRange()` function written in C++. You can see that the parameters `start` and `end` are used in the algorithm. These names are visible only within the body of this function. In addition, a *local* variable is declared inside the function declaration. The return value is stored in `sum`, and the type of the return value must be equivalent to the `<return type>` of the function.

This concludes the introduction to programmer-defined functions in C++. There will be more to learn about functions in later chapters. The next section discusses a special set of library functions that perform popular mathematical operations.

C++ FEATURE: THE MATH LIBRARY

C++ has many libraries to support your programming. You have seen the use of the iostream, string, and iomanip libraries. The square root computation program uses the math library in C++. The math library is added to your programs by using the following statement with the other #include statements:

```
#include <cmath>
```

This statement includes the C++ math library, which is actually an interface to the math library for C. The math library includes a collection of functions that you can use in your programs. The first example is found on line 43, where the condition uses the fabs function. The prototype for fabs is:

```
double fabs (double x)
```

The function computes the absolute value of a floating-point value x. This means that it returns the distance from 0 for the value. So a negative value is converted to a positive value. See Table 4.3 for examples of using the fabs function. The second function from this library is pow on line 56. This function has the following prototype:

```
double pow (double base, double exponent)
```

This function takes the base and exponent and returns the result of raising base to the exponent power. Examples of the pow function are found in Table 4.3.

Table 4.3 Examples of pow and fabs

Example	Result
fabs(5.0)	5.0
fabs(-5.0)	5.0
pow(2.0, 4.0)	16.0
pow(3.0, 3.0)	27.0

These are two examples of the many functions found in the C++ math library. There are functions in the math library for trigonometry, exponents, logarithms, and rounding. Table 4.4 summarizes the other functions found in the C++ math library.

Table 4.4 Summary of C++ Math Library Functions

Function Prototype	Description
`double cos(double x)`	Compute the cosine from trigonometry
`double sin(double x)`	Compute the sine from trigonometry
`double tan(double x)`	Compute the tangent from trigonometry
`double acos(double x)`	Compute the inverse or arccosine from trigonometry
`doublecasin(double x)`	Compute the inverse or arcsine from trigonometry
`double atan(double x)`	Compute the inverse or arctan from trigonometry
`double exp(x)`	Compute the exponential of x, which is e^x
`double log(double x)`	Compute the log of x using base e
`double log10(double x)`	Compute the log of x using base 10
`double floor(double x)`	Computes the floor of x (rounding down to the nearest integer)
`double ceil(double x)`	Computes the ceiling of x (rounding up to the nearest integer)

The C++ math library examples shown here use doubles as the parameters. However, you should be aware that these functions are overloaded to have versions that use `int` and `float` as well. For a full comprehensive set of functions, you can consult online references for the C++ library or a C++ reference manual.

C++ Feature: Counting Loops

Numerical problems like compound interest typically involve some form of counting. For example, in compound interest, you are counting the number of periods. In other programs you might be counting the number of experimental observations from which data is taken when analyzing data values, the number of exams taken by students when computing averages or standard deviations, or the number of pitches made by a pitcher in a baseball game when counting balls and strikes.

C++ has a loop that is particularly designed for counting purposes. This loop is called a for loop. The for loop has the following format:

```
for (<initialize>; <boolean expression>; <update>) {
    <statements>
}
```

The <initialize> is executed only once when entering the loop and initializes the counter for the loop. The <boolean expression> determines when the loop should continue or stop, and the <update> is where the counter is updated. The easiest way to understand the for loop is to see an example that compares it to the while loop. The following while loop would output values 1, 2, . . . , N:

```
count = 1;
while (count <= N) {
    cout << count << endl;
    count++;
}
```

This loop outputs the numbers from 1 to N. The variable count is the loop counter, and it is initialized, checked, and updated. One of the problems with using while loops in this situation is that the initialization, check, and update of the counter variable are separated. The for loop brings them all together for convenience. Consider the following equivalent for loop:

```
for (count = 1; count <= N; count++) {
    cout << count << endl;
}
```

This loop shows a for loop that also counts from 1 to N. You can see that it is more compact and places all the operations that affect the counter in the header of the loop.

Suppose you were to rewrite the compound interest program using a for loop. You would have a program like the one shown in Listing 4.4.

Listing 4.4 Compound Interest in C++ (Using for Loops)

```
1: #include <iostream>
2: #include <iomanip>    // Input/output manipulation objects
3:
4: using namespace std;
5:
```

```
6: int main () {
7:      int periods;                // The number of interest-bearing periods
8:      double rate;                // The annual interest percentage rate
9:      double interest = 0.;       // The interest in the current period
10:     double balance;             //  The current account balance
11:     int currPeriod;             //  The counter to keep track of periods
12:
13:     cout << "Please enter the number of periods: ";
14:     cin >> periods;
15:
16:     cout << "Please enter the annual interest rate: ";
17:     cin >> rate;
18:
19:     cout << "Please enter the starting balance: ";
20:     cin >> balance;
21:
22:
23:     // Two decimal places of precision
24:     cout << setprecision(2) << fixed;
25:
26:     // Set up the table header
27:     cout << setw(8) << "Period" << setw(13) << "Interest($)";
28:     cout << setw(12) << "Balance($)" << endl;
29:
30:     // This loop computes interest and balance for each period
31:     for (currPeriod = 1; currPeriod <= periods; currPeriod++) {
32:             interest = balance * rate/12.0;
33:             balance  = balance + interest;
34:
35:             cout << setw(8) << currPeriod << setw(13) << interest;
36:             cout << setw(12) << balance << endl;
37:
38:     }
39:
40:     return 0;
41: }
```

The code in Listing 4.4 is similar to the code in Listing 4.1. The difference is that the while loop is replaced by an equivalent for loop. The for loop uses the variable currPeriod as the loop counter. It is initialized, checked, and updated within the header of the for loop instead of being distributed throughout the program as it was in Listing 4.1.

Don't think of the for loop as a better loop than the while loop or vice versa. Every loop written with a while loop can be written with a for loop. Base the distinction on the context of the problem. If you are writing a loop where counting is the focus, the preference is given to the for loop. If counting is not the focus of the loop, the preference is given to the while loop.

Summary

This chapter focused on issues related to working with numerical problems in C++. Numerical problems appear in science, business, mathematics, and many other disciplines. It's useful to know how to approach solutions to numerical problems. If you pursue computer science in college, you may take a course in numerical analysis that will go deeper into this interesting field.

Discussing the solutions to numerical problems introduced C++ features that you can use in other programs but are particularly useful in numerical analysis: I/O formatting and the math library. I/O formatting requires the use of the I/O Manipulator library (iomanip). It has a collection of output manipulators that allow you to control the presentation of floating-point values as well as how values are displayed as tables with well-formatted columns. The C++ Math library (cmath) provides a collection of functions that are useful in numerical algorithms for various domains.

Exercises

The following questions test your knowledge of the material from this chapter. You can find the answers to these questions on the book's companion website at www.courseptr.com/downloads.

1. Write a C++ program that converts Celsius to Fahrenheit and Fahrenheit to Celsius. Your program should display a menu to select the type of conversion, and then the user will input the temperature and output the proper conversion. Your program should have a function for each type of conversion. The following formulas can be used:

    F = 9 / 5 C + 32
    C = 5 / 9 (F − 32)

2. Solutions for quadratic functions can be found using iterative methods, such as the function $3x^2 - 10x + 6$. Using algebra, you can get this:

   $$x_{new} = (10x - 6 / 3x)$$

   You can use this to iteratively converge on an x that is a solution for the original function. Assume that x = 4 initially, and write a program that computes the root iteratively. You should try to use functions to solve this problem.

3. Write a C++ program that computes the standard deviation for a collection of numbers. The program should ask the user how many numbers need to be entered and then input that many numbers. To compute the standard deviation, first compute the average of the numbers. Then process the numbers again to sum the difference between each number and the average, and compute the average difference. This is the standard deviation. You need an array to process the input values to compute the average and then to compute the sum of differences.

4. Write a C++ program that creates a table of the sin(x), cos(x), and tan(x) for x ranging from 0 to 2 * pi radians at increments of 0.1 radians. Your table should have a column for x that contains the radian values and a column for cos(x), sin(x), and tan(x). Your table should be formatted with 10 characters per column and 5 decimal places for all values.

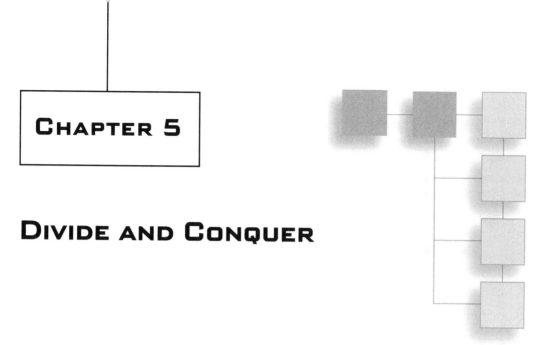

CHAPTER 5

DIVIDE AND CONQUER

In This Chapter

- Real-Life Illustrations
- Divide and Conquer in Computer Programming

> Don't be afraid to give your best to what seemingly are small jobs.
> Every time you conquer one it makes you that much stronger. If you
> do the little jobs well, the big ones will tend to take care of themselves.
>
> —Dale Carnegie, Author

Divide and conquer is a popular problem-solving technique that is frequently used in computer science. In computer science, many of the problems that we attempt to solve are complex and can be overwhelming. Divide and conquer uses the following principles:

- Divide the problem into a collection of smaller, less complex subproblems.
- Solve each subproblem, and rejoin these solutions to solve the original problem.

Developing solutions using divide and conquer is a skill that takes time to master. Divide and conquer solutions have been worked on since about 200 B.C. This approach to solving problems has many advantages, including the ability to solve difficult problems. The solutions are usually efficient for computers to execute. And it is usually possible to divide the algorithm among a collection of CPUs to solve each subproblem concurrently. (This is known as *parallel programming*.) There are some downsides to using divide and conquer, however. It can be difficult to design a solution, but this is where experience is helpful. Many of the divide and conquer algorithms employ the use of recursive function calls. Recursive functions require lots of memory and CPU resources that may be prohibitive. Recursive solutions can also be written with loops. Recursion can often be used to find the solution, which is then translated to a loop-style solution.

In this chapter, you explore real-world examples of employing this strategy to help you better understand how useful the strategy is for problem solving. You also explore the concept of recursion and recursive functions. Next, you are led through the development of a solution to a problem that uses divide and conquer. Finally, you explore some traditional algorithms that are called *divide and conquer algorithms* because of their approach to solving the problem.

REAL-LIFE ILLUSTRATIONS

Sometimes it is helpful to explain programming concepts as a relationship to everyday occurrences, because programming computers can be an abstract idea. Many people have trouble with strictly thinking in the abstract. Divide and conquer is one of these types of topics. There are two examples to illustrate the ideas behind divide and conquer. The first example is building a house, and the second is with fundraising at your school.

Building a house is a large and complex problem that requires a lot of work and coordination. A general contractor who builds a house does not do so without help. The contractor breaks down the project into smaller problems that might include the following:

■ Building the foundation

■ Framing the house

- Installing electrical
- Installing plumbing
- Installing heating and air conditioning
- Installing drywall
- Painting
- Installing fixtures

These smaller problems are much easier to understand and to complete. After completing these smaller problems, the house will be complete.

Fundraising at your school is another example of divide and conquer. The problem could be to raise $20,000 to purchase new computers. If one family in the school was asked to raise this money on its own by selling products to family members and friends, the problem would be overwhelming. However, the fundraiser committee divides the responsibility among all the families in the school. If you have 1,000 families, each family can raise $20 instead of one family raising $20,000.

In both examples, a large problem is subdivided into smaller subproblems that are easier to solve. After solving the subproblems, the results can be joined to complete the larger problem. In the next section, you learn about two common problems in programming that illustrate the use of divide and conquer.

DIVIDE AND CONQUER IN COMPUTER PROGRAMMING

In computer programming, you are working with different types of problems than the real-life examples presented in the previous section. Usually, you use divide and conquer to develop a faster algorithm. For example, the problem is that you need to search for an item in a large collection of data. Another example is that you need to take a large collection of data and sort it. Sorting means that you are putting the data in order, perhaps by organizing a list of names in alphabetical order or a list of grades in descending order.

In computer programming, divide and conquer is usually expressed using functions. Functions are a way to divide the work of a program into tasks. They operate the same way that the work for building a house was divided into tasks to solve the subproblems.

Searching: Looking for Data

The search problem is that, given a list of data, you want an algorithm that can determine if a target data item is in the list. This problem appears in many computer applications. For example, if you have a contacts list on your phone, you probably have a search feature. The search feature is where you enter the name of the person you are looking for, and the phone finds the person and displays the contact information. Another example is searching for a song in your music library or on your MP3 player. To solve this problem and to explore divide and conquer, you are introduced to two search algorithms.

Linear Search

Linear search is probably the most obvious searching algorithm. You start searching at the beginning of the list, and you compare your target with each item in the list until you have found the matching item or until you reach the end of the list. Listing 5.1 is a pseudocode algorithm for linear search.

Listing 5.1 Linear Search Algorithm

```
Given: A list of N names referenced as Name₁, Name₂,....,Nameₙ
Output "Enter the name you are looking for: "
Input target
Set position = 1
Set found = false
While found = false and position <=   Do
    If Name_position = target Then
        Output "Found name at position: ", position
        Found = true
    End If
    Increment position
End While
If found = false Then
    Output "Sorry, the name was not found"
End If
```

The algorithm in this listing is a subscript. Lists were discussed in Chapter 2, "The Nature of the Problems and Solutions," and Chapter 3, "Introduction to the Core C++ Language." The algorithm asks the user to enter a name he needs to find in the list. The position variable is used as a subscript for the names in the list. An example is in the `if` statement, where $Name_{position}$ is a name at a position in the list. The `position` variable starts with the value 1 and is incremented in the list until it reaches N. The `if` statement is `true` if there is a match to target in the list. If there is a match, the user is notified of the position of the name, and the `found` variable is set to `true`. The `found` variable exits the `while` loop if the name is found before search reaches the end of the list. If `found` is still `false`, the name was not found in the list.

How about trying the algorithm on some data so you better understand it? Suppose you have a list of 10 names:

1. Felicia

2. Erin

3. CJ

4. Marcus

5. Brian

6. Erica

7. Franklin

8. Lamar

9. Casey

10. Mary

Then you can use a table trace to see how the algorithm works. The table would have a column for each variable: `target`, `position`, $Name_{position}$, and `found`. The following is an example table trace where the user inputs the name `CJ`.

target	position	Name$_{position}$	found
CJ	1	Felicia	false
	2	Erin	
	3	CJ	true
	4		

The table trace shows how the algorithm would start by comparing CJ to Felicia. The `position` variable corresponds to the position of the names in the list used for comparison. When the names match, the found variable is set to true, and the loop exits. You should try another example, where the user searches for another name in the list. Or you could develop your own list and try it.

Playing Computer

If you have a friend who is learning to program or a friend who could help you, you can act as the computer would, which may help you understand algorithms better. Have your friend read the algorithm step by step, while you update the table after each step. This allows you to focus on how the table updates, and it keeps you from looking ahead in the algorithm, which can cause you to miss steps. You can also switch, meaning that as you read the algorithm, your friend updates the table.

You can write this algorithm in C++. Listing 5.2 is the C++ program for the algorithm shown in Listing 5.1.

Listing 5.2 C++ Program for Linear Search

```
 1: #include <iostream>
 2: #include <string>
 3:
 4: using namespace std;
 5:
 6: const int N = 10;      // Maximum size of list
 7:
 8: int main()
 9: {
10:      // Declare variables
11:
12:      // A list of names
13:      string Name[N] = {"Felicia", "Erin", "CJ", "Marcus", "Brian",
14:                        "Erica", "Franklin", "Lamar", "Casey", "Mary"};
15:      string target;          // The name to search for
16:      int position = 0;       // The current position in the list
17:      bool found = false;     // Result of search
18:
19:      cout << "Enter the name you are looking for: ";
20:      cin >> target;
21:
22:      // Examine the list from the beginning position to the end of
```

```
23:       // the list until the name is found or the end of the list is
24:       // reached.
25:       while (found == false && position < N) {
26:           if (Name[position] == target) {   // If name is found
27:               cout << "Found name at position: " << position << endl;
28:               found = true;
29:           }
30:           position++;       // Increment to the next list position
31:       }
32:
33:       // Determine if a name was not found
34:       if (found == false) {
35:           cout << "Sorry, the name was not found" << endl;
36:       }
37:
38:       return 0;
39: }
```

The linear search algorithm and program are not based on divide and conquer. To compare it to the divide and conquer versions, you should examine the algorithm or program and determine the maximum number of times the if statement is executed on a given set of data. Linear search will have its maximum number of comparisons when the name you are looking for is not in the list. This will cause the algorithm to execute the if statement 10 times, once for each name in the list. You can generalize this answer by recognizing that, for a list of length N, the maximum number of comparisons is still based on one comparison per name. There are N names, so the maximum number of comparisons is also N.

Binary Search

Binary search is an alternate search algorithm for finding an item in a list. Binary search requires that the list be sorted. For example, it can be used in the contacts example where the names are alphabetically arranged. The idea behind the algorithm is to check whether the name is in the middle of the list. If it is, you are finished; if it is not, you determine whether the item is in the left half (names that are alphabetically before the name in the middle) or in the right half (names that are alphabetically after the name in the middle). Consider looking for a word in a dictionary. You could begin by opening the book halfway and determine if the word is in the first half or the second half. If you decide it is in the first half, then you have eliminated having to search half of the book. This is a powerful concept for searching because once your decision is made, you can eliminate the half where the target name cannot be found and repeat the same algorithm on the half that can contain the target name.

Listing 5.3 is a pseudocode algorithm for binary search. The algorithm in this listing uses a function for the majority of the computation. The algorithm starts by asking the user for a name to search for. Then the algorithm calls the BinarySearch function to determine if the name is in the list of names. The algorithm then displays a message based on the result of the search.

Listing 5.3 Algorithm for Binary Search

```
Given: An alphabetical list of N names called Names(Names₁, Names₂,...,Namesₙ)
Output "Enter the name you are looking for: "
Input target
found = false
found = BinarySearch(Names, 1, 10, target)
If found = true Then
    Output "Congratulations, the name was found"
Else
    Output "Sorry, the name was not found"
End If
Stop
Function BinarySearch(List, start, end, value)
    If start > end Then
        Return false

    middle = roundDown((start + end)/2)
    If Listₘᵢddₗₑ = value
        Return true
    Else If value < Listₘᵢddₗₑ Then
        end = middle - 1
        Return BinarySearch(List, start, end, value)
    Else If value > Listₘᵢddₗₑ
        start = middle + 1
        Return BinarySearch(List, start, end, value)
    Return false
End Function
```

The `BinarySearch` function is where the divide and conquer takes place. Looking closely at the function reveals that the function is using itself. This special use of function calls makes it an example of a recursive function. A *recursive function* is one that is defined by using itself. Recursive functions were first used in mathematics in defining recurrence relations. One of the most popular recurrences is the definition of a factorial. Factorial is expressed as N! = N * (N – 1) * (N – 2) ... 2 * 1. This means that 5! = 5 * 4 * 3 * 2 * 1 = 120. A factorial can also be expressed as a recursive mathematical function:

```
factorial(0) = 1
factorial(n) = n * factorial(n-1)
```

These mathematical statements define how to compute the factorial of any number. For example, the first statement is the base rule for the factorial recurrence that states that 0! = 1. The second rule handles all other cases. You can express 5! as `factorial(5)`. The rules are applied as follows using forward substitution:

```
factorial(5) = 5 * factorial(4), and
factorial(4) = 4 * factorial(3), and
factorial(3) = 3 * factorial(2), and
factorial(2) = 2 * factorial(1), and
factorial(1) = 1 * factorial(0)
```

The last application shows `factorial(0)`, which has the value of 1 according to the base rule. There is a backward substitution that takes place, because now that you know that `factorial(0) = 1`, then `factorial(1) = 1 * 1 = 1`. If you continue to the statement above it:

```
factorial(2) = 2 * factorial(1) = 2 * 1 = 2, and
factorial(3) = 3 * factorial(2) = 3 * 2 = 6, and
factorial(4) = 4 * factorial(3) = 4 * 6 = 24, and
factorial(5) = 5 * factorial(4) = 5 * 24 = 120
```

After the backward substitution, the result is revealed as 120. This is the behavior of recursive functions in C++ as well. The set of forward substitutions is just like function calls, and the backward substitutions are the result of returning from the function calls.

If you apply this idea to the recursive `BinarySearch` function from Listing 5.3, you see how `BinarySearch` works to determine if a name is found in your list. This is the earlier list in alphabetical order:

1. Brian

2. Casey

3. CJ

4. Erica

5. Erin

6. Felicia

7. Franklin

8. Lamar

9. Marcus

10. Mary

Now, suppose you looking for the name Lamar. You would call the function as follows:

```
BinarySearch(Names, 1, 10, "Lamar")
```

Now forward substitution of the function calls can take place, which results in the following sequence of events in the first call:

```
middle = roundDown((10+1)/2) = 5
If List[middle] = "Lamar" is false
Else If "Lamar" < List[middle] is false
Else If "Lamar" > List[middle] is true
      Return Binary(List, 6, 10, "Lamar")
```

This leads to a second call, where the following happens:

```
middle = roundDown((10 + 6)/2) = 8
If List[middle] = "Lamar" is true
      Return true
```

Now backward substitution takes place:

```
Return Binary(List, 6, 10, "Lamar") => Return true
Binary(Names, 1, 10 "Lamar") => true
```

The true is then set to the variable found (see Listing 5.3). Because the found is true, the congratulatory message is displayed.

This divide and conquer algorithm can determine that Lamar is in the list with two executions of the if-then-else statement. If this were the linear search, seven if statement executions would be needed because Lamar is the seventh name in the list. This is a tremendous improvement. If you consider the worst case, as you did with the linear search, the result would be a maximum of 4 comparisons for a list of size 10. In fact, you can use mathematics to determine that the maximum number of comparisons is equal to the $\log_2(10)$. This is significant when you think of searching large lists. For example, if you have a list with 1 billion names, the worst case for linear search is 1 billion comparisons, and the worst case for binary search is 30 comparisons.

Writing this algorithm as C++ is fairly straightforward, like the linear search. Listing 5.4 is the C++ program to demonstrate binary search.

The C++ program in Listing 5.4 is the implementation of the algorithm in Listing 5.3. The call on line 25 uses 0 and 9 instead of 1 and 10. This is because arrays in C++ start at position 0 and not position 1. This is a common mistake for C++ programmers, especially in the beginning.

Listing 5.4 C++ Program for Binary Search

```
1: #include <iostream>
2: #include <string>
3:
4: using namespace std;
5:
6: bool BinarySearch(string[], int, int, string);
7:
8: const int N = 10;     // Maximum size of list
9:
10: int main()
11: {
12:     // Declaring variables
13:
14:     // List of names
15:     string Names[N] = {"Brian",  "Casey", "CJ", "Erica",  "Erin",
16:             "Felicia", "Franklin", "Lamar",  "Marcus", "Mary"};
17:
18:     string target;        // The name to search for
19:     bool found = false;   // Result of search
20:
```

```
21:
22:        cout << "Enter the name you are looking for: ";
23:        cin >> target;
24:
25:        // Calls a recursive function to search for the target in the list
26:        found = BinarySearch(Names, 0, 9, target);
27:
28:        // Display a message based on the result of the search
29:        if (found)
30:            cout << "Congratulations, the name was found";
31:        else
32:            cout << "Sorry, the name was not found";
33:
34:        return 0;
35: }
36:
37: // Name: BinarySearch
38: // Description: This function performs the binary search on an array
39: // of strings.
40: bool BinarySearch(string list[], int start, int end, string value) {
41:        int middle;
42:
43:        // When start is greater than end, value is not in the list
44:        if (start > end)
45:            return false;
46:
47:        // Determine the position of the middle of the list
48:        middle = (start + end)/2;
49:
50:        // Either the middle is the value or the search must continue
51:        // in 1/2 of the remaining list.
52:        if (list[middle] == value)
53:            return true;
54:        else if (value < list[middle]) { // Left half
55:            return BinarySearch(list, start, middle - 1, value);
56:        } else { // Right half
57:            return BinarySearch(list, middle + 1, end, value);
58:        }
59:
60: }
```

Line 28 has an `if` statement where the condition is the variable `found`. At first, this may look like an odd logical expression. However, because `found` is a Boolean variable, it will either be `true` or `false`, which satisfies the requirement to be a logical expression. Therefore, you could use either `found == true` or simply `found`, and it will accomplish the same result.

The `BinarySearch` function is defined just like any other function. It has a prototype on line 6, and the definition is on lines 39–59. The function definition resembles other definitions in the sense that it has a return type and a set of parameters. The body of the function is the same as previous functions, except it has two function calls to itself. This is the recursion implemented in C++. The `BinarySearch` function is designed to return `true` or `false`, so when a call either determines that its sublist has been exhausted or has found the name, it returns `false` or `true`. The `true` or `false` value is propagated in backward substitution to provide the result.

Recursion is a natural way to express algorithms and programs that use divide and conquer. However, this natural expression has costly side effects in implementation. Now you will explore an alternative implementation.

An Alternative Implementation

The recursive implementation of the binary search can be considered costly when executed by a computer. This is because of the number of potential function calls required to solve the problem. Calling functions in languages such as C++ requires the use of a special RAM called a *stack*. The stack manages the parameters, local variables, and function returns. Recursive functions require lots of stack usage when the successive functions are being called during the forward substitution phase. Because RAM is finite, the quantity of parameters and function calls could require more than the available RAM. This will cause your program to crash. In addition, the continuous stack manipulations come at a sacrifice to speed. Therefore, the program executes slower than an alternative implementation of binary search that does not rely on recursion. This alternative implementation replaces the repetition of the recursive calls with a looping structure.

The binary search program shown in Listing 5.5 is an example of how to implement recursion using iteration. Lines 1–35 are identical to the same lines in

Listing 5.4. The function header for the search function on line 39 is identical to the heading in Listing 5.4. The difference is in the body of the function definition. This version does not contain function calls to itself; therefore, it is not a recursive function. Instead, the recursion has been replaced by a while loop. The conditions of the while loop are the same two conditions that were used to exit the recursion:

```
if (start > end)
    return false;
...
if (list[middle] == value)
    return true;
```

These excerpts come from the BinarySearch in Listing 5.4. These two conditions are replaced by while conditions:

```
while (!found && start <= end)
```

The !found expression is true if found is still false, and it is false if found is set to true. This causes the loop to stop if the target value is found, and the variable found is set to true. However, if the target value is never found, found remains false, and the loop continues. The start <= end is related to determining whether the list is empty. In both cases, the opposite logic is used, because in recursion the condition tells the program when to stop the recursion, and in the iterative example it tells the loop when to keep iterating.

Inside the if-then-else statement of Listing 5.5 on lines 52–55, the code is the same as in Listing 5.4 minus the use of the recursive calls. This is because the loop acts as the recursive call; therefore, only the start and end need to be updated properly.

Listing 5.5 C++ Iterative Binary Search

```
1: #include <iostream>
2: #include <string>
3:
4: using namespace std;
5:
6: bool BinarySearch(string[], int, int, string);
7:
8: const int N = 10;      // Maximum size of list
```

```
 9:
10: int main()
11: {
12:     // Declaring variables
13:
14:     // List of names
15:     string Names[N] =  {"Brian",  "Casey", "CJ", "Erica",  "Erin",
16:             "Felicia", "Franklin", "Lamar",  "Marcus", "Mary"};
17:     string target;          // The name to search for
18:     bool found = false;     // Result of search
19:
20:
21:     cout << "Enter the name you are looking for: ";
22:     cin >> target;
23:
24:     // Calls a recursive function to search for the target in the list
25:     found = BinarySearch(Names, 0, 9, target);
26:
27:     // Display a message based on the result of the search
28:     if (found)
29:         cout << "Congratulations, the name was found";
30:     else
31:         cout << "Sorry, the name was not found";
32:
33:     return 0;
34: }
35:
36: // Name: BinarySearch
37: // Description: This function performs the binary search on an array
38: // of strings.
39: bool BinarySearch(string list[], int start, int end, string value) {
40:     bool found = false;
41:     int middle;
42:
43:
44:     // The loop subdivides the list using the indices. It will
45:     // end if found becomes true or if there is no more list to search.
46:     while (!found && start <= end) {
47:
48:         middle = (start + end) / 2;
```

```
49:
50:            if (list[middle] == value)
51:                found = true;
52:            else if (value < list[middle])
53:                end = middle - 1;
54:            else
55:                start = middle + 1;
56:    }
57:
58:    return found;
59:
60: }
```

Sorting: Putting Data in Order

Sorting data occurs when the data elements are arranged in numerical or alphabetical order. To use the Binary Search algorithm, you have to have sorted data; therefore, if you are given unsorted data, you can use a sorting algorithm to sort the data before using the Binary Search. Several sorting algorithms are available. The Quick Sort algorithm is a popular divide and conquer algorithm. It demonstrates the divide and conquer approach and provides another example of recursion.

The Quick Sort algorithm is based on the notion that a list of values is partially sorted if you have a median value (value that is in the middle); the smaller values are on one side, and the larger values are on the other. For example, consider the following arrangement:

5 25 2 10 15 **30** 100 45 88 76

These numbers are just partially sorted. Consider the number 30 as the median value; the numbers on the left are less than 30, and the numbers on the right are greater than 30. This means that 30 is in the correct position for when the list is sorted as shown next:

2 5 10 15 25 **30** 45 76 88 100

Therefore, because 30 is in the correct position, the objective would be to sort the left and right halves of the list. This is the divide and conquer because now the same procedure would be followed on each half: find a median, and then rearrange the list so that the lower values are to the left of the median and the upper values are to the right of the median.

The algorithm for Quicksort is shown in Listing 5.6. There are mainly three function calls. One function, called PartitionData, is where most of the work is done.

Listing 5.6 Quicksort Algorithm

```
Function Quicksort(List, left, right)
   If size(list) >= 3 Then
      medianPoint = PartitionData(List, left, right)
      Quicksort(List, left, medianPoint)
      Quicksort(List, medianPoint+1, right)
   Else
      If List[left] > List[right] Then
         Swap List[left] and List[right]
      Endif
   Endif
End Function
```

The Quicksort function is the algorithm that describes the sorting process. The if statement determines if there are at least three values in the list before doing the sort. If there are at least three values, the list can be divided and sorted. However, the Else is used when there are one or two values in the list. In the former case, you can just swap the one value with itself; in the second case, if the values are out of order, you just swap them. Now go back to where there are three or more values because this is where the work is done. The algorithm first determines where the median position is by using the PartitionData function. This function arranges the list in a partially sorted ordered, as described earlier. After that, the median point is returned. The next two steps are to recursively call the Quicksort function on the left and right halves of the list. The goal here is to sort the numbers lower than the median while also sorting the numbers higher than the median. The left half is based on the sublist from the leftmost position to the median position, and the right half is based on the sublist from the right of the median to the rightmost position. These positions are evident in the recursive function calls in the algorithm. This is the divide and conquer portion of the algorithm. The PartitionData algorithm is shown in Listing 5.7.

Listing 5.7 Partitioning Algorithm

```
Function PartitionData(List, left, right)
    psuedoMedian = List[left]
    moveRight = left+1
    moveLeft = right

    While forever Do
        While List[moveRight] < pseudoMedian and
              Not at beginning of sublist Do
            Increment moveRight
        End While

        While List[moveLeft] > pseudoMedian and
              Not at the end of the sublist Do
            Decrement moveLeft
        End While

        If moveRight < moveLeft
            Swap List[moveLeft] and List[moveRight]
        Else
            Swap List[left] and List[moveLeft]
            Return moveLeft
        End If
    End While
End Function
```

The first problem to solve in partitioning the data is determining the median value. You would have to search the entire list each time to find the actual median value, but this would make the algorithm inefficient and cancel out the efficiency gains of using a divide-and-conquer strategy. Therefore, a heuristic is used instead. A *heuristic* is an educated best guess to make a decision in an algorithm when the exact answer is either unknown or too costly. There are simple heuristics and complex heuristics. Some heuristics are good guesses, and others are poor. In this case, the algorithm opts for a simple heuristic that does not guarantee the true median is identified, so it calls it the pseudoMedian. The PartitionData algorithm assumes the first value in the list, or List[left]. This is done as the first step in the function.

The `while forever` loop is an infinite one that moves a position pointer from the right and from the left of the list. The goal from the right is to find values that are less than the median. The goal from the left is to find values that are greater than the median. When the loop finds a value on the left and one on the right that meet the criteria, it swaps them. After swapping, it goes back to moving the left and right pointer positions until they meet at the position of the `pseudoMedian`. Consider the following unsorted list as the starting point:

30 45 2 88 10 25 100 5 15 76

From the `Quicksort` function in Listing 5.6, the `left = 1` and `right = 10`. The `PartitionData` function would identify `List[left] = List[1] = 30` as the median. The `moveRight` pointer will stop at the 45 because it is greater than the median. The `moveLeft` pointer will first stop on the number 15:

30 **45** 2 88 10 25 100 5 **15** 76

The 45 and the 15 need to be swapped so that the smaller number is on the left, and the larger is on the right. This is handled by the `If` statement at the end of the outer `while` loop to obtain the following list:

30 15 2 **88** 10 25 100 **5** 45 76

The `moveLeft` and `moveRight` pointers will continue to move and stop at 88 and 5. These values are swapped:

30 15 2 5 10 **25** 100 88 45 76

The `moveLeft` and `moveRight` pointers will cross each other, and `moveLeft` will stop at 25. This will cause the algorithm to execute the `Else` clause, where the `pseudoMedian = List[left]` value is swapped with the `List[moveLeft]` value to get the following list:

25 15 2 5 10 **30** 100 88 45 76

This version of the list is where the algorithm has successfully placed the 30 in the proper position. The values to the left are less than 30, and the values to the right are greater than 30. The problem is now divided into two subproblems, one for each half of the list:

- Apply Quicksort to the sublist: **25** 15 2 5 10
- Apply Quicksort to the sublist: **100** 88 45 76

The PartitionData function is then applied to both sublists, identifying 25 and 100 (shown in bold) as the respective pseudoMedian values for the two sublists. The result of applying the partition algorithm on both of these sublists reveals that the chosen medians are actually the largest values in the sublists:

- 10 15 2 5 **25**
- 76 88 45 **100**

This happens because the selection of the median is a heuristic, which means that sometimes it makes a good choice (like the initial choice), and sometimes it makes poor choices (like these). After these sublists are partitioned, the 25 and 100 are placed in the proper positions, and the current state of the list looks like this:

10 15 2 5 **25** 30 76 88 45 **100**

Now you are left with the following subproblems to solve:

- Apply Quicksort to the sublist: **10** 15 2 5
- Apply Quicksort to the sublist: **76** 88 45

The respective pseudoMedian values will be 10 and 76 (shown in bold). After partitioning, the sublists look like the following:

- 2 5 **10** 15
- 45 **76** 88

The resulting state of the list becomes this:

2 5 **10** 15 **25** 30 45 **76** 88 **100**

The bold values are the numbers that Quicksort has placed in their proper places. This leaves the following subproblems:

- Apply Quicksort to the sublist: 2 5
- Apply Quicksort to the sublist: 15

- Apply `Quicksort` to the sublist: 45
- Apply `Quicksort` to the sublist: 88

The remaining subproblems are handled by Listing 5.6 in the `Else` clause because these sublists have fewer than three elements. The single-value sublists are in sorted order, and the values in the two-value sublists are simply swapped as needed. This then results in a list whereby all values are now placed in this list:

2 5 10 15 25 30 45 76 88 100

This example shows how you can apply divide and conquer to sorting via the `Quicksort` algorithm. It also shows how you can use a heuristic to simplify an algorithm's decision-making process. Listing 5.8 shows the C++ implementation of this algorithm.

Listing 5.8 The Quicksort Program

```cpp
1: #include <iostream>
2:
3: using namespace std;
4:
5: int PartitionData(int[], int, int);
6: void Quicksort(int[], int, int);
7:
8:
9: int main()
10: {
11:     // Random list of data
12:     int intData[] = {5, 25, 2, 30, 15, 100, 10, 45, 88, 76};
13:
14:
15:     // Sort the data
16:     Quicksort(intData, 0, 9);
17:
18:     // Output the data to verify sorting
19:     for (int i = 0; i < 10; i++)
20:         cout << intData[i] << endl;
21:
22:     return 0;
```

```
23: }
24:
25:
26: // This function partitions data around the value that is assumed
27: // to be the median value. It places values greater than the median
28: // to the right and values less than the median to the left. The
29: // median is always assumed to be the leftmost value in the array.
30: // Left and right are the indices of the bounds for the partition.
31: int PartitionData(int data[], int left, int right)
32: {
33:     int pseudoMedian;
34:     int moveLeft;
35:     int moveRight;
36:     int temp;
37:
38:     pseudoMedian = data[left];      // Choose median as the leftmost value
39:     moveRight = left+1;      // Start moving from the left position
40:     moveLeft = right;        // Start moving from the right position
41:
42:
43:     // This loop continues until the left and right pointers
44:     // meet. This means that all elements have been partitioned
45:     while (true) {
46:
47:         // This loop moves the pointer to the right as long as
48:         // the number at that position is less than the
49:         // pseudoMedian
50:         while (data[moveRight] < pseudoMedian &&
51:             moveRight < right) {
52:             moveRight++; // Move to the right one element
53:         }
54:
55:         // This loop moves the pointer to the left as long as
56:         // the number at that position is greater than the
57:         // pseudoMedian
58:         while (data[moveLeft] > pseudoMedian &&
59:             moveLeft > left) {
60:             moveLeft-; // Move to the left one element
61:         }
62:
```

```
63:              // If the moving left and right pointers have not
64:              // crossed, the two values should be swapped
65:              // to their proper sides
66:              if (moveRight < moveLeft) {
67:                  temp = data[moveRight];
68:                  data[moveRight] = data[moveLeft];
69:                  data[moveLeft] = temp;
70:              }
71:              else {
72:                  // Swap the pseudoMedian into place
73:                  temp = data[moveLeft];
74:                  data[moveLeft] = data[left];
75:                  data[left] = temp;
76:                  return moveLeft; // The position of the median
77:              }
78:
79:      }
80: }
81:
82:
83:
84: // This function executes the Quicksort algorithm. The
85: // left and right are the indices representing the bounds of
86: // the array that are to be sorted.
87: void Quicksort(int data[], int left, int right)
88: {
89:      int splitPoint;   // Position of the pseudoMedian
90:      int temp;         // used for swapping
91:
92:      // If left passes right, there is nothing to process
93:      if (left > right)
94:              return;
95:
96:      // If there are three or more elements in the list, then Quicksort
97:      if (left < (right - 1)) {
98:
99:          // Find a pseudoMedian
100:         splitPoint = PartitionData(data, left, right);
101:
102:         // Sort around the pseudoMedian
```

```
103:            Quicksort(data, left, splitPoint);
104:            Quicksort(data, splitPoint+1, right);
105:
106:    } else {
107:        // Swap the two elements if they are out of order
108:        if (data[left] > data[right]) {
109:            temp = data[right];
110:            data[right] = data[left];
111:            data[left] = temp;
112:        }
113:    }
114: }
```

For the most part, this is a direct translation of the algorithm into C++. One of the differences is that the algorithm used the Swap abstraction to indicate that the values need to be swapped. In C++ and many other languages, the swapping of values requires three lines of code:

```
Temporary = A
A = B
B = Temporary
```

These three lines of code are the template for swapping the values in variables A and B. First, the value in A is copied to the Temporary variable so that the second instruction does not destroy the value stored in A. This technique is used in Listing 5.8 on lines 67–69, 73–75, and 109–111.

SUMMARY

In this chapter, you learned about a strategy called divide and conquer. The chapter started by discussing some examples of divide and conquer in real-life problems. Then you learned how to perform search using both linear and divide and conquer algorithms. These algorithms are called linear search and binary search. The linear search is implemented using a brute-force approach that starts at the beginning of the list and checks each value until the target is found. The binary search is implemented using divide and conquer to eliminate half of the list after each comparison. In addition, the Quicksort algorithm was shown as an example of a divide and conquer algorithm. It sorts a list of values by subdividing the list and sorting the resulting sublists.

Divide and conquer solutions lend themselves naturally to recursion, which the binary search algorithm demonstrated. You can then change recursive solutions to iterative solutions with some minor adjustments. This is done because recursive implementations in languages such as C++ can be extremely inefficient for large values.

EXERCISES

The following questions test your knowledge of the material from this chapter. You can find the answers to these questions on the book's companion website at www.courseptr.com/downloads.

1. Compare the number of comparisons for linear search and binary search. Add code to the linear search and binary search programs to count the number of times the equals-to comparison is performed. Your program should output the number of comparisons when the program is complete. Then run each program several times, and examine your results.

2. This problem is based on the result of exercise 1. Take the result from exercise 1 and change the programs to search for integer values in arrays of 100,000. Use the rand() function to fill the arrays with random integers using a loop at the start of the program. Then run 10 experiments, and compare the results.

3. Recursion is used for many mathematical functions. Use the pseudocode algorithm for factorial, and produce a C++ version of factorial that uses recursion.

4. Build an iterative version of factorial based on the recursive pseudocode presented in this chapter.

5. Write a recursive function that can count the number of nonzero elements in an array. Test your function in a program with zeros placed in random locations.

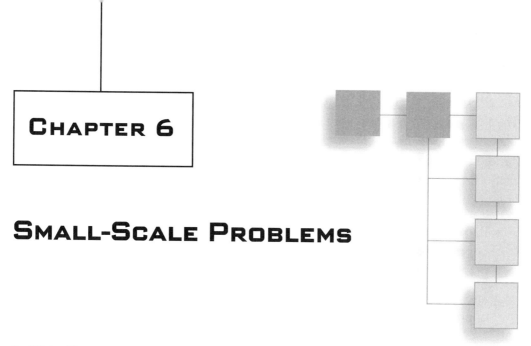

CHAPTER 6

SMALL-SCALE PROBLEMS

In This Chapter

- Problem 1: Paper, Scissors, Rock!
- Problem 2: Demographic Analysis

Inside every well-written large program is a well-written small program.

—C.A.R. Hoare

In the previous chapters, you learned about C++ core statements, functions, basic program design and pseudocode, and divide and conquer. You can use all these ideas to solve small-scale problems. The scale of a problem is based on several factors:

- The difficulty of the solution
- The number of functions in the solution
- The amount and diversity of the data in the solution

Starting with small-scale problems helps you master the use of the core C++ language and functions while applying some basic analysis ideas. Large, complex programs are made up of smaller, less complex programs; therefore, this mastery will be valuable as the scale and complexity of the problems increase.

Problem 1: Paper, Scissors, Rock!

The first problem you will look at is a popular game called Paper, Scissors, Rock, which you have undoubtedly played with friends. The game is played with one hand. Each player makes a fist and moves his fist up and down while saying to each other, "Paper, Scissors, Rock!" When the players say, "Rock!" they form one of three symbols with their hands:

- **Paper.** The hand is held out flat, with all fingers pointing to the opponent.
- **Scissors.** The hand is held like a pair of scissors, where the index finger and middle finger form the blades of the scissors pointing to the opponent.
- **Rock.** The hand is held out while it is balled into a fist.

The winner is determined by the following criteria:

- **Rock Wins.** Rock is the winner against scissors because rock can crush scissors.
- **Paper Wins.** Paper wins against rock because paper can cover rock.
- **Scissors Wins.** Scissors wins against paper because scissors cuts paper.

The game should support a human-versus-human mode and a human-versus-computer mode.

This game is a perfect example of a small-scale problem because it has a small amount of data to manage and a small number of functions. In the next section, you are taken through the analysis of the problem to develop a solution using techniques you have been exposed to previously.

Analyze the Problem

In Chapter 2, "The Nature of the Problems and Solutions," you learned a basic analysis technique that involved modeling the problem using pencil and paper or having friends help you identify the major tasks to be performed. You also learned that looking for verbs in the description helps to identify these tasks.

Your analysis should start by answering the four basic questions:

- What would be considered the input data?
- What would be considered the output information?
- What are the formulas/processes you have to use to solve this by hand?
- Are there special conditions?

The input data for this problem would be the mode (1 player versus 2 player), the names of the players, and their choice of paper, rock, or scissors. The output of the program would be the winner of the game.

The processes and formulas are based on the tasks to be performed. You should examine the problem before reading further to see what tasks you identify. After looking at the program, you could identify the following tasks:

- Determine the winner and display the result.
- Compute the computer's move.
- Get the user's move.
- Get the name of the user.

Why Should You List the Tasks?

Listing the tasks in an unordered fashion allows you to focus on identifying the tasks in the problem instead of focusing on how you will perform each task and what order the tasks will be performed in. The list allows you to track which tasks you have already considered and can serve as a checklist as you move forward in the analysis and design phase. Checking off tasks you have completed may seem like an old-fashioned technique, but it is one that works for all levels of programmers, including advanced professionals.

In professional settings, a group of software developers/programmers meet and use a whiteboard to make these types of lists. There is usually discussion about what the tasks will do and how they relate to one another.

Notice that the tasks are not labeled in any particular order. This should only be a brainstorming exercise, free from algorithm development.

The next step in the analysis is to organize these tasks into the order that you want them to happen. You can do this as another list:

1. Get the name of the user.

2. Compute the computer's move.

3. Get the user's move.

4. Determine the winner and display the result.

This list shows the order. You may be wondering about the computer and the human choosing at the same time. The computer is going to make its selection at random, so it does not matter whether it goes first or second. Now it's time to write algorithms for each task and determine whether the tasks need to be functions.

Design the Algorithms

Now you will look at each task in your list and determine the pseudocode algorithm that is needed for the task. You will also determine whether you think the task should be a function. In general, a function should require about a handful of lines in the algorithm. If you think the task will be used more than once, it should be a function. A one- or two-line task does not need to be a function. You will see what this means as you follow this example.

The first task is to get the user's name. You can accomplish this task with just two lines of code to prompt the user and get the information. Therefore, this can be part of the main algorithm and not a separate function. Listing 6.1 shows this part of the main algorithm.

Listing 6.1 Algorithm to Get Name (Portion of Main Algorithm)

```
Output "Welcome to Paper, Scissors, Rock. Please enter your name: "
Input username
```

The next task is to compute the computer's move. This requires randomly selecting between rock, paper, and scissors, which should be done as a function. The call to the function is in the main algorithm after the input statement (after reviewing all the tasks, the main algorithm is shown in its entirety), but the definition of the function is shown in Listing 6.2.

The function in Listing 6.2 computes a random value between 1 and 3, which acts as code for a particular string. The if statements determine which string is returned for each random value.

Listing 6.2 The Algorithm for the Computer's Move

```
Function ComputerMove()
    number = Random Number between 1 - 3
    If number is 1 Then
        Return "Paper"
    If number is 2 Then
        Return "Scissors"
    If number is 3 Then
        Return "Rock"
End Function
```

The next task is to get the user's move in the game. The user selects paper, scissors, or rock. There are several ways to handle this type of task. Some programs present a menu to the user to make his selection from. A menu would look like this:

```
Please choose from the following:
1. Paper
2. Scissors
3. Rock
Enter choice:
```

The other option is for the user to enter names such as Paper, Scissors, or Rock; enter numbers such as 1, 2, or 3 (no menu); or enter abbreviations such as P, S, and R. As a programmer, you have the choice of how you would like to have the user perform the input. There are a few considerations to make:

- When you have the user enter strings, you can use his input as direct output; however, there is a high probability that the user will make errors on the input, and your program will have to detect the errors.

- If you have the user input numbers or abbreviations, you must convert that input to a string value for output purposes.

- Menus are user friendly as long as they are short; long menus can be difficult for users to follow.

These options show the various trade-offs in your choices. In this example, the algorithm uses numbers without a menu. (Later in this chapter, you will see a menu.) The task for getting the user's move should be a function because it will require several lines of code and will be sufficiently complex.

The algorithm in Listing 6.3 shows the function for handling the user's input. The do-while loop validates the user's input. If the user enters a value that is not 1, 2, or 3, the loop continues to ask the user to input an appropriate value. This algorithm asks the user to input values of 1, 2, or 3 and then returns the appropriate string based on the input value.

Listing 6.3 The Algorithm for the User's Move

```
Function UserMove()
    Do
        Output "Please enter 1=Paper, 2=Scissors, 3=Rock: "
        Input choice
    While choice < 1 or choice > 3
    If choice is 1 Then
        Return "Paper"
    If choice is 2 Then
        Return "Scissors"
    If choice is 3 Then
        Return "Rock"
End Function
```

Input Validation

Input validation is important for your programs, and it's a good idea to start putting it in your algorithms so that you will view it as part of the algorithm. Input validation is important because your program's execution depends on the input data. If your program receives input data that it cannot use, your program produces incorrect results or crashes. Would you keep using a program that crashes even if you were the one who made the mistake inputting the information? The answer is usually no. Users prefer to be reminded of the proper input values instead of watching the program exit or produce unexpected results.

In some cases, you may provide more help information to the user when he supplies incorrect data instead of simply repeating the prompt. This is usually appropriate when you realize that a user may have forgotten some key information about the input constraints that requires further explanation. These types of reminders require you to write your code differently:

```
Input value
While value is improper Do
    Display a more detailed help message
    Display a prompt to try again
    Input value
End Do
```

This code gets the input value. If it's incorrect, it goes into the error loop where more detailed instructions are given. The do-while loop does not work in this situation because you enter the do-while loop when input is correct and incorrect. In this case, you only enter the while loop when the input is incorrect.

The final task is to determine the winner and display the result. This task requires a function because it needs to implement the three criteria for determining a winner or determine that there is a tie.

The algorithm in Listing 6.4 computes the winner of the game. The idea behind the algorithm is to first check for a tie and then determine if the human player has won. If there is no tie and the human player did not win, the computer must have won. There are several ways to write this algorithm. How would the algorithm change if you wanted to determine if the computer won after checking for a tie instead of determining if the human won? How would the algorithm change if you wanted to determine if the computer won, determine if the human won, and then settle for the tie? These are good questions for you to explore.

Listing 6.4 Algorithm for Determining a Winner

```
Function DetermineWinner (name, human, computer)
   If human = computer Then
      Display "Result: A Tie"
   Else If human = "Rock" and computer = "Scissors" or
            human = "Paper" and computer = "Rock"    or
            human = "Scissors" and computer = "Paper" Then
      Display "Result: ", name, " Wins!"
   Else
      Display "Result: Computer Wins!"
End Function
```

Now that all the tasks are completed, it's time to complete the main algorithm. Listing 6.5 shows the main algorithm, starting with the welcome message and getting the user's move. The do-while loop is there to allow the user to play the game as many times as he wants. Inside the loop, you see that the human and the computer make their moves using the functions UserMove and ComputerMove. Then the algorithm echoes their choices to the screen and determines the winner. The DetermineWinner function outputs the result. After a round of the game is over, the user is asked if he wants to play again.

Listing 6.5 Main Algorithm

```
Output "Welcome to Rock, Paper, Scissors. Please enter your name: "
Input username
Do
    humanMove = UserMove()
    opponentMove = ComputerMove()
    Output "You played the ", humanMove
    Output "The computer played the ", opponentMove
    DetermineWinner(username, humanMove, opponentMove)
    Output "Do you want to play again? (y/n)"
    Input answer
While answer = y
Output "Thank you for playing our game"
Stop
```

The algorithm is complete. You should test it by using a name like Alice for the username. Then execute the functions in order and check that it produces the correct results. You can use table tracing that was introduced in Chapter 2 and has been demonstrated in previous chapters. The next step is to implement this algorithm in C++.

Implement in C++

You can write the C++ program by translating the pseudocode into C++. The thought and difficulty are in developing the algorithm. If you do a good job with the algorithm, the programming becomes more enjoyable. The following is sample output of the complete C++ program:

```
Welcome to Rock, Paper, Scissors. Please enter your name: Charles
Please enter 1=Paper, 2=Scissors, 3=Rock: 1
You played the Paper
The computer played the Rock
Result: Charles Wins!
Do you want to play again? (y/n) y
Please enter 1=Paper, 2=Scissors, 3=Rock: 2
You played the Scissors
The computer played the Scissors
Result: A Tie
Do you want to play again? (y/n) y
Please enter 1=Paper, 2=Scissors, 3=Rock: 3
```

```
You played the Rock
The computer played the Paper
Result: Computer Wins!
Do you want to play again? (y/n) n
Thank you for playing our game
```

Before you examine see the C++ code that produces this result, there are a few C++ concepts that need to be covered.

C++: Random Numbers

You can generate random numbers in C++ by using the functions `srand()` and `rand()`. They are standard functions in C++ that do not require special header files. The `srand()` function seeds the random number generator. Seeding the random number generator is the way of initializing the random number generator. The `rand()` function returns a random integer each time it is executed.

The `srand()` function is executed only once in a program. Typically, this is done near the start of `main()` or in an initialization function for the program. If you use `srand()` more than once, you may experience unexpected results, such as the randomness not occurring. Table 6.1 states that the `seed` value should come from a random source. This `seed` value could come from the user, but you

Table 6.1 Random Number Library Functions

Usage	Description
`void` **srand(** unsigned seed **)**	Initializes the random number generator using `seed` as the initializing value. The `seed` should be generated from a random source.
`int` **rand()**	Returns a random integer between 0 and RAND_MAX (usually the largest integer value).
`time_t` **time(** time_t *time_save **)**	Gets the current time and stores it in `time_save` or returns the current time in seconds if NULL is passed as the parameter. You must use `#include <ctime>` or `#include <time.h>` to use this function.

cannot guarantee the user will provide a random value each time the program is executed. The customary source for the seed is to use the time() function:

```
srand(time(NULL));
```

This line of code returns the current time as the number of seconds from January 1, 1970. This date is the timestamp for the start of the UNIX operating system, which is when the time library was implemented. To this day, this function always returns the number of seconds elapsed from that date. Because the number of seconds changes each time the program is executed, time(NULL) is a suitable random source for srand().

The rand() function is called each time you need a random integer generated. This can be called from any other place in your program; it always returns a random integer if the seeding has been done properly.

C++: Character Library

There is a library derived from the C-Libraries to provide character manipulations. It's handy for programs that need to input, process, or output character data. The library is composed of several functions for either testing the values of character variables or transforming the values. Every function in the library accepts an integer argument and returns an integer argument. This allows the values passed in and returned to be either ASCII values for the characters or actual characters.

Table 6.2 shows popular functions that are a part of the C character manipulation library. The first few functions are typically used in conditional statements:

```
if (isdigit(choice) == 0)
    cout << "The value of choice is not a numeric value" << endl;
```

The isdigit function can be used in while loops, do-while loops, and any other location for a conditional expression or integer expression.

The C++ Program for Paper, Scissors, Rock

The program that produces this output is found in Listings 6.6 and 6.7. Listing 6.6 is where the main algorithm is shown, and Listing 6.7 is where the functions are shown.

Table 6.2 Character Library Functions

Usage	Description
int **isalnum**(int c)	Determines if the character c is alphanumeric. Returns 0 for false and any other integer for true.
int **isalpha**(int c)	Determines if the character c is alphabetic. Returns 0 for false and any other integer for true.
int **isdigit**(int c)	Determines if the character c is numeric. Returns 0 for false and any other integer for true.
int **islower**(int c)	Determines if the character c is a lowercase alphabetic character. Returns 0 for false and any other integer for true.
int **ispunct**(int c)	Determines if the character c is punctuation. Returns 0 for false and any other integer for true.
int **isspace**(int c)	Determines if the character c is white space, such as a space or tab. Returns 0 for false and any other integer for true.
int **isupper**(int c)	Determines if the character c is an uppercase alphabetic character. Returns 0 for false and any other integer for true.
int **tolower**(int c)	Converts the character c to lowercase if possible. The lowercase version is returned if the conversion is possible; otherwise, an unchanged value is returned.
int **toupper**(int c)	Converts the character c to uppercase if possible. The uppercase version is returned if the conversion is possible; otherwise, an unchanged value is returned.

Listing 6.6 The main( ) Function for Paper, Scissors, Rock

```
1: #include <iostream>          // C++ I/O
2: #include <string>            // C++ string class
3: #include <cctype>            // C++ Character Manipulation
4: #include <ctime>             // time() function
5:
6: using namespace std;
7: // Function prototypes
8:
9: // Handles the move for the user
10: string UserMove();
11:
12: // Determines the move for the computer player
13: string ComputerMove();
14:
15: // Determines who wins the match
```

```
16: void DetermineWinner(string, string, string);
17:
18:
19: int main()
20: {
21:     // Data dictionary
22:     string username;            // Name of the user
23:     string humanMove;           // The move of the user
24:     string opponentMove;        // The move of the computer
25:     char answer;                // Answer for y/n to play again
26:
27:     // Initialize the random number generator
28:     srand(time(NULL));
29:
30:     // Get the player's name
31:     cout << "Welcome to Paper, Scissors, Rock. Please enter your name: ";
32:     cin >> username;
33:
34:     // This loop plays one match paper, scissors, rock per iteration.
35:     do {
36:
37:         // Get choice from user and computer
38:         humanMove = UserMove();
39:         opponentMove = ComputerMove();
40:
41:         cout << "You played the " << humanMove << endl;
42:         cout << "The computer played the " << opponentMove << endl;
43:
44:         // Evaluate the choices to show a winner
45:         DetermineWinner(username, humanMove, opponentMove);
46:
47:         cout << "Do you want to play again? (y/n) ";
48:         cin >> answer;
49:
50:         // Use toupper to accept lower/upper case answers
51:     } while (toupper(answer) == 'Y');
52:
53:
54:     cout << "Thank you for playing our game" << endl;
55:
```

```
56:     system("pause");
57:     return 0;
58: }
```

The code in Listing 6.6 is the main() function for the Paper, Scissors, Rock game. Translating the main algorithm generates this code. Lines 1–4 show #includes for libraries needed for the program, including the need to use character manipulation and the time function. Lines 9–16 show the prototypes for the functions that were created in the analysis and design. The definitions for these functions are shown in Listing 6.7. The main() function initializes the random number generator on line 28. In general, this is how early you always want to initialize the random number generator. After the input of the user's name, lines 34–51 are the main game loop. Inside the game loop, each player makes a move, and the winner is determined for that match. On line 51, the toupper function converts the input from the user to uppercase. Therefore, if the user inputs y, then it will be converted to Y, and likewise with n. Doing this allows you to have one comparison rather than comparing against y and Y using the || operator.

Listing 6.7 Supporting Functions for Paper, Scissors, Rock

```
1: // This function asks the user to enter his choice for paper, scissors,
2: // or rock and returns result to the caller.
3: string UserMove() {
4:     int choice;
5:
6:     // Loop validates the input is 1, 2, or 3
7:     do {
8:         cout << "Please enter 1=Paper, 2=Scissors, 3=Rock: ";
9:         cin >> choice;
10:     } while (choice < 1 || choice > 3);
11:
12:     // Maps input values 1, 2, and 3 to appropriate user plays
13:     if (choice == 1)
14:         return "Paper";
15:     else if (choice == 2)
16:         return "Scissors";
17:     else
18:         return "Rock";
19: }
20:
```

```
21: // This function uses a random number generator to have the computer play
22: // random choices. It returns the result as a string.
23: string ComputerMove() {
24:      int number;
25:
26:
27:      // Obtains a random number in range 1 - 3
28:      number = (rand() % 3) + 1;
29:
30:      // Maps random choice to appropriate user plays
31:      if (number == 1)
32:         return "Paper";
33:      else if (number == 2)
34:         return "Scissors";
35:      else
36:         return "Rock";
37:
38: }
39:
40:
41: // This function uses the human and computer moves to determine the
42: // winner. The function outputs the winner or a tie.
43: void DetermineWinner(string name, string human, string computer) {
44:
45:      // This if statement evaluates for a tie first. Second, it
46:      // evaluates having the user win. Lastly, it proclaims the
47:      // computer as the winner.
48:      if (human == computer)
49:         cout << "Result: A Tie" << endl;
50:      else if ((human == "Rock" && computer == "Scissors") ||
51:              (human == "Paper" && computer == "Rock") ||
52:              (human == "Scissors" && computer == "Paper"))
53:         cout << "Result: " << name << " Wins!" << endl;
54:      else
55:         cout << "Result: Computer Wins!" << endl;
56: }
```

Listing 6.7 follows Listing 6.6 in the same file. This part of the program consists of the three functions that are called from the main() function in Listing 6.6 on lines 38, 39, and 45. Lines 61–79 show the function UserMove() that defines how a user makes a move. This function asks the user to input a 1, 2, or 3. It uses a `do-while` loop to validate the input of the user. If the input is valid, the function returns a string for `Paper`, `Scissors`, and `Rock` for values of 1, 2, or 3, respectively.

Lines 81–98 show the definition for the `ComputerMove()` function. This function is similar to the `UserMove()` function. However, the `ComputerMove()` function uses the random number generator on line 88 to compute the move for the computer. This line may seem confusing at first. The `rand()` function returns values from 0 to `RAND_MAX`. The modulus operator commonly keeps the random numbers within a range. The expression `rand() % 3` ensures that only three values are shown because there are only three possible remainders when you divide by 3: 0, 1, and 2. At this point, the problem is that you want the values to be 1, 2, or 3. If you examine the sequence, you see that you need to add 1 to each value to get the desired result. Therefore, the expression `(rand() % 3) + 1` generates values 1, 2, and 3. After this, the function selects a move just like the `UserMove()` function.

Lines 101–116 show the definition for the `DetermineWinner()` function. This function uses the strategy explained in the analysis and design section with the pseudocode in Listing 6.4. The overall strategy is to determine if a tie exists first. If there is no tie, the function determines if the player is the winner; if that is not `true`, the winner must be the computer.

This completes the Paper, Scissors, Rock game. This example showed how to use your analysis and design techniques to create a program solution for a small-scale problem. After completing your algorithm, you can use it as a guide in writing the C++ program.

PROBLEM 2: DEMOGRAPHIC ANALYSIS

In the social sciences, it is common to need to work with demographic data. Demographic data is information about the subjects that are being studied. For example, if you have a study that is examining how having a pet in the home affects the well-being of the family members, you will be studying various people. Demographic data on people might be their age, gender, and ethnicity. Social scientists concern themselves with the characteristics of the population in their study to determine if it matches the intended population of the study. If they plan to say something about how this relates to America, the population of the study would need a ethnicity distribution of about 65% white, 14% black, 10% Hispanic, 4% Asian, and 7% other. If the analysis of their data shows that it's 50% white, 30% black, 10% Hispanic, and 10% Asian, the population of the study does not correlate with the population of the United States.

These scientists need a software tool that lets them determine these types of percentages for the ethnicity demographics in their study. They want a menu-driven program that can be used to enter data, view the data, and provide the distribution analysis.

Analyze the Problem

First you analyze the problem by answering the basic four questions:

- What would be considered the input data?
- What would be considered the output information?
- What are the formulas/processes you have to use to solve this by hand?
- Are there special conditions?

The input data would be the ethnicity information and the number of people in the population of the study. The output would consist of displaying the data and the distribution table.

The special processes would be being able to count the number of times a particular ethnicity appears in the list. In Chapter 5, "Divide and Conquer," there was a discussion about searching for an element. You can adapt the linear search here to count the number of times an ethnicity appears instead of just finding the first occurrence. There are no special conditions for this problem.

Now you have to develop a task list. You can develop your list out of order as in the first problem and then order it. Or you can develop it in order. The ordered task list follows:

1. Display a menu.
2. Get the user's selection.
3. Execute the selection.
4. Display a list of data.
5. Enter data into the list.
6. Compute the diversity distribution.

This task list has a few items that belong together. Items 1, 2, and 3 are related to the functioning of the menu. Items 4, 5, and 6 are the particular tasks the program performs when the menu option is selected.

Design the Algorithms

Menu-driven programs have a similar structure. The main function is typically responsible for managing the menu, and then there is at least one function created for each menu selection. The analysis shows that there will be three primary tasks handled in the main function, and the other three tasks will be assigned to individual functions.

The first algorithm is the main algorithm shown in Listing 6.8. This algorithm is responsible for managing the menu and launching the other functions as needed. Notice that the loop will loop forever until option 4 is chosen to exit the program. This is another common way of handling menus. This way, the menu will display after correct and incorrect selections.

Listing 6.8 Main Algorithm

```
Output "Demographic Analysis Program"
Do
    Output "1. Enter Data"
    Output "2. View Data"
    Output "3. Show Demographics"
    Output "4. Quit"
    Output "Enter your selection: "
    Input choice

    If choice = 1 Then
        newSize = EnterData(List, oldSize)
    Else If choice = 2 Then
        DisplayData(List, Size)
    Else If choice = 3 Then
        DisplayDemographics(List, Size)
    Else If choice = 4 Then
        Output "Thank you for using our program"
        Exit loop
```

```
        Else
            Output "Incorrect option selected"
        End If
While forever
Stop
```

The next algorithm is for the function to enter data. This function must allow the user to input data into the list even if data is in the list. This means that the list changes size after this function is executed. There also needs to be a special value to enter when the user has finished entering data. This special value is called a *sentinel value*. In this algorithm, the sentinel value is Done.

The algorithm in Listing 6.9 shows the EnterData() function. This function uses currentSize to determine the position for the new data value. All data values are added to the end of the list. The while loop determines if the sentinel value has been entered. The sentinel value is Done, and when it's entered, the function stops allowing input. Also, the list has a maximum capacity; when that capacity is reached, a message is displayed, and the function is exited.

Listing 6.9 EnterData Algorithm

```
Function EnterData(List, currentSize)
    Output "Enter your ethnicity data one at a time (Enter Done) when finished"
    Output "Enter Item", currentSize + 1, ": "
    Input race

    While race not equal "Done" Do
        Increment currentSize
        List[currentSize] = race
        If currentSize = MAXSIZE Then
            Output "Capacity has been reached"
            Return currentSize
        End If
        Output "Enter Item", currentSize + 1, ": "
        Input race
    End While
    Return currentSize
End Function
```

The next function to be written is the one to display the contents of the data list. This function is displayed in Listing 6.10. It's a straightforward function that iterates over each element in the list, starting at the first position and stopping at the last position. It outputs each value in the list with its position in the list outputted prefixing the data value.

Listing 6.10 DisplayData Algorithm

```
Function DisplayData(List, currentSize)
   Output "The current data:"
   position = 1
   While position <= currentSize Do
      Output currentSize,". ",List[position]
      Increment position
End Function
```

The last function computes and displays the demographic information based on the linear search. It is common to build new algorithms based on familiar algorithms. The linear search is designed to look for values in a list and can be modified to find all occurrences of values and count those occurrences.

Listing 6.11 is based on the linear search. It does not need a found variable because the goal is not to find only one occurrence, and the algorithm should visit each data item. There are four if statements—one for each category. When a race category is found, the counter is incremented. Finally, the percentages are displayed. Multiplying by 100 shows percentages with values between 0.0 and 100.0.

Listing 6.11 DisplayDemographics Algorithm

```
Function DisplayDemographics(List, currentSize)
   position = 1
   While position <= currentSize Do
      If List[position] = "Black"
         Increment blackCount
      End If
      If List[position] = "White"
         Increment whiteCount
      End If
      If List[position] = "Asian"
         Increment asianCount
```

```
            End If
            If List[position] = "Hispanic"
                Increment hispanicCount
            End If
        End While
        Output "Demographic Summary"
        Output "White Population: ", whiteCount/currentSize*100,"%"
        Output "Black Population: ", blackCount/currentSize*100,"%"
        Output "Asian Population: ", asianCount/currentSize*100,"%"
        Output "Hispanic Population: ", hispanicCount/currentSize*100,"%"
End Function
```

The C++ Solution for Demographic Analysis

This C++ solution shows how to use C++ for menu-driven programs. It also shows how to pass array data to functions. It is translated from the pseudocode algorithms, and its output is shown here:

```
Demographic Analysis Program
1. Enter Data
2. View Data
3. Show Demographics
4. Quit
Enter your selection: 1

Enter your ethnicity data one at a time (Enter Done when finished)
Enter Item 0: White
Enter Item 1: Black
Enter Item 2: Hispanic
Enter Item 3: Asian
Enter Item 4: Done

1. Enter Data
2. View Data
3. Show Demographics
4. Quit
Enter your selection: 2

The current data:
0. White
1. Black
```

```
2. Hispanic
3. Asian

1. Enter Data
2. View Data
3. Show Demographics
4. Quit
Enter your selection: 3

Demographic Summary
White Population: 25.00%
Black Population: 25.00%
Asian Population: 25.00%
Hispanic Population: 25.00%

1. Enter Data
2. View Data
3. Show Demographics
4. Quit
Enter your selection: 1

Enter your ethnicity data one at a time (Enter Done when finished)
Enter Item 4: Black
Enter Item 5: White
Enter Item 6: Done

1. Enter Data
2. View Data
3. Show Demographics
4. Quit
Enter your selection: 3

Demographic Summary
White Population: 33.33%
Black Population: 33.33%
Asian Population: 16.67%
Hispanic Population: 16.67%

1. Enter Data
2. View Data
```

```
3. Show Demographics
4. Quit
Enter your selection: 4
Thank you for using our program
```

The execution of the program shows how the menu is redisplayed after each selection from the menu. It also shows that after there is data in the list, more data can be entered. The item numbers pick up from where they left off. This program uses a menu, and switch statements usually implement menus.

C++ *Feature: switch Statements*

The switch statement is another C++ conditional statement that is used primarily with menu processing, command-line argument processing, and state machines. Up to this point, you have been introduced to the if statement and if-else statement as the conditional statements in C++. The switch statement is a specialized statement that tests for equality only on ordinal data types. This means that if the data you are testing can map to integer values, you can use the switch statement for decision-making. The switch statement tests only for equality.

The format of the switch statement is the following:

```
switch (<int expression>) {
    case <int label 1>:
        <statements 1>
        break;
    case <int label 2>:
        <statements 2>
        break;
...
    default:
        <statements last>
        break;
};
```

The switch statement uses an integer-type compatible expression in its header. This expression is evaluated and then compared to each of the <int label x> labels. If there is a match, the statements listed after the corresponding colon are executed. There can be more than one C++ statement in any of the <statements x> blocks. Any C++ statement can be there that you would put in a C++ program. The

Table 6.3 switch Statement and if-else Equivalent

switch Statement	if-else Statement
| ```
switch (value) {
  case 1:
    cout << "value is 1";
    break;
  case 2:
    cout << "value is 2";
    break;
  default:
    cout << "value is unknown";
    break;
}
``` | ```
if (value == 1) {
  cout << "value is 1";
} else if (value == 2) {
  cout << "value is 2";
} else {
  cout << "value is unknown";
}
``` |

switch statement provides a compact and elegant approach to perform equality testing. You can achieve the same result with if-else statements using a more cluttered syntax.

Table 6.3 shows how switch statements and if-else statements can provide the same function using equality. Why have switch statements? It's the same reason for having specialized tools in many professions. For example, you could use a skillet with high sides to fry fish, or you could use a deep fryer to fry the fish. The skillet is a versatile tool that you can use for many tasks, and frying fish is one of them. It does it well, but not as well and as easily as a deep fryer. The deep fryer is not as versatile, but it's the best tool for frying the fish because that is its specialty. In the same way, the switch statement provides a nice compact way to compare equality with less syntax than the if-else statement. Some would say that switch is more elegant and better suited for expressing the concept of a program.

The break in the switch statement is optional and may be removed if you want to combine the result of more than one case.

The code in Listing 6.12 demonstrates the fall-through case in a switch statement. If value is equal to a or b, it executes the same statements. The fall-through case is where you want to express the idea of <option 1> || <option 2> || ...<option n>. You can mix fall-through cases with normal cases, and you have as many fall-throughs as you would like. You can even have statements

immediately following a fall-through case as long as none of those statements is
break.

Listing 6.12 The Fall-Through Cases in switch Statements

```
switch (value) {
  case 'a':
  case 'b':
     cout << "value is a or b";
     break;
  case 'c':
     cout << "value is c";
     break;
  default:
     cout << "value is not a, b nor c";
     break;
  }
```

C++ Source Code

This section shows the C++ source code for the solution to the demographic
analysis program and discusses the implementation features. There are two
listings in this section; Listing 6.13 shows the main() function, and Listing 6.14
shows the supporting functions.

Listing 6.13 The main( ) Function for Demographic Analysis

```
1: #include <iostream> // C++ I/O
2: #include <string>    // The string class
3: #include <iomanip>  // I/O manipulation
4:
5: using namespace std;
6:
7: const int MAXSIZE = 10;
8:
9:
10: // Function prototypes
11:
12: // This function enters data into the list
13: int EnterData(string[], int);
14:
```

```
15: // This function displays data from the list
16: void DisplayData(string [], int);
17:
18: // This function computes and displays demographic data
19: void DisplayDemographics(string [], int);
20:
21:
22:
23:
24: int main()
25: {
26:     int choice;            // The menu choice
27:     int size = 0;          // The size of the data list
28:     string list[MAXSIZE];  // The data list
29:
30:     cout << "Demographic Analysis Program" << endl;
31:
32:     do {
33:
34:         // Display the menu
35:         cout << endl;
36:         cout << "Menu" << endl;
37:         cout << "1. Enter Data" << endl;
38:         cout << "2. View Data" << endl;
39:         cout << "3. Show Demographics" << endl;
40:         cout << "4. Quit" << endl;
41:         cout << "Enter your selection: ";
42:         cin >> choice;
43:
44:         // Determine what choice was selected. The default case
45:         // is invoked if something other than 1 - 4 is selected.
46:         switch (choice) {
47:             case 1:
48:                 cout << endl;
49:                 size = EnterData(list, size);
50:                 break;
51:             case 2:
52:                 cout << endl;
53:                 DisplayData(list, size);
54:                 break;
```

```
55:                case 3:
56:                    cout << endl;
57:                    DisplayDemographics(list, size);
58:                    break;
59:                case 4:
60:                    cout << endl;
61:                    cout << "Thank you for using our program" << endl;
62:                    // Exit the program
63:                    exit(0);
64:                default:
65:                    cout << endl;
66:                    cout << "Incorrect option selected" << endl << endl;
67:                    break;
68:            };
69:
70:            // Infinite loop caused by true conditional expression
71:        } while (true);
72:
73:
74:        return 0;
75: }
```

Listing 6.13 has a constant named MAXSIZE that determines the maximum capacity of the list. In the loop, lines 46–68 show the switch statement. This statement is typically used with menus because a menu has options labeled as integer values or character values, which are still integers. The default case for the switch statement displays an error message before the loop redisplays the menu. Each case in the switch statement executes a function to carry out the tasks. The case 4: uses the exit() function to exit the program immediately. The 0 being passed to the exit() function signifies successful completion of the program. The use of functions for the menu options provides nice modularity for the program.

Listing 6.14 shows the functions that perform each menu operation. Each of these functions shows that passing an array to a function simply requires the [] (empty square brackets) on the argument to state that it's a function. Because C++ arrays start at position 0 instead of position 1, all the code from the pseudocode has to be slightly updated to reflect this. There are three major changes:

- The initial position in the list should be set to 0 when a loop is iterating over the elements in the array. (See lines 43 and 56 in Listing 6.14.)

- The loops should iterate from 0 to currentSize -1 since the last element is at the position currentSize - 1 and not currentSize because the array starts at 0. Therefore, < is used instead of <=. (See lines 44 and 65 in Listing 6.14.)

- The next position to get a value in a list of size equal to currentSize is position currentSize. Therefore, the increment of the currentSize should follow the data insertion. Again, this is related to the starting position of the array being 0. (See line 20 in Listing 6.14.)

This problem is also considered a small-scale problem because it does not have a large number of functions or a diverse dataset. You can also see that sometimes your solutions are made up of variations on algorithms that you have seen before.

Listing 6.14 The Supporting Functions for Demographic Analysis

```
1: // This function allows the user to enter data into the list until
2: // there is no more data to enter or until the list is full. The
3: // word "Done" is used to end data input
4: int EnterData(string list[], int currentSize) {
5:
6:       string race;
7:
8:       // Greet the user and accept a data item
9:       cout <<   "Enter your ethnicity data one at a time (Enter Done";
10:      cout <<   " when finished" << endl;
11:
12:      cout << "Enter Item " << currentSize << ": ";
13:      cin >> race;
14:
15:      // If the data time is not "Done," continue to accept data
16:      // items
17:      while (race != "Done") {
18:          // Put item in list and increment the current size
19:          list[currentSize] = race;
20:          currentSize++;
```

```
21:
22:              // If capacity is reached, stop adding data to the list
23:              if (currentSize == MAXSIZE) {
24:                  cout ≪ "Capacity has been reached" ≪ endl ≪ endl;
25:                  return currentSize;
26:              }
27:
28:              cout ≪ "Enter Item " ≪ currentSize ≪ ": ";
29:              cin ≫ race;
30:
31:
32:          }
33:
34:      return currentSize;
35:
36: }
37:
38: // This function displays the current list of data
39: void DisplayData(string list[], int currentSize) {
40:      int position;
41:      cout ≪ "The current data:" ≪ endl;
42:
43:      position = 0;
44:      while (position < currentSize) {
45:          cout ≪ position ≪ ". " ≪ list[position] ≪ endl;
46:          ++position;
47:      }
48: }
49:
50:
51:
52: // This function computes the demographic information by scanning
53: // the list for matching data. It then outputs the demographic data
54: // summary.
55: void DisplayDemographics(string list[], int currentSize) {
56:      int position = 0;
57:      double blackCount, whiteCount, asianCount, hispanicCount;
58:
59:      // Initialize the counters
60:      blackCount = whiteCount = asianCount = hispanicCount = 0;
```

```
61:
62:        // Iterate over all values in the list. If a value
63:        // matches a category, increment the associated
64:        // counter.
65:        while (position < currentSize) {
66:
67:            if (list[position] == "Black")
68:                blackCount++;
69:
70:            if (list[position] == "White")
71:                whiteCount++;
72:
73:            if (list[position] == "Asian")
74:                asianCount++;
75:
76:            if (list[position] == "Hispanic")
77:                hispanicCount++;
78:
79:            ++position;
80:
81:        }
82:
83:
84:        // Output the summary as percentages. The output is set to
85:        // display floating-point values in fixed point and two
86:        // decimal places.
87:        cout << "Demographic Summary" << endl;
88:        cout << fixed << setprecision(2);
89:        cout << "White Population: " << whiteCount/currentSize*100;
90:        cout << "%" << endl;
91:        cout << "Black Population: " << blackCount/currentSize*100;
92:        cout << "%" << endl;
93:        cout << "Asian Population: " << asianCount/currentSize*100;
94:        cout << "%" << endl;
95:        cout << "Hispanic Population: " << hispanicCount/currentSize*100;
96:        cout << "%" << endl;
97:
98: }
```

SUMMARY

This chapter introduced you to small-scale problems and showed you how you can use the basic analysis and design techniques of previous chapters to create interesting programs.

You also learned more features about the C++ language. Some library functions allow you to generate random numbers and manipulate character data. In addition, you learned that C++ offers a specialized control structure called the switch statement that allows you to test for equality in more elegant fashion. The switch statement is popular for implementing menu-driven programs.

EXERCISES

The following questions test your knowledge of the material from this chapter. You can find the answers to these questions on the book's companion website at www.courseptr.com/downloads.

1. Add another option to the Paper, Scissors, Rock game. This option can be anything that you can think of for this new game. Perhaps paper does not beat rock. Instead, paper beats your new item, and your new item beats rock. Implement your new rule in a C++ program by modifying the program that was created in this chapter.

2. The demographic analysis program does not perform input validation on the data that the user enters. Create a new function called InputValidation that has a string as a parameter and returns a Boolean value. This function should make sure that data values are entered using the same case as expressed in the program (uppercase first letter) and with the same spelling. If the data value is valid, the function returns true. If it's not, it returns false. Use your new function to implement input validation in the ReadData function.

3. Write a program that uses a menu to enter grades for a student. The menu provides options to enter grades, display grades, and compute the average grade.

4. Add two menu options to the grade program to display the lowest and highest grades.

5. Write a program to play a number guessing game, where the user chooses a number, and the computer must guess the number in fewer than seven guesses. The range of numbers is 1 to 100. (Hint: Use a binary search.)

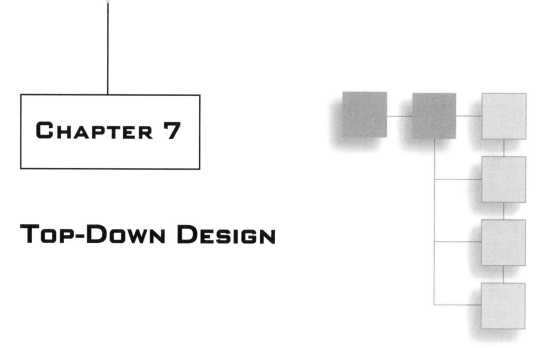

CHAPTER 7

TOP-DOWN DESIGN

In This Chapter

- Top-Down Design Principles
- Example of Stepwise Refinement

The function of good software is to make the complex appear to be simple.

—Grady Booch

Top-down design is a technique that professional programmers use when they have to go beyond simply identifying tasks and instead need to define the task within tasks. Small-scale problems are usually composed of tasks at the same level. This means that there are few opportunities for a task to contain several other tasks that turn into functions. As the complexity of your problems grows to medium-scale problems, you will notice that the first list of tasks usually breaks down even further into more tasks that can be as complex as a single function in C++.

Top-down design is introduced to direct your problem-solving process to create efficient designs even though the problems are more complex. In fact, you have seen some ideas of top-down design in previous chapters. In Chapter 5, "Divide and Conquer," you saw algorithms that used this approach and recursive functions. In that chapter, the problem was divided into smaller but equivalent subproblems. In Chapter 2, "The Nature of the Problems and Solutions," you learned the basic approach to developing solutions. This process involved identifying the smaller tasks that make up the larger solution to the problem.

In this chapter, you explore the more general approach to top-down design and see how to apply it to medium-scale and large-scale problems.

TOP-DOWN DESIGN PRINCIPLES

Top-down design is also known at *stepwise refinement*. Nicklaus Wirth introduced the idea of stepwise refinement to the software development community. Stepwise refinement is also applied in other disciplines where complex systems need to be developed.

In stepwise refinement, the solution to the problem is found by breaking down the problem into solvable subproblems. However, these subproblems are not smaller versions of the large problem like you saw in Chapter 5 when learning about recursion. These subproblems have the following characteristics:

- Each subproblem must be solvable by an algorithm.
- Each subproblem should be independent of the other subproblems.
- Solving a subproblem should be significantly less complex than the main problem.
- Solving the subproblems should lead to solving the main problem by jointly composing the solutions to the subproblems.

If this list of characteristics seems to be related to functions, you have a keen understanding of the previous chapters. Performing stepwise refinement will lead to functions or groups of related functions called *modules*.

Figure 7.1 depicts one of the key ideas of the stepwise refinement technique. You start with a problem and a solution to that problem. Then you refine the problem/solution until you reach a final problem/solution that is a computer program. Each version of the problem/solution represents different levels of abstraction. High-level abstraction has few details, whereas low-level abstraction has many. The first version of the problem/solution is the highest abstraction level, and the final version is the lowest abstraction level.

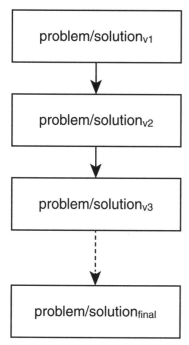

Figure 7.1
A pictorial example of stepwise refinement progression.

Figure 7.2 shows the other key idea of stepwise refinement that each iteration involves breaking down the problems/solutions of the previous iterations into smaller problems/solutions. The problem/solution in version 1 is divided into the subproblems/solutions in version 2. These problems are broken down to the

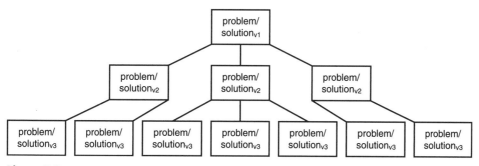

Figure 7.2
A pictorial example of stepwise refinement showing the breaking up of problems/solutions into subproblems/solutions.

problems/solutions of version 3. The number of subproblems/solutions that are created in each iteration is based on the problem/solutions of the previous level. The lowest level of this chart would result in a final problem/solution that correlates to parts of the final program that solves the version 1 problem/solution.

This process may take several iterations to complete, so you must be patient and organized as you go through these iterations. The number of iterations increases with the complexity of the problem/solution. There is no minimum or maximum number of iterations; you just keep doing them until you have subproblems/solutions that can easily be made into functions and modules.

Note

It is common to feel as though you are wasting time executing these iterations of design to break down the problem instead of programming right away. However, the more complex the problems, the more important it is to use techniques such as stepwise refinement. This process organizes your thoughts and enables more efficient and productive programming.

Example of Stepwise Refinement

In this section, you explore stepwise refinement in the context of a sample application. Suppose you are responsible for building a Blackjack game that allows up to four players and a computerized dealer. Blackjack is a card game in which each player, including the dealer, is dealt two cards. Each player looks at his cards and determines if the sum of the values of the cards is equal to 21. If a player has 21, that player wins. If a player has less than 21, he has the option of taking more cards or staying with the cards he has. The game is over when someone has exactly 21 or until everyone either goes over 21 (a bust) or stays. The winner is the player with the highest total that is less than 21. The card values are based on the number on the card for cards 2–10; all face cards are valued at 10, and aces are either 1 or 11. Therefore, you could be dealt an ace and a queen, and your total would be 21 (10 points for the queen + 11 for the ace). In addition, if you have a king and a 10 of diamonds in your hand and are dealt an ace, you also have 21 because 10 + 10 + 1 is 21. In this case, the ace is used as 1 instead of 11.

The rules of Blackjack are not difficult. However, writing the program to play the game is nontrivial. Your first attempt at developing this game may look something like this:

1. Determine the names of the players.

2. Display the instructions.

3. The dealer deals two cards to each player. If someone has 21, the game is over.

4. The players decide to stay with the cards they have or take an additional card(s).

5. After the players have all the cards they want, evaluate the hands for a winner.

This first iteration captures a lot of what we might want to do in the program. It is a list of subproblems for the program. The problem is that these steps are not detailed enough to write a program. You may think that each of these steps is an algorithm on its own or a function. However, it is more likely that some of the steps are actually more than one function. In short, there are a lot of uncertainties and missing details.

In this iteration, each step is considered a problem because each one is independent enough to stand on its own as a problem without its being a part of Blackjack. For example, step 3 states, "The dealer deals two cards to each player," and step 4 states, "Players decide to stay with the cards they have or take an additional card(s)." You can design these steps independently because the dealer dealing cards to the players is an independent activity from players examining their hands for the next move.

In the second iteration, each subproblem generated by the first iteration is treated as its own problem.

Determine the Names of the Players

This subproblem is where the program must obtain the names of each player in the game. You might write the following in the second iteration:

1. Ask the user for the names of the players.

2. Input the names into a list of player names.

This is the refinement to the first subproblem of the first iteration. It is not quite an algorithm; however, based on your prior experience, you can probably see that another iteration is needed to get to an algorithm.

The pseudocode in Listing 7.1 shows an algorithm after a third iteration on this subproblem. This algorithm solves the first subproblem presented as a problem. This solution will be a function in the final program.

Listing 7.1 Algorithm for Determining the Names of Players

```
Function GetUserData(listOfNames, numPlayers)
    count = 0
    While count < numPlayers Do
        Output "Please enter the name of Player #",count,": "
        Input nameOfPlayer
        listOfNames[count] = nameOfPlayer
        increment count
    End While
End Function
```

The next subproblem is display the instructions. Writing a function called DisplayInstructions that outputs the rules of the game solves this problem. Due to its simplicity, it is left as an exercise for the user. The next subproblem is the first round of dealing cards in Blackjack.

Deal Two Cards to Players

This subproblem requires the program to deal two cards to each player in the game, including the dealer. You also need to determine if anyone has 21 at this point in the game.

Note

You should realize that it is impossible for a player to bust at this point in the game. The highest possible card combination with just two cards is to get a face card or a card with a 10 and an ace. In this case, you have $10 + 11 = 21$, and you win the game. All other card combinations will be less than 21. You may be thinking about having two aces and getting $11 + 11 = 22$. Remember, however, that the ace can be 1 or 11. Therefore, the player would have either $11 + 1 = 12$ or $1 + 1 = 2$, but not 22.

The second iteration of this subproblem produces the following:

1. Randomly select two cards from a deck of cards.

2. Give two cards to a player.

3. Repeat steps 1–2 until all players have a hand of two cards.

4. Examine the two cards in a player's hand.

5. Convert the cards to numeric values, and compute the sum.

6. If the sum is equal to 21, the player is a winner.

7. Repeat steps 4–6 until all hands have been evaluated.

These steps are a refinement of the subproblem and have introduced a few more subproblems. For example, the deck of cards needs to be defined at this point in the problem, as does randomly selecting from the deck. Also, the problem of converting cards to numeric values is a subproblem. Finally, it feels as though there are two major tasks being completed here, with a few subtasks.

Figure 7.3 shows a task hierarchy diagram, which shows the relationship between tasks and subtasks. In this case, the dealing of cards is the task that contains two subtasks: pulling random card, and assigning cards to a hand. Figure 7.3 also shows that the task for evaluating a hand depends on two tasks: converting hands to a sum and determining if the hand is a winning one.

Selecting Cards from the Deck

Your problem states that you need to deal two random cards from the deck and assign them to the player's hand. One observation to make at this time is that

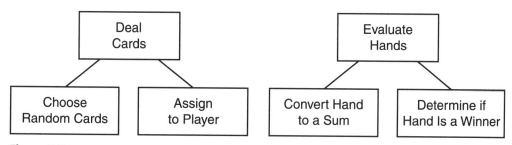

Figure 7.3
A task hierarchy for dealing cards and evaluating a hand.

you have to deal one card at a time later in the game. Therefore, you are going to build an algorithm to deal one card and then use it twice here and use it again later in the program.

Listing 7.2 shows the function algorithm for dealing a single card. The algorithm uses two lists with 52 entries (one for each card): deckOfCards and deckStatus. The deckOfCard is a list of strings that represent the cards, using abbreviations. For example, ace of hearts is "AH", three of spades is "3S", and jack of diamonds is "JD". The function returns one of these strings for the card that is selected randomly. The deckStatus is a list of Boolean values that correlate with the cards in the deck. If entry in the deckStatus is true, the card is in the deck; if it's false, the card is not in the deck. For example, suppose the ace of spades, "AS", is located in the deckOfCards[1]; deckStatus[1] will tell you if the ace of spades is in the deck. The loop will iterate forever unless a random card is found in the deck that has not already been selected. The assumption here is that the deck will be reset after each game.

Listing 7.2 Algorithm for Dealing a Card

```
Function DealCard(deckOfCards, deckStatus)
   Do
      choice = randomNumber(1, 52)
      If deckStatus[choice] is true Then
        deckStatus[choice] = false
        return deckOfCards[choice]
      End If
   While forever
End Function
```

You have to use this function to deal a hand for a player. The player's hand will also be a list. This iteration also produces pseudocode, as shown in Listing 7.3. This function updates one player's hand twice using the DealCard function to generate a hand of two cards.

Listing 7.3 Algorithm for Dealing Two Cards

```
Function DealTwoCards(deckOfCards, deckStatus, playerHand, PlayerName)
   playerHand[1] = DealCard(deckOfCards, deckStatus)
   playerHand[2] = DealCard(deckOfCards, deckStatus)
```

```
    Output "Player: ", PlayerName, " has the following hand"
    Output playerHand[1] and PlayerHand[2]
End Function
```

Following are the subproblems that you are focused on now:

1. Randomly select two cards from a deck of cards.

2. Give two cards to a player.

3. Repeat steps 1 and 2 until all players have a hand of two cards.

Because this appears to be a task separate from the evaluation, there should be an algorithm that uses Listings 7.2 and 7.3 to complete these steps.

Listing 7.4 shows how your main algorithm looks to this point as a series of function calls that handle getting the names of players, showing the game rules and instructions, and dealing the hands for the four players. The main algorithm is not complete at this time, but this shows how stepwise refinement solves the first part of the problem.

Listing 7.4 Main Algorithm

```
// Get user information and display rules (see Listing 7.1 for details)
GetUserData(listOfNames, numPlayers)
DisplayInstructions()
// Deal two cards to each participant (see Listing 7.3 for details)
DealTwoCards(deckOfCards, deckStatus, DealerHand, "Dealer")
i = 1
While i <= numPlayers Do
    DealTwoCards(deckOfCards, deckStatus, PlayerHand[i], listOfNames[i])
    Increment i
End While
```

This completes the solution to the card-dealing subproblem. The next subproblem is to evaluate the hands.

Evaluating Hands

Evaluating hands is another key subproblem to solve. This subproblem comes from the following second iteration of the stepwise refinement derived at the start of this section. (Note that the original numbering is kept here.)

4. Examine the two cards in a player's hand.

5. Convert the cards to numeric values, and compute the sum.

6. If the sum is equal to 21, the player is a winner.

7. Repeat steps 4–6 until all hands have been evaluated.

The first subproblem in step 4 is simply accessing the list entry for the player's hand. The second subproblem shown in step 5 is much more complex. To convert cards to values, you need to look at a card and determine its value. In addition, remember that the value of an ace depends on the total value of the hand. The conversion and summing subproblem requires another iteration:

1. Look for and count the aces in the hand.

2. Examine non-ace cards, and add the value of the card or 10 for the face cards to the sum.

3. Add 1s to sum for each ace for the first sum.

4. Add 1 ace as an 11 to the sum and other aces as 1s for the second sum.

5. Determine which of the sums is the greatest and not over 21 and return the greater sum.

6. If neither sum is less than 21, return the lower value.

This third iteration shows the logic involved in determining the value to use for the hand. The goal is to return the highest possible value for the hand that is not greater than 21. If that is not possible, the algorithm returns a sum that is greater than 21.

The fourth iteration of this problem/solution is the algorithm that is shown in Listing 7.5. The while loop at the start of the function evaluates the card of the player's hand. If the card is an ace, the algorithm counts the card; otherwise, it adds the card value to the sum. The card values can be determined with a single operation, so no special pseudocode is needed for this. (You will see how this is done in Chapter 9, "Medium-Scale Problems.") The handSum holds the value of the sum for the hand. If there are no aces, that is the sum that is returned.

Listing 7.5 Evaluating a Hand

```
Function HandEvaluation(playerHand, numberOfCards)
    position = 1
    aceCount = 0
    handSum = 0
    While position <= numberOfCards
        If playerHand[position] is an ace Then
            Increment aceCount
        else
            handSum = handSum + cardValue(playerHand[position])
        increment position
    End While

    // If there are no aces
    If aceCount is 0 Then
        Return handSum

    // If there are aces, follow these steps
    handSumFirst = handSum + aceCount
    handSumSecond = handSum + 11 + (aceCount - 1)

    If handSumFirst >= handSumSecond Then
        If handSumFirst <= 21 Then
            Return handSumFirst
        Else
            Return handSumSecond

    If handSumSecond > handSumFirst
        If handSumSecond <= 21 Then
            Return handSumSecond
        Else
            Return handSumFirst
End Function
```

If there are aces, two sums are computed: handSumFirst and handSumSecond. The first sum contains the sum if all the aces are treated as 1s. The second sum is for when one of the aces is treated as an 11. The if statements that follow determine the value to return. The first if statement determines if handSumFirst is the best sum. It's the best sum if it's greater than handSumSecond and it's less than or equal to 21; otherwise, handSumSecond is the best sum. The second if statement determines if handSumSecond is the best sum using similar logic.

This ends the solution to the hand evaluation subproblem. You can incorporate this new function from Listing 7.5 into the main algorithm that is shown in Listing 7.6. The newly added lines determine if there are winners after the first two cards are dealt. There can be more than one winner. The dealer's hand is checked first; if his hand value is equal to 21, a message is outputted, and the gameover flag is set to true to stop the game. However, the player's hands are also evaluated. For each player who has a hand equal to 21, a congratulatory message is outputted, and the gameover flag is set. The gameover flag is used later; it signals to the program that the game has completed.

Listing 7.6 Main Algorithm

```
// Get user information, and display rules (see Listing 7.1 for details)
GetUserData(listOfNames, numPlayers)
DisplayInstructions()
// Deal two cards to each participant (see Listing 7.3 for details)
DealTwoCards(deckOfCards, deckStatus, DealerHand, "Dealer")
i = 1
While i <= numPlayers Do
    DealTwoCards(deckOfCards, deckStatus, PlayerHand[i], listOfNames[i])
    Increment i
End While
// Evaluate hands (see Listing 7.5 for details)
handValue = HandEvaluation(DealerHand, 2)
If handValue equals 21 Then
    Output "Dealer Wins :("
    gameOver = true
End If
i = 1
While i <= numPlayers Do
    handValue = HandEvaluation(PlayerHand[i], 2)
    If handValue equals 21 Then
        Output listOfNames[i], " is a Winner! :)"
        gameOver = true
    End If
    Increment i
End While
```

You have completely solved at least half of the original subproblems. These are the original subproblems from the first iteration:

1. Determine the names of the players.

2. Display the instructions.

3. The dealer deals two cards to each player. If someone has 21, the game is over.

4. The players decide to stay with the cards they have or take additional card(s).

5. After the players have all the cards they want, evaluate the hands for a winner.

The subproblems 1–3 have now been solved with algorithms that can be converted to C++ code. However, if you look carefully, you see that more than that has been solved. The subproblems in 4 and 5 are based on dealing cards and evaluating hands, which is already done! So now you get to reuse the work that has been done to solve these subproblems.

Allow Players to Take More Cards

There are two subproblems to be addressed to complete the design of the Blackjack game. The first of the subproblems is to allow players to take more cards to try to reach 21. The second subproblem is to evaluate the final hands and determine winners. The second iteration on the first subproblem produces the following thoughts:

1. Display the player's hand.

2. Ask the player to take a hit or stand.

3. If the player takes a hit, he is dealt as many cards as he wants.

4. Repeat steps 1–3 for each player.

This refinement is much closer to the level of detail needed to write an algorithm. In this iteration, notice that you can use the DealCard function again.

Listing 7.7 shows the algorithm for a player move. This algorithm is for use by human players. The algorithm starts by asking if the user wants a hit. If the user answers yes, the card is dealt, and the number of cards in the user's hand is increased. This continues until the player says no; then the algorithm says the player stands.

Listing 7.7 Algorithm for Dealing More Cards

```
Function DealToPlayer(deckOfCards, deckStatus, playerHand, cardsInHand, pla-
yerName)
    Output "Player turn: ",playerName
    Output "Hand: ", playerHand[1], playerHand[2]
    Do
        Output "Do you want a hit? (y/n)"
        Input answer
        If answer equals "y" Then
            Increment cardsInHand
            playerHand[cardsInHand] = DealCard(deckOfCards, deckStatus)
        End If
    While answer equals "y"
    Output "Player Stands"
End Function
```

This is only half the algorithms needed for dealing extra cards. The dealer must also take extra cards if desired. Because the computer will be the dealer, the function must have some decision-making built into it.

The algorithm in Listing 7.8 shows the dealer's approach to taking hits. The dealer keeps taking hits until the total card value is greater than 16. This means the dealer's total will be at least 17. The done flag is there to allow cards to be dealt until the goal is reached. Notice that HandEvaluation is used in this algorithm to determine whether the dealer should continue drawing cards or stop.

Listing 7.8 Algorithm for Dealer to Take Cards

```
Function Dealer(deckOfCards, deckStatus, playerHand, cardsInHand, playerName)
    Output "Player turn: ",playerName
    Output "Hand: ", playerHand[1], playerHand[2]
    done = false
    Do
        value = HandEvaluation(playerHand, cardsInHand)
        If value < 16 Then
```

```
            Increment cardsInHand
            playerHand[cardsInHand] = DealCard(deckOfCards, deckStatus)
        Else
            done = true
        End If
    While not done
    Output "Dealer Stands"
End Function
```

The algorithm in Listing 7.9 is an updated version of the main listing that allows the players to take more cards and the dealer to take more cards. This additional part of the algorithm uses the DealToPlayer and Dealer algorithms from Listings 7.7 and 7.8, respectively.

Listing 7.9 Main Algorithm

```
// Get user information and display rules (see Listing 7.1 for details)
GetUserData(listOfNames, numPlayers)
DisplayInstructions()
// Deal two cards to each participant (see Listing 7.3 for details)
DealTwoCards(deckOfCards, deckStatus, DealerHand, "Dealer")
i = 1
While i <= numPlayers Do
    DealTwoCards(deckOfCards, deckStatus, PlayerHand[i], listOfNames[i])
    Increment i
End While
// Evaluate hands (see Listing 7.5. for details)
handValue = HandEvaluation(DealerHand, 2)
If handValue equals 21 Then
    Output "Dealer Wins :("
    gameOver = true
End If
i = 1
While i <= numPlayers Do
    handValue = HandEvaluation(PlayerHand[i], 2)
    If handValue equals 21 Then
        Output listOfNames[i], " is a Winner! :)"
        gameOver = true
    End If
    Increment i
End While
```

```
If gameOver equals false Then
    // Allow players to take more cards in turn (see Listing 7.7 for details)
    i = 1
    While i <= numPlayers Do
        playerNumOfCards[i] = 2
        DealToPlayer(deckOfCards, deckStatus, PlayerHand[i],
                     playerNumOfCards[i] ,listOfNames[i])
        Increment i
    End While
    // Allow dealer to obtain more cards (see Listing 7.8 for details)
    dealerCards = 2
    Dealer(deckOfCards, deckStatus, dealerHand, dealerCards, playerName)
End If
```

Evaluate Hands for Winners

The final subproblem is to determine the winners of the game and display the final hands. This subproblem can use some of the work that is already done. For instance, the HandEvaluation function can evaluate each hand. After evaluating the hands, the hands must also be displayed. This can be done as a separate function or within the main algorithm.

The final main algorithm is presented in Listing 7.10. It repeats some of the code from the evaluation subproblem for when each player has two cards. This repeated code is a hint that the design can be improved. This is not uncommon when writing software. Even after completing a design down to the algorithm level, you will see other places to simplify the software by creating new functions for code that is used more than once. You will have an opportunity to do this as part of the exercises in this chapter.

Listing 7.10 Final Main Algorithm

```
// Get user information and display rules (see Listing 7.1 for details)
GetUserData(listOfNames, numPlayers)
DisplayInstructions()
// Deal two cards to each participant (see Listing 7.3 for details)
DealTwoCards(deckOfCards, deckStatus, DealerHand, "Dealer")
i = 1
```

```
While i <= numPlayers Do
    DealTwoCards(deckOfCards, deckStatus, PlayerHand[i], listOfNames[i])
    Increment i
End While
// Evaluate hands (see Listing 7.5. for details)
handValue = HandEvaluation(DealerHand, 2)
If handValue equals 21 Then
    Output "Dealer Wins :("
    gameOver = true
End If
i = 1
While i <= numPlayers Do
    handValue = HandEvaluation(PlayerHand[i], 2)
    If handValue equals 21 Then
        Output listOfNames[i], " is a Winner! :)"
        gameOver = true
    End If
    Increment i
End While
If gameOver equals false Then
    // Allow players to take more cards in turn (see Listing 7.7 for details)
    i = 1
    While i <= numPlayers Do
        playerNumOfCards[i] = 2
        DealToPlayer(deckOfCards, deckStatus, PlayerHand[i],
                    playerNumOfCards[i] ,listOfNames[i])
        Increment i
    End While
    // Allow dealer to obtain more cards (see Listing 7.8 for details)
    dealerCards = 2
    Dealer(deckOfCards, deckStatus, dealerHand, dealerCards, playerName)

   // Evaluate hands (see Listing 7.5 for details)
    handValue = HandEvaluation(DealerHand, dealerCards)
    If handValue equals 21 Then
        Output "Dealer Wins :("
    End If
    i = 1
    While i <= numPlayers Do
        handValue = HandEvaluation(PlayerHand[i], playerNumOfCards[i])
```

```
    If handValue equals 21 Then
        Output listOfNames[i], " is a Winner! :)"
    End If
    Increment i
  End While
End If
```

SUMMARY

In this chapter, you learned about top-down design concepts and principles. This chapter also demonstrated top-down design using a medium-scale problem: The Blackjack game. During the process, stepwise refinement was put into action, and you read about the various decisions that are made along the way.

The framework, tools, and concepts are the same for any problem, but the steps in the process are not. The design process requires more creativity as the problems grow in scale. There are several ways to design a Blackjack game. The differences could start with the first iteration of the stepwise refinement. Therefore, the best way to truly understand the process is to practice solving larger problems using the process.

The next chapter discusses another design approach named bottom-up design. This approach will complement the top-down approach from this chapter.

EXERCISES

The following questions test your knowledge of the material from this chapter. You can find the answers to these questions on the book's companion website at www.courseptr.com/downloads.

1. The Blackjack problem could be improved and made more modular by creating more functions to exploit code reuse. This is especially evident in the main algorithm. Write a function to evaluate all the hands in the game using the code from the main algorithm as a guide. Call the function EvaluateWinners. This function should output if the player wins, loses, or busts. Then rewrite the main algorithm to use this function.

2. It would be useful to have a DisplayHand function that displays the contents of a given player's hand, including the dealer's hand. Write this function, and find good places to use it in the algorithm to make the

program more user friendly. You should use your function in any functions that currently exist.

3. Create a top-down design using stepwise refinement for a microwave oven program. You should examine your own microwave oven for the features and use a menu-based approach for your program.

4. Create a top-down design for a money management program. The program should allow you to keep track of deposits and withdrawals for your bank account. Withdrawals can be cash or checks. Deposits can also be cash or check. Your program can be a menu-driven program or a command-based one.

5. Create a top-down design using stepwise refinement for the Uno card game. Your design should use the rules for Uno at www.unorules.com/. Your game should work for 2–4 players.

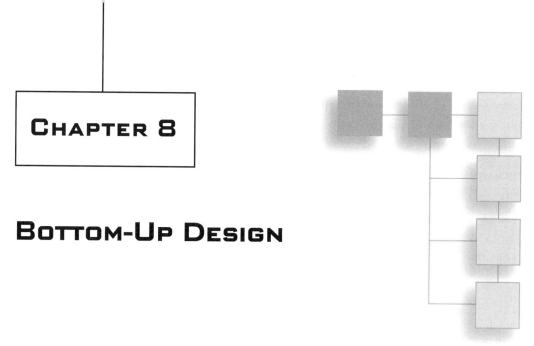

CHAPTER 8

BOTTOM-UP DESIGN

In This Chapter

- Bottom-Up Design Principles
- Bottom-Up Design Example
- Top-Down Versus Bottom-Up

"There are two ways to write error-free programs; only the third one works."

—Alan J. Perlis

The previous chapter introduced top-down design. The top-down design process is one way to tackle the problem solving for larger-scale problems. The complement to top-down design is bottom-up design. Bottom-up design occurs when you determine what programming assets are available to you, and you use them to build up your program instead of creating them yourself. To better understand this approach, consider what happens when you build with Legos or any other building set. If you want to build a car, you start looking for parts that you know are part of a car:

- Wheels and tires
- Seats
- Doors

- Windshield

- Engine

- Hood and trunk

If you have the right sets of parts, you will find many of these parts that are prefabricated for you to use in your car. This does not mean that every car will look the same; it just means that you get to reuse parts and possibly save time and effort because you do not have to build these components yourself. As you can see, bottom-up design can be efficient. However, it does require that you have enough components to build with.

The next section introduces the bottom-up process. It requires a set of assets that are presented as a library designed for making card games. Then the Blackjack game is presented again using bottom-up principles.

BOTTOM-UP DESIGN PRINCIPLES

Bottom-up design is popular in industry because many times, you are not building software from scratch. Instead, you are adding features to an existing software application. In this situation, it is important for the developer to learn the current design and the collection of components that is available as a library. Then the programmer writes solution for the feature using the available components.

Bottom-up design promotes certain characteristics in the software development process:

- **Bottom-up design promotes code reuse.** During the design process, you are exploring the various functions and data structures (that is, lists and arrays) that you can use in the program you are working on. You can find these components in libraries. These libraries can be standard C++ libraries, company-specific libraries, third-party libraries found online, or your personal library. If you are using library components, you know you are reusing code, and you are doing bottom-up design.

- **Bottom-up design typically leads to shorter programs.** Bottom-up design encourages the use of functions and other components that will do a lot of work for you. Therefore, you do not have to create it from scratch, you will ultimately have less code to write, and your programs will be shorter. Imagine having a program that is composed mostly of function calls because the logic of the program is embedded within the functions you are using.

- **Programs are typically easier to read.** The programs you write are usually shorter, and that leads to better readability. In addition, there is less to write because your program is using abstractions that hide the algorithmic details. Therefore, there are also fewer details for you to understand.

BOTTOM-UP DESIGN EXAMPLE

In Chapter 7, "Top-Down Design," Blackjack illustrated the process of top-down design. To maintain some consistency, this chapter also uses Blackjack as an example. However, you can now see how the same program would be built using bottom-up design. This provides a nice comparison and contrast experience of the two-design processes.

To demonstrate bottom-up design, there is a short introduction to a library to assist with card game software. The library is called the Card Game library, and it is presented using pseudocode. However, it could easily be the framework for a library in many languages.

Card Game Library

Suppose there exists a library that helps you build card games in C++. This library contains special data types for cards, decks, hands, and players and has functions that allow you to build any card game with them. Is this a far-fetched idea? Absolutely not. There are many libraries out there you can use to build programs in bottom-up fashion. You can find libraries online that may be able to help you with your own projects. The only problem with some libraries is that you may not know enough C++ to use them in some cases. However, if the library uses C++ ideas that you are comfortable with, you should consider using it in one of your projects.

The Card Game library contains a Deck data type and a Card data type that have several functions to operate on decks. These functions, which perform their actions on a deck of cards, are shown in Table 8.1. The first parameter in each function represents the deck of cards. The second parameters are the target of the actions. For example, `DealAll(deck, players, number)` is a function that deals cards from the deck. The other two parameters tell the function who gets the cards and how many cards they get. This pattern is followed throughout all portions of this library presentation.

Table 8.1 The Card Library for Decks

Name of Function	Description
`Shuffle(deck)`	This function shuffles the deck variable to have a random ordering.
`card Getcard(deck)`	This function returns the next card in the deck.
`PutCardTop(deck, card)`	This function puts the card on the top of the deck.
`PutCardBottom(deck, card)`	This function puts the card on the bottom of the deck.
`Deal(deck, player, number)`	This function deals one or more cards to a player.
`DealAll(deck, players, number)`	This function deals cards from the deck to each player in the list of players. The number says how many cards each player gets.

The `Card` data type has a set of specialized functions, shown in Table 8.2, that allow you to manipulate information about standard playing cards. There are functions to identify the suit of the card (spades, hearts, diamonds, or clubs) as well as the numeric value of the card. This data type also has a function that outputs the card information as an output statement would do.

Table 8.2 The Card Library for Cards

Name of Function	Description
`SuitName SuitOf(card)`	This function obtains the suit of a card.
`Value ValueOf(card)`	This function returns the value of the card. Cards are numbered 1–13 for ace–king.
`DisplayCard(card)`	This function displays the card on the screen.

The functions for the Hand data type are summarized in Table 8.3. This data type simulates a player's hand. A player's hand is considered a collection of `Card` typed data. The functions allow you to manage the hand of a player by adding

Table 8.3 The Card Library for Hands

Name of Function	Description
AddToHand(Hand, card)	This function adds a card to the hand.
RemoveFromHand(Hand, card)	This function removes a card from the hand.
DisplayHand(Hand)	This function displays the cards in the HAND variable.
number NumberOfCards(Hand)	This function returns the number of cards in the hand.
card GetCard(Hand, position)	This function allows you to get the card at a particular position. It does not remove the card from the hand.

and removing cards. There are also ways to show the entire hand or retrieve a copy of one of the cards in the hand. The GetCard function is useful for obtaining a card for processing. For example, there may be a need to discard a card from the hand. You use the GetCard function to get a card, and then you can remove the card from the hand.

```
myCard GetCard(myHand, 5)
// Processing myCard
RemoveFromHand(myHand, myCard)
```

The previous lines of pseudocode remove the fifth card from the player's hand. The first instruction obtains the fifth card in the hand. You can then analyze the card to determine if it should be discarded. The last instruction discards the card from the hand. If you want to put this card back into the deck, you can add the following instruction to the end:

```
PutCardBottom(theDeck, myCard)
```

This last instruction takes the myCard variable that was just removed from the hand and puts it on the bottom of the deck of cards referred to by the theDeck variable.

Table 8.4 summarizes the functions you can perform on the Player data type and the Players data type. The Player type represents a single player, whereas players is a list of players that a card game would want to manage. You can add and remove from the list, and you can set attributes of a player, such as the name and hand.

Table 8.4 The Card Library for Players

Name of Function	Description
players CreatePlayers(number)	This function creates a collection of players for the game.
player GetPlayer(players, position)	This function returns the player at a given position in the list of players.
RemovePlayer(players, player)	This function removes a player from the list of players.
AddPlayer(players, player)	This function allows you to get the card at a particular position. This does not remove the card from the hand.
setNames(players)	This function sets the names of the players in the list of players.
setHand(player, Hand)	This function sets the hand of the player to Hand.
name GetName(player)	This function returns the name of the player.
Hand GetHand(player)	This function allows access to the hand of the player.

The Card Game library has a rich collection of functions and types that you can use to design card games. In the next section, this library demonstrates how bottom-up design would be done for Blackjack.

Bottom-Up Design of Blackjack

The bottom-up design process uses assets such as the Card Game library to build a solution instead of deriving each component, as you saw in the top-down design. The bottom-up design process starts by looking for assets that relate to the problem you are trying to solve. In this case, you would have come across something like the Card Game library as a starting point. If you are planning to have graphics in your game, perhaps you can find other libraries that assist with graphics and graphical user interfaces (the buttons, menus, and so on). However, for this exercise, the assumption is that you are building a simple version of the game that you saw in Chapter 7, so the card library is sufficient.

The next step in the process is to write down the game-playing process. This is the same step that the top-down design process starts with. The following is a list of that process from Chapter 7:

1. Determine the names of the players.

2. Display the instructions.

3. The dealer deals two cards to each player. If someone has 21, the game is over.

4. The players decide to stay with the cards they have or take an additional card(s).

5. After the players have all the cards they want, evaluate the hands for a winner.

The next step is to start building the code for each of these subproblems using the library. The card library has functions for creating the players in the game.

The algorithm in Listing 8.1 shows how the Card Game library can simplify the design of the same function from Chapter 7. The function gets the user information and adds a dealer to the game as a player, because the dealer is also playing Blackjack. The function is so short that you may not even need to make it a function in the main algorithm. You could have the body of this function written directly in the main algorithm.

Listing 8.1 Algorithm to Obtain User Information

```
Function GetUserData(thePlayers)
    Output "Enter the number of players"
    Input num
    thePlayers = CreatePlayers(num)
    setNames(thePlayers)
    AddPlayer(thePlayers, Dealer)
End Function
```

The next part of the algorithm is to deal the initial two cards to the players in the game. The top-down design had two functions created to perform this task: DealCard and DealTwoCards. You can replace the statement in the first iteration by a single function found in Table 8.1. The Deal function deals a set number of cards to each player in the game. You can use the Deal function in the main algorithm; therefore, you do not need to create functions.

The main algorithm is shown in Listing 8.2. If you compare this to Listing 7.4, you see the simplicity that is created by this bottom-up design. The top-down design included function calls and a while loop. However, now you just have function calls, and two functions were eliminated from the code because the Deal library function solved the problem.

Listing 8.2 Main Algorithm for Blackjack

```
Shuffle(deckOfCards)
// Get user information and display rules (see Listing 8.1 for details)
GetUserData(thePlayers)
DisplayInstructions()
// Deal two cards to each participant (see Table 8.1 for details)
DealAll(deckOfCards, thePlayers, 2)
```

Listing 8.3 shows the function that evaluates a hand. The beginning of this function is made more readable by using the Card Game library. In the previous version, there were references to the hand as playerHand[position]. The while loop was also arguably more difficult to read and understand. However, the remainder of the code is the same. This is because the rules of Blackjack are encoded in this part of the algorithm. Typically, libraries contain concepts that are generic. The card game class contains functions that are useful to any card game, not specific games; this class is intended to help you write *any* card game.

Listing 8.3 Evaluating a Hand

```
Function HandEvaluation(playerHand)
    position = 1
    aceCount = 0
    handSum = 0
    numberOfCards = NumberOfCards(playerHand)
    While position <= numberOfCards
        theCard = GetCard(playerHand, position)
        If ValueOf(theCard) is an ace Then
            Increment aceCount
        else
            handSum = handSum + ValueOf(theCard)
        increment position
    End While

    // If there are no aces
    If aceCount is 0 Then
        Return handSum

    // If there are aces, follow these steps
    handSumFirst = handSum + aceCount
```

```
        handSumSecond = handSum + 10 + (aceCount - 1)

    If handSumFirst >= handSumSecond Then
        If handSumFirst <= 21 Then
            Return handSumFirst
        Else
            Return handSumSecond

    If handSumSecond > handSumFirst
        If handSumSecond <= 21 Then
            Return handSumSecond
        Else
            Return handSumFirst
End Function
```

Note

> Some libraries may have more specific features targeted toward popular uses. For example, a card library may have a hand evaluation function that has options to choose from popular games such as Blackjack and Poker. Therefore, when you are looking for libraries, you should try to choose one that will provide you as many features to support all aspects of your program as possible, but also remember that generality is typically the goal of library design.

The evaluation portion of the main algorithm has been added in Listing 8.4. This part of the algorithm is different from Listing 7.4 because of the Card Game library, and because dealers are considered players. Now all the hands of the players can be evaluated. The GetPlayers function retrieves a player from the list of players in the game. Then the GetHand method retrieves the hand for each player. When you use abstractions, it is common to have to chain together several function calls to get the data that you require. The main algorithm does not usually add much code, and it makes the result a lot more readable in the process.

Listing 8.4 Main Algorithm for Blackjack

```
// Get user information and display rules (see Listing 8.1 for details)
GetUserData(thePlayers)
DisplayInstructions()
// Deal two cards to each participant (see Table 8.1 for details)
DealAll(deckOfCards, thePlayers, 2)
```

```
// Evaluate hands (see Listing 8.3 for details)
i = 1
While i <= numPlayers Do
    thePlayer = GetPlayer(thePlayers, i)
    handValue = HandEvaluation(GetHand(thePlayer))
    If handValue equals 21 Then
        Output getName(thePlayer), " is a Winner! :)"
        gameOver = true
    End If
    Increment i
End While
```

Listing 8.5 performs the same task as the function in Listings 7.7 and 7.8 combined. This must be written as a combined function because the dealer is treated like another player. Therefore, it would not make sense to have separate functions for dealing more cards to the player and the dealer.

Listing 8.5 Algorithm for Dealing More Cards

```
Function DealToPlayer(thePlayer, deckOfCards)
    Output "Player turn: ", GetName(thePlayer)
    DisplayHand(GetHand(thePlayer))
    If thePlayer is the theDealer Then
        value = HandEvaluation(theDealer)
        While value < 21 Do
            Deal(deckOfCards, theDealer, 1)
            value = HandEvaluation(theDealer)
        End While
    Else
        Do
            Output "Do you want a hit? (y/n)"
            Input answer
            If answer equals "y" Then
                Deal(deckOfCards, thePlayer, 1)
            End If
        While answer equals "y"
        Output "Player Stands"
    End If
End Function
```

The number of parameters is down from five to just one. The references to list elements are removed as well. The result is a simpler and easier-to-read function. Also, you can see the power of code reuse up to this point. The functions GetName and GetHand have been used several times in Listings 8.1 through 8.5.

The final version of the main algorithm is shown in Listing 8.6. If you compare this version to Listing 7.10, you see that this main algorithm is shorter and could be made even shorter by creating a function to evaluate all players. In addition, this main algorithm has higher readability. Someone who has no experience with programming could probably make much better sense out of this version than the version in Listing 7.10.

Listing 8.6 Final Main Algorithm for Blackjack

```
// Get user information and display rules (see Listing 8.1 for details)
GetUserData(thePlayers)
DisplayInstructions()
// Deal two cards to each participant (see Table 8.1 for details)
DealAll(deckOfCards, thePlayers, 2)

// Evaluate hands (see Listing 8.3 for details)
i = 1
While i <= numPlayers Do
    thePlayer = GetPlayer(thePlayers, i)
    handValue = HandEvaluation(GetHand(thePlayer))
    If handValue equals 21 Then
        Output getName(thePlayer), " is a Winner! :)"
        gameOver = true
    End If
    Increment i
End While
If gameOver equals false Then
    // Allow players to take more cards in turn (see Listing 8.5 for details)
    i = 1
    While i <= numPlayers Do
        thePlayer = GetPlayer(thePlayers, i)
        DealToPlayer(thePlayer, deckOfCards)
        Increment i
    End While
    // Evaluate hands (see Listing 8.3 for details)
    i = 1
    While i <= numPlayers Do
```

```
        thePlayer = GetPlayer(thePlayers, i)
        handValue = HandEvaluation(GetHand(thePlayer))
        If handValue equals 21 Then
            Output getName(thePlayer), " is a Winner! :)"
        End If
        Increment i
    End While
End If
```

Top-Down Versus Bottom-Up

You might be wondering which design philosophy is the best one for you to adopt and use: top-down or bottom-up. In reality, neither is better than the other. These processes are complementary. When you have to design software from scratch or add to existing software, you are likely to use both processes to help you achieve your best design. For example, in Chapter 7 you saw a top-down design of the Blackjack game. Once the design was done, there was an exercise pointing out opportunities to create more functions and make a more modular design. Once the design was completed, you had assets that you created. You could then use these assets to create a more modular design and increase the code reuse. This is a bottom-up mentality. Some problems are difficult to solve using only bottom-up because the assets you have do not match closely enough with the problem you are solving. In other words, the abstractions provided by your assets are far enough below the abstraction of the problem that you have to perform a few iterations of stepwise refinement to break down the abstractions of the problem far enough to meet the level of the assets.

For example, Figure 8.1 shows that the Blackjack game is one-level of abstraction from the Card Game library. This means that the Blackjack design can directly use the Card Game library to solve problems. It also implies that, in some cases, the Card Game library can replace the need to build entire functions from scratch. For example, in the top-down design, the card-dealing functions had to be written from scratch, but because the Card Game library has a dealing function, there is no need to create one from scratch.

In contrast, Figure 8.2 shows that if you have only a game library, you will be missing all the goodies in the Card Game library. This means that you have to

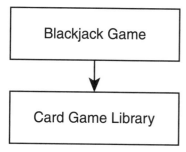

Figure 8.1
One level of abstraction between the Blackjack game and Card Game library.

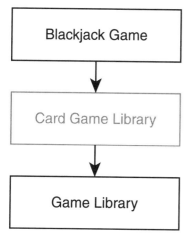

Figure 8.2
At least one level of abstraction between the Blackjack game and a game library.

build the concepts of cards, decks, and hands. You may be able to find a player abstraction in the game library that you can use. In this case, the game library does not have enough abstractions for everything that needs to be created for the Blackjack game. Therefore, you need to use some top-down methodology to generate the missing functions and other components. Bottom-up methodology would take advantage of the Player type that the game library supplies.

Finally, you will use a top-down approach to determine what the assets should be. After determining the assets, you will realize that you need some that are not available to you. Therefore, you will create the remainder of the assets and then use a bottom-up approach to assemble them for a solution. This is the approach used by object-oriented programming, which is a topic covered later in this book.

So, there really is no competition between top-down and bottom-up. In fact, you should look at these methods as teammates to help you solve complex problems.

SUMMARY

This chapter is the third chapter focused on design in this book. It presented the bottom-up method for solving problems and building algorithmic solutions and programs. The bottom-up process is used where you are solving a problem and you are aware of a library of programming components that can do some of the work for you. Your goal is to reuse these components and build your program like you would use Lego bricks to build a house, vehicle, or other structure.

In this chapter, you saw how to take a basic library that was designed for card games and build the Blackjack game, which resulted in different algorithms than the top-down version of the game. You saw examples of how to employ code reuse and asset abstractions to create more readable designs.

Finally, you learned about the relationship between top-down and bottom-up design. You saw that these two methods are not opposites in conflict with one another; actually, they are complementary and can be used together to create elegant, modular, efficient, and creative designs.

EXERCISES

The following questions test your knowledge of the material from this chapter. You can find the answers to these questions on the book's companion website at www.courseptr.com/downloads.

1. Use the Card Game library and build a Go Fish game.

2. The Card Game library presented in this chapter is just a small version of what else is possible. List three other features that you think would be good for a Card Game library. List your features as a function with parameters and a short description.

3. Create more modularity by removing the redundant code in the main algorithm that evaluates all the players in the game. Write a function called EvaluateWinners. This function should examine all the players and output if each player wins, loses, or busts. Then rewrite the main algorithm to use this function.

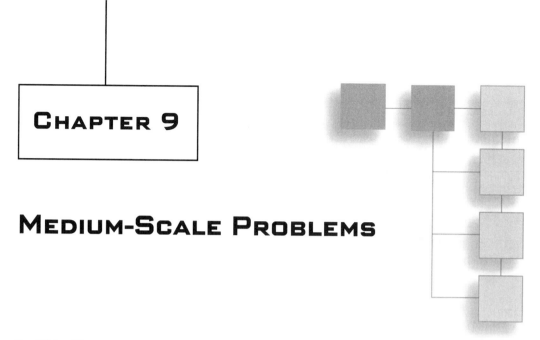

CHAPTER 9

MEDIUM-SCALE PROBLEMS

In This Chapter

- Blackjack Game
- Data Representation: Single and Multidimensional Arrays
- Functions: Pass-By-Reference in C++
- The Complete Blackjack Functions in C++
- Case Study: Expense Report Program
- Records in C++
- Files in C++
- Complete Expense Report Program

There are two ways of constructing a software design. One way is to make
it so simple that there are obviously no deficiencies. And the other way
is to make it so complicated that there are no obvious deficiencies.

—C.A.R. Hoare

Chapter 7, "Top-Down Design," and Chapter 8, "Bottom-Up Design," discussed
important software design practices that are typically needed to solve medium-
scale problems. These are problems that require more data and more functions

to solve. In Chapters 7 and 8, you explored the two complementary design processes within the context of creating a solution to the Blackjack game.

In this chapter, you discover how to implement the Blackjack design from Chapter 7 into C++, while also learning about some new C++ features and expanding your knowledge of some previously covered features such as functions. In addition, a simple database application is presented to display new C++ features.

The new C++ features introduced in this chapter include pass-by-reference, multidimensional arrays, parallel arrays, pointers and dynamic memory allocation, and records using classes.

Blackjack Game

The Blackjack game designed in Chapter 7 has been implemented in this chapter. An example of its output is shown in Listing 9.1.

Listing 9.1 Output from Blackjack Program

```
Enter the number of players to play: 2
Please enter the name of Player #1: Dawn
Please enter the name of Player #2: Jimmy
-----------------------------------------------------------
Player: Dealer has the following hand: 3S, JC
Player: Dawn has the following hand: JS, JD
Player: Jimmy has the following hand: 7C, 6H
-----------------------------------------------------------
Player turn: Dawn
Dawn's current hand: JS, JD
Dawn's current total: 20
Do you want a hit? (y/n) n
Dawn Stands
-----------------------------------------------------------
Player turn: Jimmy
Jimmy's current hand: 7C, 6H
Jimmy's current total: 13
Do you want a hit? (y/n) y
Jimmy's new Card: AD
Jimmy's current total: 23
-----------------------------------------------------------
```

```
Dealer's turn
Hand: 3S, JC
Dealer's new card: 5D and current total: 23
-----------------------------------------------------------
Dealer busts!
Dawn beat the dealer and wins!
Jimmy busts and did not win.
```

The output in Listing 9.1 shows one round of Blackjack. The program asks for the players' names and then uses those names through the game as part of the prompts. Two characters are combined to represent the value and the suit of the cards. For example, the first character is A (ace), 2–10, J (jack), Q (queen), or K (king) to represent the value of the card, and the second character is C (clubs), D (diamonds), S (spades), or H (hearts) to be the suit of the card. Players are given the option to take a hit unless their hands are equal to 21 or over 21. All hands are evaluated at the end of the game to determine the winner.

The next section covers the data structures used in this program.

Data Representation: Single and Multidimensional Arrays

The data representation in the Blackjack program demonstrates the use of single-dimensional and multidimensional arrays. The single-dimensional arrays are not a new concept for this book; however, they are used as parallel arrays. Parallel arrays represent how multiple arrays can hold collections of data in different arrays that are correlated with each other. Multidimensional arrays have more than one subscript; there is one subscript for each dimension.

Parallel Arrays in Other Languages

Parallel arrays are not just a C++ concept; they are a programming concept that you can implement in any programming language that supports arrays. The example in Figure 9.1 shows three arrays: firstName, lastName, and Age. The first two arrays would be arrays of strings, and the third array would be an array of integers.

	firstName	lastName	Age
[0]	Charles	Jones	25
[1]	Stacy	Mills	34
[2]	Larry	Smith	19
[3]	Aaron	Thomas	30
[4]	Margaret	Johnson	38
[5]	Tom	Washington	55
[6]	Zachnary	Hill	45

Figure 9.1
An example of three arrays being used as parallel arrays to store data about people.

The arrays in Figure 9.1 are parallel because the data stored at a location in the firstName array is associated with the data at the same location in the other two arrays. The following would be a sample C++ declaration:

```
string firstName[100];
string lastName[100];
int    age[100];
```

Note that parallel arrays must be the same length, and typically, these arrays are used together. For example, if you needed to print all the data, you may have a loop like the following:

```
for (int i = 0; i < 100; i++) {
    cout << setw(15) << firstName[i] << setw(20) << lastName[i]
        << setw(4) << age[i] << endl;
}
```

All three arrays are accessed independently for the cout statement that will make it appear that the record of information about the person is stored together when it is outputted to the screen. You can also write the functions for adding new people or removing people; these functions require all three arrays to update in a coordinated fashion.

Parallel Arrays in C++

In the Blackjack game implementation, there are several instances of parallel arrays. The first instance keeps track of each player's name and the number of cards each player has. The declarations for these arrays follow:

```
string listOfNames[MAX_PLAYERS];
int playerNumOfCards[MAX_PLAYERS];
```

These two arrays store strings and integers, respectively. They have the same size based on the `MAX_PLAYERS` constant. These two arrays are used cooperatively in several function calls throughout the body of the `main` function:

```
DealToPlayer(deckOfCards, deckStatus, playerHand[i], playerNumOfCards[i] ,
listOfNames[i]);
DealTwoCards(deckOfCards, deckStatus, playerHand[i], listOfNames[i]);
```

Both `DealToPlayer` and `DealTwoCards` are responsible for updating the number of cards in the player's hand. These functions use the player's name to personalize the prompts and output so that it's clear which player is being dealt cards.

Introduction to Multidimensional Array Concepts

Multidimensional arrays are arrays that have more than one subscript. The most common multidimensional array is a two-dimensional array, which is sometimes called a *matrix*. Figure 9.2 shows graphic examples of a 2D array and a 3D array.

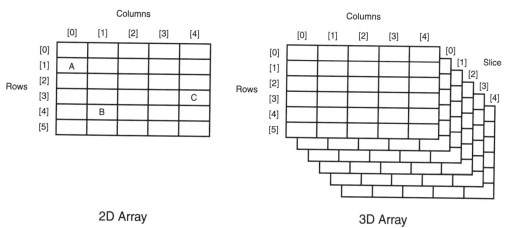

2D Array   3D Array

Figure 9.2
Examples of multidimensional arrays: 2D array and 3D array.

The 2D array has rows (horizontal cells) and columns (vertical cells). To identify an element in a 2D array, you have to use a row and column location. In Figure 9.2, the 2D array contains three elements: A, B, and C. The letter A is found at position (1, 0), which is row 1 and column 0. The letter B is found at position (4, 1), and C is found at position (3, 4).

The 3D array is built as multiple 2D arrays, where each 2D array is sometimes called a *slice*. To reference an element in the 3D array, you have to have three values (row, column, slice). The slice selects which of the 2D array slices is being referenced. See Figure 9.2, where the slices are labeled. For example, the location (3, 4, 2) would correspond to the cell on the fourth row, fifth column, and third slice. (Remember: all references start at 0.)

Multidimensional Arrays in C++

The Blackjack game provides an example of a two-dimensional array. Its declaration is the following:

```
string playerHand[MAX_PLAYERS][MAX_CARDS_PER_HAND];
```

The declaration for a 2D array is an extension of the single-dimensional array. The same rules apply to the second dimension as to the first dimension. In this case, `playerHand` maintains the hands of cards for each player. Each row represents the cards in a player's hand. Player 1 is at row 0, player 2 is at row 1, and so on. When you declare a two-dimensional array, the first index is always the maximum number of rows, and the second index is the maximum number of columns.

Suppose you want to display all the cards for each player's hand. Then you can use nested loops like the ones in Listing 9.2.

Listing 9.2 Examples to Display Contents of 2D Arrays

```
1: for (int row = 0; row < MAX_PLAYERS; row++) {
2:      for (int col = 0; col < MAX_CARDS_PER_HAND; col++) {
3:              cout << playerHand[row][col] << " ";
4:      }
5:      cout << endl;
6: }
7:
```

```
8:
9:
10: row = 0;
11: while (row < MAX_PLAYERS; row++) {
12:     col = 0;
13:     while (col < MAX_CARDS_PER_HAND) {
14:             cout << playerHand[row][col] << " ";
15:             col++;
16:     }
17:     cout << endl;
18:     col++;
19: }
```

Listing 9.2 shows two loop nests that do the same thing. The first loop nest in lines 1–6 uses the `for` loop. The outer loop controls the rows, and the inner loop controls the columns. The second loop nest is shown in lines 10–19. This loop nest uses `while` loops to perform the same task. Notice that the `cout` on lines 3 and 14 prints the cards for a given player on one line of output. Each player's hand is shown on a separate line because of the `cout << endl` on lines 5 and 17.

Multidimensional arrays can be passed to functions as well. Recall that you can pass a single-dimensional array using this template for the function definition header:

```
return-type function-name(element-type array-name[])
```

The `array-name[]` does not require that you specify the size of the array within the brackets. This allows the function to be used for arrays of different sizes. In the case of multidimensional arrays, you have to specify the maximums for the other dimensions after the first dimension:

```
return-type function-name(element-type array-name[][max-columns][max-slices])
```

This template shows that if you were to write a function to display the contents of a 2D array like the `playerHand` array, you would have to specify the maximum number of columns. The function `DisplayHands` is shown in Listing 9.3.

Listing 9.3 DisplayHands Function to Demonstrate 2D Array Parameter

```
1: void DisplayHands(string 2dArray[][MAX_CARDS_PER_HAND], int numPlayers) {
2:
3:     for (int row = 0; row < numPlayers; row++) {
```

```
4:                  for (int col = 0; col < MAX_CARDS_PER_HAND; col++) {
5:                      cout << 2dArray[row][col] << " ";
6:                  }
7:                  cout << endl;
8:          }
9: }
```

The function in Listing 9.3 shows how to pass a 2D array as a parameter. This function would be called like the following:

```
DisplayHands(playerHand, 2);
```

This function call would display the cards in the hands for two players. Although the Blackjack game does not have this function, it does use the playerHand array in dealing cards and evaluating hands. The following three function calls show a different way to use a 2D array in a program:

```
DealTwoCards(deckOfCards, deckStatus, playerHand[i], listOfNames[i]);
DealToPlayer(deckOfCards, deckStatus, playerHand[i], playerNumOfCards[i] ,
listOfNames[i]);
handValue = HandEvaluation(playerHand[i], playerNumOfCards[i]);
```

Each of these function calls is using the playerHand 2D array by passing one row at a time. The [i] is the first index of the 2D array that determines the row of the array. All three of these functions have headers that would remind you of single-dimensional arrays being passed to them:

```
void DealTwoCards(const string deck[], bool status[], string hand[], string
name)
void DealToPlayer(const string deck[], bool status[], string hand[], int& num-
Cards, string name)
int HandEvaluation(const string hand[], int numCards)
```

These examples have the parameter for the playerHand row indicated in bold. Each parameter refers to a single-dimensional array. The functions themselves do not care whether the single-dimensional array comes from the row of a multidimensional array or an actual single-dimensional array. This is an example of how the contract between the function calls and function definitions is based on the structure of the data type and not the name of the data type.

The data structures in the Blackjack game are both single dimensional and two dimensional arrays. In the next section, you examine how the functions in the Blackjack game introduce new behaviors for functions in C++.

FUNCTIONS: PASS-BY-REFERENCE IN C++

Until this chapter, you have worked with functions that pass parameters and return values using the `return` statement. If you needed to return more than one value, you had to split the functions into multiple functions. In general, pass-by-value functions are the safer ones to use whenever possible. However, in some cases you have a function that must return or update more than one value. This is not possible using pass-by-value. Recall that pass-by-value occurs when the value of the parameters is passed from the calling function to the function by copying the values. Pass-by-reference occurs when the values are not copied; instead, a reference is made between the calling function and the called function. A diagram comparing pass-by-value and pass-by-reference is shown in Figure 9.3.

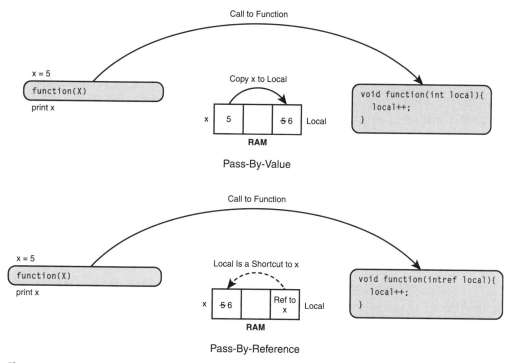

Figure 9.3
Diagrams of pass-by-value versus pass-by-reference.

Figure 9.3 shows some details to illustrate how pass-by-value is different from pass-by-reference. In the pass-by-value diagram (top of Figure 9.3), the program assigns 5 to x and then calls `function(x)`. The call invokes the system to copy the value from the variable x to the variable local. The view of RAM is that now there are two copies of the value 5: one for x and one for local. After the copy, the two values are independent. When function increments local, it changes local from 5 to 6, but it does not affect x. This is pass-by-value where a copy is used.

Alternatively, you can use a pass-by-reference, as shown in the pass-by-reference diagram (bottom of Figure 9.3). Everything executes the same until the function is called. At this time, a reference is made from local to x. The reference means that when local is changed in function, x is also updated. Therefore, the diagram shows that there is only one 5, and it is stored in x. After function updates local, the print x prints the value of 6 and not 5.

Notice that in Figure 9.3, the pseudocode indicates that the type of local is an int in the pass-by-value version, but it is an intref in the pass-by-reference version. In C++, the intref is written as int&, where the & means reference. You can use the ampersand with any type of parameter. The Blackjack program has several examples of pass-by-reference:

```
void GetUserData(string names[], int& num)
```

In the preceding examples, the GetUserData function asks for the number of players and the names of the players. That means this function updates the num parameter with the number of players. It also updates the names array. In C++, all arrays are passed to functions using pass-by-reference because of efficiency and not because it changes.

Note

In a program, arrays can be large. Larger arrays would cause the program to execute slowly if they were copied during a function call using pass-by-value. Instead, arrays are always pass-by-reference, because setting up the reference takes the same amount of time regardless of the size of the array.

If arrays are always pass-by-reference, how do you protect a function from altering an array the way x is protected in pass-by-value of Figure 9.3? If you do not want the function to update the array, you add the keyword const to the function prototype and definition. The headers for DealToPlayer and Dealer use the word const for the deck parameter. This is because you cannot change the contents of the deck of cards during the function call.

The other examples of pass-by-reference are in these headers:

```
void DealToPlayer(const string deck[], bool status[], string hand[],int&
numCards, string name)
void Dealer(const string deck[], bool status[], string hand[],int& numCards)
```

These two functions allow the players to take a hit and obtain more cards and for the dealer to do the same. The numCards parameter in both of these functions may change after the calls to these functions; therefore, this parameter is passed by reference. The calls to functions using pass-by-reference do not change, as shown in Listing 9.4 on lines 25, 53, and 59.

Listing 9.4 The main() Function for Blackjack

```
1: /*
2:  * Name: main
3:  * Description: The main program for playing Blackjack.
4:  */
5: int main()
6: {
7:      string listOfNames[MAX_PLAYERS];    // Names of players
8:      int playerNumOfCards[MAX_PLAYERS]; // Number of cards held by a player
9:      bool deckStatus[CARDS_IN_DECK];     // Determines what cards are taken
10:      string dealerHand[MAX_CARDS_PER_HAND];   // The dealer's hand
11:      // Maintains hands for all players

12:      string playerHand[MAX_PLAYERS][MAX_CARDS_PER_HAND];
13:
14:
15:      int numPlayers;                 // The number of players in the game
16:      int handValue;                  // The value of a player's hand
17:      bool gameOver = false;          // Set to true when game is over
18:      int numDealerCards;             // The number of cards the dealer has
19:      int dealerHandValue;            // The value of the dealer's hand
20:
21:
22:      srand(time(NULL));              // Support random card dealing
23:
24:      // Get user information and display rules
25:      GetUserData(listOfNames, numPlayers);
26:
```

```
27:
28:     // Deal two cards to the dealer and each player
29:     numDealerCards = 2;
30:     DealTwoCards(deckOfCards, deckStatus, dealerHand, "Dealer");
31:
32:     for (int i = 0; i < numPlayers; i++){
33:         playerNumOfCards[i] = 2;
34:         DealTwoCards(deckOfCards,deckStatus, playerHand[i],
35:                     listOfNames[i]);
36:     }
37:
38:     // Evaluate hands
39:     handValue = HandEvaluation(dealerHand, 2);
40:
41:     // Game is over if the dealer has 21
42:     if (handValue == 21) {
43:         cout <<   "Dealer has 21 and the game is over" << endl;
44:         gameOver = true;
45:     }
46:
47:
48:     // If the dealer does not have 21, the game continues
49:     if (gameOver == false) {
50:
51:         // Allow players to take more cards in turn
52:         for (int i = 0; i < numPlayers; i++) {
53:             DealToPlayer(deckOfCards, deckStatus, playerHand[i],
54:                         playerNumOfCards[i] ,listOfNames[i]);
55:         }
56:
57:
58:         // Allow dealer to obtain more cards
59:         Dealer(deckOfCards, deckStatus, dealerHand, numDealerCards);
60:
61:
62:         cout << "-------------------------------------------------------\n";
63:
64:         // End of game: Evaluate hands
65:
66:         // Compute the dealer's hand
```

```
67:        dealerHandValue = HandEvaluation(dealerHand, numDealerCards);
68:
69:
70:        // First, evaluate the dealer's hand value
71:        if (dealerHandValue == 21) {
72:            cout <<   "Dealer has 21" << endl;
73:        } else if (dealerHandValue > 21) {
74:            cout << "Dealer busts!" << endl;
75:        }
76:
77:        // Each player is compared to the dealer's hand and to 21
78:        // to determine his status.
79:        for (int i = 0; i < numPlayers; i++) {
80:
81:            // Compute the value of the player's hand
82:            handValue = HandEvaluation(playerHand[i], playerNumOfCards[i]);
83:
84:            // Evaluate the player's hand
85:            if (handValue == 21) {
86:                cout << listOfNames[i] << " has 21! Great Job :)" << endl;
87:            } else if (handValue > 21) {
88:                cout << listOfNames[i] << " busts and did not win." << endl;
89:            } else if (handValue > dealerHandValue || dealerHandValue > 21) {
90:                cout << listOfNames[i] << " beat the dealer and wins!" << endl;
91:            } else {
92:            cout << listOfNames[i] << " did not beat the dealer and loses!"
93:                << endl;
94:            }
95:        }
96:    }
97:
98:    return 0;
99: }   // End of main
```

Listing 9.4 shows the main function for the Blackjack implementation. You can compare this listing to the pseudocode in Chapter 7 for Blackjack. It starts by getting the user information in line 25. Lines 28–36 deal two cards to the dealer and each player. These lines also determine if the dealer has 21; the game then ends by setting gameover to true and skipping the large if statement on lines 48–96. The code on lines 52–59 allows each player and the dealer to take hits or to stand. Lines 67–92 determine the winner of the game by evaluating the dealer's hand and then comparing the dealer's hand to each player's hand.

THE COMPLETE BLACKJACK FUNCTIONS IN C++

The remainder of the Blackjack implementation is shown in Listings 9.5 to 9.11 to complete the process of taking the Blackjack problem from idea to algorithm to C++ implementation. Each function is explained in some detail here to point out how C++ implements some of the algorithmic ideas from the pseudocode and to display more programming techniques.

The GetUserData function in Listing 9.5 is called from main. Its job is to obtain the number of players and their names from the user. The function has two parameters: an array for the player names (names) and the number of players (num). The first parameter is used in lines 10–13 to ask the user for the number of players. A do-while loop ensures that the user enters a value that is not greater than the maximum number of players. In lines 17–23, the loop is executed to retrieve the name of each player from the user. The num variable serves as the upper bound for the loop.

Listing 9.5 GetUserData Function

```
1: /* Name: GetUserData
2:  * Parms: names          array of player names
3:  *          num           The number of players
4:  * Description: Gets the number and names of players from
5:  * the user.
6:  */
7: void GetUserData(string names[], int& num) {
8:
9:      // Get the number of players less than the max possible
10:     do {
11:             cout << "Enter the number of players to play: ";
12:             cin >> num;
13:     } while (num > MAX_PLAYERS);
14:
15:
16:     // Gets the names of each player
```

```
17:        for (int count = 0; count < num; count++) {
18:            string nameOfPlayer; // Localized use and declaration
19:
20:            cout << "Please enter the name of Player #"<< count + 1 << ": ";
21:            cin >> nameOfPlayer;
22:            names[count] = nameOfPlayer;
23:        }
24:        cout << "----------------------------------------------------------\n";
25:
26: }
```

Listing 9.6 shows two functions: `DealTwoCards` and `DealCard`. The `DealTwoCards` function is built to accept a player's hand as an array. It also takes the deck of cards and the `status` array. The `status` array entries are `true` if the card has been dealt, and they are `false` if the card has not been dealt. It is maintained in parallel with the `deck` array. This function uses the `DealCard` function to deal one card at a time and assign it to the first and second positions of the hand: `hand[0]` and `hand[1]`.

The `DealCard` function is the second function in Listing 9.6. It is called in lines 10 and 11 as a part of the `DealTwoCards` function. It randomly selects a card from the `deck` array. However, it only returns the card to the calling function if the card has not been dealt. This prevents having the same card show up more than once from the deck. It is achieved by checking the corresponding location in the `status` array first to see if the card has been dealt. If the status is `true`, the card has been dealt, so the loop forces the program to choose another card at random. If the status is `false`, the card's status is set to `true`, and it is returned to the calling function.

Note

The loop that chooses the card has the potential for executing a long time if the random number generator continues to choose cards that have already been selected. The probability of an abnormal delay is remote. However, you could alter this algorithm to try random seeking some fixed number of times, such as 25. If it continues to fail to find a card, you could perform a linear search until it either finds a card or determines all cards have been dealt and then reshuffles the deck.

Both of these functions use pass-by-reference to optimally pass the arrays to the functions. However, you shouldn't change the `deck`, so its parameter is preceded by a const. The status array changes because cards are dealt, so it does not have the const qualifier.

Listing 9.6 DealTwoCards and DealCard Functions

```
* Parms: deck    arrays of cards
1: /* Name: DealTwoCards
2:   * Parms: deck    array of cards
3:   *          status array of bools to determine if card has been dealt
4:   *          hand    array of cards in the player's hand
5:   *          name    the name of the player
6:   * Description: This function deals the first two cards of a player's hand.
7:   */
8: void DealTwoCards(const string deck[], bool status[],
9:                                       string hand[], string name) {
10:      hand[0] = DealCard(deck, status);
11:      hand[1] = DealCard(deck, status);
12:      cout << "Player: " << name << " has the following hand: ";
13:      cout << hand[0] << ", " << hand[1] << endl;
14: }
15:
16:
17: /* Name: DealCard
18:   * Parms: deck    arrays of cards
19:   *          status array of bools to determine if card has been dealt
20:   * Description: Uses an array as the deck of cards and randomly selects
21:   * a card that has not been dealt.
22:   */
23:
24: string DealCard(const string deck[], bool status[]) {
25:      int choice;
26:
27:      // Selects a card at random and checks its dealt status
28:      do {
29:              choice = rand() % CARDS_IN_DECK;
30:
31:              // If not dealt, then deal it
32:              if (status[choice] == false) {
33.                      status[choice] = true;
34:                      return deck[choice];
35:              }
```

```
36:    } while(1);
37: }
```

Listing 9.7 contains the two functions that compute the value of a hand of cards in Blackjack. The first function, named HandEvaluation, scans the hand and computes its value. The second function, named CardValue, uses ASCII codes to determine the value of individual cards. Lines 22–33 count the number of aces and compute the sum of the cards in a hand, omitting the aces in the sum. The aces are dealt with next by determining how many of them exist. If there are no aces, the function is finished on line 37. Two sums are computed if aces are involved. In the first sum, all the aces are considered 1s. In the second sum, one ace is considered 11, and all others are 1s. Lines 48–55 determine which sum should be the value of the hand. It uses the same rules any player would use for the decision. The value of the hand is the higher of the two sums that is 21 or less. If both are over 21, the player has busted, and the first sum is returned.

The CardValue function is designed to only process cards that are 2–10, jack, queen, or king. This is because the aces are filtered out in the HandEvaluation function on line 25. The main goal is to convert characters into integers. Line 72 handles cards 2–9. In this case, the ASCII codes for characters 2–9 are 50–57. Therefore, the subtraction of the codes from 48, which is 0, reveals the numeric value of the character. For example, the character 5 has an ASCII code of 53; subtracting 48 from 53 results in the integer 5. The else clause on lines 74–75 returns the integer 10 for all the other cards considered by this function (that is, tens, jacks, queens, and kings.

Listing 9.7 HandEvaluation and CardValue Functions

```
1: /* Name: HandEvaluation
2:  * Parms: hand array of cards in the player's hand
3:  *        numCards the number of cards in the hand
4:  * Description: Computes the point value for the player's hand.
5:  * It does this by computing the value of the hand where all
6:  * the aces are 1s and where one ace is an 11 and the rest
7:  * are 1s. The function returns the highest value that is
8:  * not over 21.
9:  */
10:
11: int HandEvaluation(const string hand[], int numCards) {
```

```
12:        int position = 0;    // Position in the hand
13:        int aceCount = 0;    // Number of aces in the hand
14:        int handSum = 0;     // The total value of the hand
15:        int handSumFirst;    // Total value: aces are all 1's
16:        int handSumSecond;   // Total value: 1 ace is an 11
17:
18:        // Scan the entire hand and count the number of aces and
19:        // sum the non-ace cards
20:        while (position < numCards) {
21:                string card = hand[position];
22:
23:                // The first character of a card is the value.
24:                // The ace begins with the letter A.
25:                if (card[0] == 'A')
26:                        aceCount++;
27:                else {
28:                        // Each card has a value determined by CardValue
29:                        handSum = handSum + CardValue(hand[position]);
30:                }
31:                position++;
32:
33:        }
34:
35:
36:        // If there are no aces, no special sum is needed
37:        if (aceCount == 0)
38:                return handSum;
39:
40:        // If there are aces, two sums are computed
41:        handSumFirst = handSum + aceCount;
42:        handSumSecond = handSum + 11 + (aceCount - 1);
43:
44:
45:        // Determines which hand value to return:
46:        // returns 21, the largest value under 21, or
47:        // a bust value.
48:        if (handSumFirst <= 21 || handSumSecond <= 21)
49:                if (handSumFirst >= handSumSecond)
50:                        return handSumFirst;
51:        else
```

```
52:                          return handSumSecond;
53:        else
54:                     return handSumFirst;
55: }
56:
57:
58: /* Name: CardValue
59:  * Parms: card a playing card with value and suit
60:  * Description: compute the Blackjack value of the
61:  * card based on the first character of the card string.
62:  */
63:
64: int CardValue(string card) {
65:      char charVal;
66:
67:      // Gets the first character to determine value
68:      charVal = card[0];
69:
70:      // Numeric characters are converted using ASCII values
71:      // All others are considered 10s
72:      if ( (charVal >= '2') && (charVal <= '9') )
73:                return (int)charVal-48;
74:      else
75:                return 10;
76: }
```

Listing 9.8 shows the function `DealToPlayer`. This function is responsible for allowing the player to take hits or stay with the current card total. The function uses pass-by-reference parameters for efficiency in passing arrays. But it also uses it because the parameter may be updated. The `status` and `hand` arrays are updated if the player takes a hit. The `numCards` parameter is updated if the player takes a hit also. Line 27 determines if the player is eligible to take a hit, meaning that the cards in the current hand must be less than 21. Lines 33–36 process a hit that a player takes. The `DealCard` function returns a card, and it is placed in the next available position in the hand.

Listing 9.8 DealToPlayer Function

```
1: /* Name: DealToPlayer
2:  * Parms: deck         array of cards
```

```
3:  *         status    array of bools to determine if card has been dealt
4:  *         hand      array of cards in the player's hand
5:  *         numCards  the number of cards in the player's hand
6:  *         name      the name of the player
7:  * Description: This function allows a player to take hits or
8:  * stand.
9:  */
10:
11: void DealToPlayer(const string deck[], bool status[], string hand[],
12:                   int& numCards, string name) {
13:     char answer;   // Answer to take a hit or stand
14:
15:     cout << "----------------------------------------------------------\n";
16:     cout << "Player turn: " << name << endl;
17:     cout << name << "'s" <<   " current hand: " << hand[0] << ", "
18:          << hand[1] << endl;
19:
20:     // Loop continues for the player to take hits
21:     do {
22:             cout << name << "'s current total: "
23:                  << HandEvaluation(hand, numCards) << endl;
24:
25:             // If player has less than 21, he has the option
26:             // to take a hit or stand.
27:             if (HandEvaluation(hand, numCards) < 21) {
28:                     cout << "Do you want a hit? (y/n) ";
29:                     cin >> answer;
30:
31:                     // Taking a hit here
32:                     if (answer == 'y') {
33:                             numCards++;
34:                             hand[numCards-1] = DealCard(deck, status);
35:                             cout << name << "'s" << " new Card: "
36:                                  << hand[numCards-1] << endl;
37:                     }
38:             } else {
39:                     // Hand value is 21 or greater.
40:                     // No more cards can be taken.
41:                     return;
```

```
42:                    }
43:
44:        } while (answer == 'y');
45:
46:        cout << name << " Stands" << endl;
47: }
```

The function in Listing 9.9 is the Dealer function, which is the dealer equivalent of the DealToPlayer function. The function contains parameters that serve the same purpose as they did in the DealToPlayer function. The primary difference is that the dealer must stay when the hand value reaches at least 17.

Listing 9.9 Dealer Function

```
1: /* Name: Dealer
2:  * Parms: deck       array of cards
3:  *        status     array of bools to determine if card has been dealt
4:  *        hand       array of cards in the player's hand
5:  *        numCards the number of cards in the player's hand
6:  * Description: This function acts as the dealer in taking hits. The dealer
7:  * will always take a hit when the hand is less than 17. If 17 or above the
8:  * dealer will stand.
9:  */
10:
11: void Dealer(const string deck[], bool status[], string hand[],
12:              int& numCards) {
13:
14:      bool done = false;       // Set when the dealer limit is reached
15:      int handValue;         // The value of the hand
16:
17:      cout << "----------------------------------------------------------\n";
18:      cout << "Dealer's turn" << endl;
19:      cout << "Hand: " << hand[0] << ", " << hand[1] << endl;
20:
21:      // The loop continues while dealer value is less than 17
22:      do {
23:              handValue = HandEvaluation(hand, numCards);
24:
25:              // Stop taking cards if at least 17
26:              if (handValue >= 17)
```

```
27:                          done = true;
28:            else {
29:                      // The dealer takes a hit
30:                      numCards++;
31:                      hand[numCards-1] = DealCard(deck, status);
32:                      cout << "Dealer's new card: " << hand[numCards-1]
33:                              << " and current total: ";
34:                      cout << HandEvaluation(hand, numCards) << endl;
35:
36:                  }
37:
38:        } while (!done);
39:
40:        cout << "Dealer Stands" << endl;
41: }
```

This concludes the Blackjack implementation. You are encouraged to test the program on your own and try rewriting parts of it to see if you can get the same results. This also concludes a case study that has spanned three chapters to show the analysis and design process to the implementation. Undoubtedly, you will see some slight variations in the implementation from the algorithm in the design. The reasons for this may be that C++ provides different ways to handle parts of the algorithms, or during implementation you sometimes determine other ways to write the solution that are cleaner or more efficient when written in the implementation language. Remember: your algorithms guide you in writing the implementation, but feel free to explore alternative approaches to parts of the algorithm during implementation.

CASE STUDY: EXPENSE REPORT PROGRAM

This section discusses some more advanced features of C++, but within the context of an expense report program. This program is a simple database application, where the expense report is maintained in a database of records. Each record in the database contains the expense date, budget category, and amount. The program allows the user to interact with the expense database via a menu. It loads saved expenses from a file and then allows the user to use a menu to add expenses, remove expenses, generate an expense report, and search expenses. When the program ends, the expense data is saved to the expense report data file. The data file has the following format:

```
<number of expense records>
<date₁> <category₁> <amount₁>
<date₂> <category₂> <amount₂>
...
<dateₙ> <categoryₙ> <amountₙ>
```

This file format shows that the first line of the file is the number of expense records in the file. The expense records follow that number. Each expense record has its own line and contains the date, budget category, and amount of the expense.

The file shown in Listing 9.9 is a sample expense data file used to test the expense report program and generate the output shown in Listing 9.10.

Listing 9.9 The Contents of the Expenses.exp File

```
6
4/7/2011        mortgage            2000.00
4/8/2011        dining              36.00
4/9/2011        car                 300.00
4/9/2011        insurance           66.00
4/10/2011       groceries           150.00
4/10/2011       gas                 45.00
```

Listing 9.10 Sample Output from the Expense Report Case Study

```
                Expense Menu

1. Add an expense
2. Remove an expense
3. Search for an expense
4. Generate an expense report
5. Exit
Please enter your menu selection(1-5): 4


                Expense Report

1:      4/7/2011        mortgage        $2000
2:      4/8/2011          dining        $36
```

3:	4/9/2011	car	$300
4:	4/9/2011	insurance	$66
5:	4/10/2011	groceries	$150
6:	4/10/2011	gas	$45

Expense Menu

1. Add an expense
2. Remove an expense
3. Search for an expense
4. Generate an expense report
5. Exit
Please enter your menu selection (1-5): 2

Expense Report

1:	4/7/2011	mortgage	$2000
2:	4/8/2011	dining	$36
3:	4/9/2011	car	$300
4:	4/9/2011	insurance	$66
5:	4/10/2011	groceries	$150
6:	4/10/2011	gas	$45

-1: To Return to main menu
Enter the number of the row you would like to remove: 2
Date: 4/8/2011
Category: dining
Amount: $36.00
Are you sure you want to delete the above entry?(y/n) y
Expense Report

1:	4/7/2011	mortgage	$2000.00
2:	4/9/2011	car	$300.00
3:	4/9/2011	insurance	$66.00
4:	4/10/2011	groceries	$150.00
5:	4/10/2011	gas	$45.00

-1: To Return to main menu
Enter the number of the row you would like to remove: -1

Expense Menu

1. Add an expense
2. Remove an expense

```
3. Search for an expense
4. Generate an expense report
5. Exit
Please enter your menu selection(1-5): 1

Enter date: 4/12/2011
Enter category: lunch
Enter amount: $10.00
You entered the following:

Date: 4/12/2011
Category: lunch
Amount: $10.00
Is the data entered correctly (y/n)? y

                Expense Menu
1. Add an expense
2. Remove an expense
3. Search for an expense
4. Generate an expense report
5. Exit
Please enter your menu selection(1-5): 3

Enter a search text: lunch
1:    4/12/2011            lunch        $10.00

                Expense Menu
1. Add an expense
2. Remove an expense
3. Search for an expense
4. Generate an expense report
5. Exit
Please enter your menu selection(1-5): 5
Thank you for using expenses!
```

This output shows how a user can generate an expense report that shows all the records, add an expense to the database, remove an expense from the database, and perform a search. As you learn how this program is constructed, you will also learn how to use dynamic memory allocation and records in C++.

Introduction to Dynamic Memory Allocation Concepts

Medium-scale problems usually present issues with using arrays. These issues revolve around allocating enough memory for the arrays in the program to support the needs of the user. For example, suppose you are writing a banking program that maintains a history of bank transactions. If you have an array of bank transactions for each month, your array would be different lengths each month, depending on the number of transactions. In both of these cases, you will not know the size of the array until your program is executing.

Consider the banking program, and one way you may be thinking of doing this is to make MAX_TRANSACTIONS a large value so that the programs could handle any number of transactions. For example, suppose that you set MAX_TRANSACTIONS to 1,000. This would mean that you would be setting your computer to allocate enough memory to handle 1,000 transactions for each month. Suppose a client that has one month with 950 transactions is using your program, but the other 11 months are less than 100 transactions each. This means that you have allocated memory for thousands of transactions that were never made. This is a wasteful method for allocating memory because your guess was too high for the needs of the client. On the other hand, suppose your bank account program is servicing a business that requires more than 1,000 transactions in several months, and your program keeps reporting memory errors because the arrays are not large enough. This scenario means that you have not allocated enough memory for transactions to satisfy this client's needs.

In both situations, your program was not compatible with the memory needs of the user. You want your program to provide the right amount of memory in each situation. If the client needs a small amount of memory, your program should allocate that. If your client needs a large amount of memory, you should allocate a large amount of memory. However, when you have to allocate array sizes at the time of compiling the program, you have to make guesses that will not be appropriate for all clients. The alternative is to use dynamic memory allocation.

Dynamic memory allocation occurs when the program allocates memory based on the needs of the user during the program execution. Therefore, it allows your arrays to grow and shrink as necessary. If the user needs memory for 2,000 transactions in one month and memory for 100 transactions in the next month, that is the amount of memory that the program provides for each month. On the other hand, if the client needs memory for 20 allocations each month, the program only allocates memory for 20 allocations each month. Dynamic memory allocation allows your programs to be flexible by allocating memory as directed by the individual user's needs and not wasting memory by allocating too much.

Dynamic memory allocation systems also allow you to deallocate memory during the execution of the program. This is important in programs where information may be added and removed. When data is removed, the array can shrink to prevent waste. Removing data requires you to deallocate memory in your program.

Note

Dynamic memory allocation seems to provide you with an infinite supply of memory. However, this is a false assumption. Your computer is equipped with a certain amount of memory. The amount of memory that can be allocated to your program depends on the amount of memory on your computer and the allocation procedures of your operating system software.

Any dynamic memory allocation system provides ways for the programmer to allocate and deallocate memory during the execution of the program. In the next section, you learn how this is done in C++.

Dynamic Memory Allocation in C++

Dynamic memory allocation in C++ is done using pointers. A *pointer* is a memory location that contains the address of another memory location. A *pointer variable* is a variable that can hold the value of a memory address. Are you still not sure what a pointer is? Think about pass-by-reference shown in Figure 9.3. The memory cell for `local` says Ref to x. You would reference another variable by placing the address of the variable you are trying to reference in another variable, as `local` is in the example. If you know where x is, you can locate the value stored there. A pointer is simply a way to reference another memory location or variable. Now you know a secret: pass-by-reference is done by using memory pointers, or just pointers for short.

Pointers are powerful because they can refer to any memory location. Because a variable can represent them, while a program is executing, a pointer variable can be updated to point to a new memory address. The following are sample pointer variable declarations:

```
int* anIntPtr;
char* aCharPtr;
double* aDoublePtr;
```

The pointer variable declarations require a type to define what kind of memory location the pointer variable can point to. The * (asterisk) is the symbol used in the variable declaration to show that a pointer variable is being declared. A pointer can reference dynamically allocated memory if its address is assigned to the pointer variable.

C++ programs have a special part of memory known as the *heap*. The heap is where dynamic memory allocation takes place. You can think of the heap as a large basket of available memory locations. The operator called new retrieves the address of one of these locations and takes it out of the basket because it is no longer available. You can use the new operation like this:

```
anIntPtr = new int;
aDoublePtr = new double;
```

These examples create pointers to memory locations from the heap. The new operator returns NULL if the heap has no available memory locations. These examples allocate a single memory location. If you allocate an entire array of memory locations, the same operator that is used for array declarations is used here for allocation. Some examples include the following:

```
anIntPtr = new int[100];
aDoublePtr = new double[max_nums];
```

These examples create arrays dynamically and use the square bracket operator [ ]. The first example creates an array of 100 integers using the heap for the memory. The second example creates an array of size max_nums; it also uses the heap for its memory. The second example illustrates how a user's input may dictate the size of the array. Suppose there was a prompt earlier in the program where the user enters a maximum value and the input statement stores the request in the variable max_nums. Then, later in the program, the new operator creates an array of that size.

Dynamic Memory Allocation in Expense Report

The expense report program uses dynamic memory allocation to allow the user to enter as many expense records as needed. The expense records are maintained within an array. A pointer is used to refer to the dynamic array. The following is the declaration:

```
ExpenseRec *allExpenses;
```

Notice that this is a pointer to a new type: ExpenseRec. You learn how this is created in the next section, but for now assume it represents a record in your database that contains the date, budget category, and amount of a particular expense. The fact that allExpenses is a pointer is what allows the dynamic memory allocation in the program.

It is a good idea to initialize your array with a reasonable number of locations. You determine this as the programmer. In this program, maxSize is set to a good starting size for the array, and then the allocation is performed with the new operation as shown here:

```
allExpenses = new ExpenseRec[maxSize];
```

Later in this chapter, you will see how logic is added in the main function and addExpense function to adjust the size of the array based on the size of the input file and user additions, respectively. The next topic to discuss is how the expense records are implemented.

RECORDS IN C++

Most programming languages have a way of representing a record; C++ is no exception. A record is composed of data fields, where a data field contains one value that contributes to the record. Records are usually organized to form a database. For example, a school might have a database that contains records for the students in the school. Each student record could contain at least the following fields:

- Last Name
- First Name
- Middle Name

- Age

- Grade Level

- Homeroom Teacher

- GPA

There are many other fields that would make up a database record for a student, but this gives you an idea of the type of information that can be stored there and provides examples of fields.

C++ is a superset of the C language; therefore, it contains some antiquated constructs because it must support the C language. C defines records using the struct, which is short for structure. It allows you to define the fields of the record and the name of the record. However, C++ uses another construct called the class that defines user-defined data types and supports object-oriented programming, which will be discussed in Chapters 11, "Object-Oriented Programming in C++: Part I," and 12, "Object-Oriented Programming in C++: Part II."

Note

The standard language description for C++ states that structs and classes have the same capabilities. Therefore, when learning C++, it is more appropriate to learn how to use a class than to learn how to use a struct.

Defining Records in C++

A C++ class defines a data type that does not currently exist. For example, a record in a database is one data type you might want to create. The basic syntax for the class to define a record data type follows:

```
class <classname> {
public:
    <constructor>
    <type1> <data member name1>
    <type2> <data member name2>
    . . .
    <typen> <data member namen>
};
```

This definition introduces a new data type that is now named <classname>. The <type> and <data member> combinations define the types and the names of the fields in the database record. The <constructor> is a special function that is created to set initial values of new records.

For example, you could create the student record from earlier in this section by using the code in Listing 9.11.

Listing 9.11 Sample Record for a Student Database

```
class StudentRec {
public:
    StudentRec();
    string lastName;
    string firstName;
    string middleName;
    int age;
    int gradeLevel;
    string homeroomTeacher;
    double gpa;
};
```

The class in Listing 9.11 defines a data type called StudentRec that you can use to define an array of student records. The function StudentRec() is the constructor function for this record that will initialize it. The constructor function would be defined as follows:

```
StudentRec::StudentRec(): lastName(""), firstName(""), middleName(""), age(0),
gradeLevel(0), homeroomTeacher(""), gpa(0.0) {}
```

The constructor must have the same name as the class name. The :: is called a *scope* operator. The scope operator demonstrates ownership. It shows that the class StudentRec owns the constructor StudentRec(). You must include the scope operator in this function definition because the constructor belongs to the class. When you are initializing a database record, the values you choose to initialize each field are up to you. In this case, all the strings are initialized using the empty string, the integer fields are initialized with 0, and the real number fields are initialized with 0.0. Notice the {} at the end, which indicates the constructor is a function. In the case of database records, the body of the constructor is always empty. You will use the body of the constructor for object-oriented programming.

The expense report program has an expense report record defined to contain the information for one expense. This record is defined in Listing 9.12.

Listing 9.12 Expense Record for Expense Report Case Study

```
class ExpenseRec {
public:
    ExpenseRec();         // Constructor to initialize records
    string date;          // The date of the record
    string theCategory;   // The category of the record
    double value;         // The amount spent
};
```

The expense record is composed of two strings for the date and budget categories and a double that is the dollar amount spent. The constructor function is ExpenseRec(), and it has the following definition:

```
ExpenseRec::ExpenseRec(): date(""), theCategory(""), value(0.0) {}
```

This constructor initializes the data fields of the record and contains an empty body. It is executed whenever a new expense record needs to be created. The next section discusses how to use these record data types.

Using Records in C++

The class is the template for the records that you want to create in your program. Remember that these records are new data types in C++. You can use the names of these records in the same way you would use data types. For example, to create one record, you can define a variable:

```
StudentRec yourRecord;
StudentRec aFriendsRecord;
```

These examples define the variables named yourRecord and aFriendsRecord that are using the StudentRec data type to define what values they can hold. You can also use these data types for parameters of functions:

```
void UpdateRecord(StudentRec& aRec) { . . .}
void DisplayRecord(const StudentRec& aRec) { . . . }
```

These function definition headers are for functions that expect to receive `StudentRec` data as parameters. In both cases, pass-by-reference is being used because records can be arbitrarily large. Also, it is costly to copy the records for the same reasons it is costly to copy arrays, as discussed earlier in this chapter. The `const` modifier in the `DisplayRecord` parameter list protects the parameter from being changed even though it is passed-by-reference. This is the same concept used for arrays earlier in this chapter.

You can also create arrays of records. Using the class name as the data type for the array does this:

```
StudentRec arrayOfRecords[100];
```

The array declaration has no special rules. It now contains a collection of `StudentRec` data values instead of integers, floats, and strings.

Note

> The constructors of the classes are being executed when variables of their type are being declared. For example, when `yourRecord` is declared, the program executes the constructor for the `StudentRec` type. Constructors are also executed when they're used as parts of arrays or as part of dynamic memory allocation.

This summarizes the various ways that you can use records in a C++ program. Just remember that your record is a new type in your C++ program; therefore, you can use it in the same way that you used other data types.

Accessing Fields in C++ Records

Records are not that useful unless you are able to access the individual fields of the database records. These fields are accessed using the dot operator. The dot operator is a period (.) that shows something being a component of a data type. Consider the following examples:

```
yourRecord.firstName = "Jessica";
cout << yourRecord.firstName << endl;
if (yourRecord.age > "16") . . .
arrayOfRecords[5].firstName = "James";
cin >> arrayOfRecords[5].gpa;
cout << arrayOfRecords[i].lastName << endl;
```

This is a representative list of ways you might use the dot operator. The period separates the record variable from the field variable. For example, `yourRecord` is the record variable declared earlier, and `firstName` is the field variable. Another example is with arrays; `arrayOfRecords[5]` is the record variable, and `gpa` is the field variable. These examples demonstrate the flexibility of the dot operator. In essence, you employ the dot operator to access a field, which is essentially a variable that represents data. Therefore, you can use the fields of the record just like other data variables: in arithmetic expressions, as parameters, for input and output, and more.

FILES IN C++

Input and output has been done using the keyboard and console screen, respectively. However, if you have a program that requires a large amount of data for input, it is better to have the program read the input from a file instead of having a user enter the data. In addition, the output from your program may be required at a later time, or you might like to share with others, so you would want your program to output to a file instead of the screen. In both of these cases, you need to allow your program to manipulate files, which is what this section explains.

File Data Types in C++

Files in C++ are manipulated by variables declared in your program. These variables have to be defined using a file access data types. There are three primary file access data types:

- `ifstream`: Input file stream data type for declaring variables to manipulate input files

- `ofstream`: Output file stream data type for declaring variables to manipulate output files

- `fstream`: Input/output stream data type for declaring variables to manipulate files for input and output

These data types are accessed by using the #include directive to include the fstream header file as shown here:

```
#include <fstream>
```

This single header is used for all the file data types. The file data types are then used to declared file variables. Declaring a file variable resembles other variable declarations, as shown here:

```
ifstream inputFile;    // Input file variable
ofstream outputFile;   // Output file variable
```

These file variables become the interface for accessing data files on your computer. These data files contain all ASCII characters and are used in the same way as `cin` and `cout`. Before you get to that, you have to associate the file variable with a file. For example, suppose you created a data file that contains a list of names called `names.dat`. You would use the `open` function for files to open the file:

```
inputFile.open("names.dat");
```

The `open` function belongs to all the `fstream` data types, and it requires you to give it a string, string literal, or string variable that gives the name of the file it should open and associate with the file variable.

Using Data Files in IDEs

IDEs treat data files differently, so it is important for you to determine where the data file is in relationship to the binary program that is generated. Typically, an IDE compiles your program and places the binary version of the program in a folder separate from the source code that you typed in. However, your data file is still in the folder with the source code. Therefore, when you try to open the file

```
inputFile.open("names.dat");
```

it assumes the file is in the same folder as the binary. However, it is not in the same folder as the binary, so the program appears not to work because the file could not be opened.

In Microsoft Visual Studio, your executable binary program is placed in the `Debug` folder in the project folder. Suppose your project is called `playingWithFiles`. Then your executable will be in the folder `playingWithFiles/Debug`, but your source code and data files will be in `playingWithFiles/playingWithFiles`. Therefore, you have to alter the opening in the following way:

```
inputFile.open("../playingWithFiles/names.dat");
```

The `..` symbol means parent directory, which is the project folder. Then you have to go down one level into the project subfolder that has the same name as the project folder to access the data file.

In Xcode, the problem is solved in a different way. You do not have to change the open code, but you do change the configuration of the build process in the project. Locate the `targets` folder in the project window, and right-click on it and choose Add->New Build Phase->New Copy Files Build Phase. You choose the executables location and click OK. A build phase is a step that the IDE follows when building your program. This new build phase is for copying files to the location of the executable program. The final step is to drag your data file into this newly created build phase. Now when you build and run your program, the data file is copied to the same directory as the executable binary program.

After the names.dat file is opened, it is associated with the inputFile variable. After a file is opened, you can process the data in the file using several operations and techniques. When that is done, the file is closed using the close function as shown here:

```
inputFile.close();
```

A file must be closed when the program does not need to access it anymore. In some programs, the file is closed right after the processing of the file is completed, and in other programs the file may be closed just before the program ends. If you do not close files properly, you risk losing data in the files and causing problems for your operating system to function properly.

The next section covers how you read from and write to data files using C++.

File Processing in C++

Once you open a data file, you can read from the file (input) or write to the file (output). Files can be read using any of the input operations and functions used to read data from the keyboard, and the same is true for writing files. For example, consider having the names.dat file opened using the inputFile variable from the previous section. Suppose the file has the following contents:

```
Ralph
Jason
Alice
Mary
Mark
Rebecca
```

You could read the first three names from the file employing three uses of the extraction operator:

```
inputFile >> name1;
inputFile >> name2;
inputFile >> name3;
```

The variables name1, name2, and name3 must be declared as string variables, and these lines of code will extract the name Ralph into the variable name1, the name Jason into name2, and the name Alice into name3. Similarly, the insertion operator can output these names to an output file (assuming the outputFile variable is declared and used to open an output file) using the following lines of code:

```
outputFile << name1;
outputFile << name2;
outputFile << name3;
```

You should have noticed that file processing with the extraction and insertion operators requires replacing the cin with an input file variable and replacing the cout with an output file variable.

Note

You can practice using files for input and output by taking programs from previous chapters and altering them to read/write files instead. Input files are created using the same sequence of data that you typed as input. Place the data into the file using the exact pattern as the input. Then include fstream, declare a file variable, and open the file. After that, replace all occurrences of cin with the file variable. Now compile and run your program; the program outputs all the same prompts, but instead of waiting, it reads the data from the file and generates output. You can add output files to the program by declaring an output file variable, opening the file, and then replacing all the cout statements that you want to output to the file with the output file variable.

These are the basic ways to process a file. However, if you need to read every name from the file, you do not want a statement for each data item. In this case, use a while loop to read the data from the file. Consider the following loop:

```
inputFile.open("names.dat");
while (inputFile >> name) {
    cout << name << endl;
}
inputFile.close();
```

This loop reads all the names from the input file named names.dat. It does not matter how many names are in the file; each one is read. This is accomplished because the while loop is based on the expression inputFile >> name. This operation returns `true` when there is still data to read, but when it reaches the end-of-file marker, it returns `false`. The end-of-file is a special nonprintable character at the end of each file. No data can appear after the end-of-file marker. Because the expression `inputFile >> name` returns `true` when the marker has not been reached, the loop continues to read data and output data until the expression reaches the end-of-file marker and forces the loop to exit.

Sometimes you want to read the data into an array. Suppose you have an array of strings named `allNames`. You could alter the previous loop in the following way to read the data from the file into the array:

```
inputFile.open("names.dat");
i = 0;
while (inputFile >> allNames[i]) {
    i++;
}
inputFile.close();
```

This loop uses an index named `i` to access each element of the array. The input is done directly to the array. When the loop is completed, all the names in the file will be added to the array.

You can write data to output files using a loop in a similar fashion. Suppose you have the same array of names called `allNames`. It is currently filled with 100 names, and you want to output them to a file. The following loop is one way to achieve this:

```
outputFile.open("outputnames.dat");
for (int i = 0; i < 100; i++) {
    outputFile << allNames[i] << endl;
}
outputFile.close();
```

The opening of the output file is followed by the processing of the file. Notice that the insertion operators are used just like they would be for a `cout`. The `for` loop controls access to the array and outputs the contents of the array one element at a time. There is no need to test for end-of-file because you are writing the data to the file. The end-of-file marker is moved down each time you add data to the file.

File Error Handling in C++

One common problem with using files is that the program cannot open the file. This might happen for several reasons:

- The filename is misspelled.

- The file is not located where the program is attempting to access it.

- The file is currently being used by another program that has locked access to the file.

- The file is corrupt.

The easiest method for verifying that a file has been opened is to test the file variable after the open has been attempted. If the file variable evaluates to `true`, the file has been opened properly. If it evaluates to `false`, the file could not be opened. The following is an example of a typical `if` statement that is used for this verification:

```
inputFile.open("names.dat");
if (!inputFile) {
    cout << "The program was not able to open the file" << endl;
}
```

This code tests the value of the `inputFile` file variable. If the `inputFile` variable is `false`, there was an error opening the file. Therefore, the expression `!inputFile` will be `true`, and the program will notify the user of the problem.

Now it is time to examine the entire expense report program. The next section takes you through each function of the expense report case study program.

COMPLETE EXPENSE REPORT PROGRAM

The key functions for the expense report program are discussed in this section. They demonstrate the use of dynamic memory allocation and records. The prototypes for the key functions in addition to `main` follow:

```
bool AddExpense(ExpenseRec[], int&, int&);
bool RemoveExpense(ExpenseRec[], int&, int&);
bool ExpenseReport(const ExpenseRec[], int);
bool SearchExpenses(const ExpenseRec[], int);
```

From the prototypes, you can see that these functions also use pass-by-reference because data changes when expenses are added or removed. In addition, each function must access the array of expense records that is more efficiently passed using pass-by-reference.

The program starts with the main function that is shown in Listing 9.13. This function initializes the program and processes the menu selections. Lines 8–14 declare the variables needed in this program. Line 9 is particularly interesting because this is where the pointer is declared to support the dynamically allocated array expense records. Lines 32–37 determine the initial size of the array. The logic here is to set the array to a predefined minimum size if there are no records in the input file, but to double the size if there are records in the input file. The rationale is that if records are in the input file, the array needs to be large enough to hold those records, while also providing memory for the user to add additional records. The array is allocated on line 40, and then a for loop is used to read the data from the file into the newly allocated array. Lines 56–99 process the menu selections. The loop is set to loop indefinitely because the quit option from the menu ends the program. The switch statement processes each menu option. Each menu option calls a function to process the request. The only exception is the exit option on line 82. It could be done as a function, but it is done this way to show a variation. This option exits the program, but before it exits, it saves the data stored in the array of expense records to the expense file. By doing that, the next time the program loads, it can access the file.

There are examples of accessing fields of records in lines 46–48 and lines 91–93. The lines show how you can use the dot operator to read data into the fields and output data from the fields, respectively.

Listing 9.13 Main Function

```
1: /* Name: main
2:  * Description: This is the main function that initializes
3:  * the program and processes menu selections.
4:  */
5:
6: int main()
7: {
```

```
8:        int command;      // The command from the menu
9:        ExpenseRec *allExpenses; // Dynamic array of all expense records
10:       int noOfRecords;   // The number of expense records
11:       int maxSize;        // The current maximum size of the dynamic array
12:       fstream expenseFile; // The file handle for the expense file
13:
14:       string filename = "myexpenses.exp"; // Default expense filename
15:
16:
17:       // Open the expense file
18:       expenseFile.open(filename.c_str());
19:
20:       // The loop ensures that the file is opened before allowing
21:       // the program to continue
22:       while (!expenseFile) {
23:           cout << "Expense file could not be opened. ";
23:           cout << "Check file name and reenter the name" << endl;
24:           cin >> filename;
25:           expenseFile.open(filename.c_str());
26:       }
27:
28:       // Read the first line of the file with the number of records
29:       expenseFile >> noOfRecords;
30:
31:       // Adjust the size of the array to accommodate the records
32:       if (noOfRecords == 0) {
33:           maxSize = MIN_SIZE;
34:       }
35:       else {
36:           maxSize = 2 * noOfRecords;
37:       }
38:
39:       // Allocate an array big enough for the records
40:       allExpenses = new ExpenseRec[maxSize];
41:
42:       // Read all records from the file
43:       for (int i = 0; i < noOfRecords; i++) {
44:
45:           // Read one record
46:           expenseFile >> allExpenses[i].date
```

```
47:                          >> allExpenses[i].theCategory
48:                          >> allExpenses[i].value;
49:      }
50:
51:      // Close the file when reading is complete
52:      expenseFile.close();
53:
54:      // This loop runs infinitely to keep displaying the menu after
55:      // processing an option
56:      while (1) {
57:
58:          // The menu function displays the menu and returns the selection
59:          command = Menu();
60:
61:          // Process menu selection
62:          switch (command) {
63:              case 1:
64:
65:                      AddExpense(allExpenses, noOfRecords, maxSize);
66:                      break;
67:              case 2:
68:
69:                      RemoveExpense(allExpenses, noOfRecords, maxSize);
70:                       break;
71:
72:                case 3:
73:
74:                      SearchExpenses(allExpenses, noOfRecords);
75:                      break;
76:
77:                case 4:
78:
79:                      ExpenseReport(allExpenses, noOfRecords);
80:                      break;
81:
82:                case 5: // Exit and save the file
83:                      cout << "Thank you for using expenses!" << endl;
84:
85:                      // Reopen the file
86:                      expenseFile.open(filename.c_str());
```

```
87:                              // Write the number of records to the file
88:                              expenseFile << noOfRecords << endl;
89:                              // Save all records from the file
90:                              for (int i = 0; i < noOfRecords; i++) {
91:                                  expenseFile << allExpenses[i].date << "\t"
92:                                              << allExpenses[i].theCategory << "\t"
93:                                              << allExpenses[i].value;
94:                              }
95:
96:                              return 0;
97:
98:                  default:
99:                      break;
100:              }
101:      }
102:
103:      return 0;
104: }
```

The ExpenseReport function shown in Listing 9.14 is executed for number 4 on the menu. It is called from main (Listing 9.13, line 82) when the user selects the option. This function displays a table of expenses that might resemble the following output:

Expense Report

```
1:    4/7/2011        mortgage      $2000
2:    4/8/2011          dining      $36
3:    4/9/2011             car      $300
4:    4/9/2011       insurance      $66
5:   4/10/2011       groceries      $150
6:   4/10/2011             gas      $45
```

You can see that the output is placed in neatly arranged columns. Each record is prefixed with its position in the array of expense records. It is common to display position values starting from 1 even though the array starts at 0. This is accomplished in the output statement in line 13 of Listing 9.14.

You access the data values in the fields using the dot operators in lines 14–16. The allExp[i] is accessing the i'th expense record of the array.

Listing 9.14 ExpenseReport Function

```
1: /* Name: ExpenseReport
2: * Parms: allExp    The list of expense records
3: *          numRecs The number of expense records in the list
4: * Description: This function generates an expense report as
5: * a table. Each report is numbered.
6: */
7:
8: bool ExpenseReport(ExpenseRec allExp[], int& numRecs) {
9:      cout << setw(33) << "Expense Report\n\n";
10:
11:      for (int i = 0; i < numRecs; i++) {
12:              // Columns are set up for the data
13:              cout << i + 1 << ":";
14:              cout << setw(12) << allExp[i].date;
15:              cout << setw(15) << allExp[i].theCategory;
16:              cout << setw(8)  << "$" << allExp[i].value << endl;
17:      }
18:
19:      return true;
20: }
```

Listing 9.15 shows the SearchExpenses function, which allows the user to enter a keyword and the program to find matching records. To reemphasize the fact that a search function should not change the contents of the array, the const modifier is used on the parameter.

The search text is inputted on line 16, followed by a loop to compare the search text with each record. The records are divided into fields, and a nifty concept combines the fields to allow easier searching. The fields are combined using the string concatenation operation on line 23. This allows you to use the find function for strings to locate the search text. The statement aRecord.find (searchText) finds the searchText in the string named aRecord. This function returns the position where the searchText is found, or it returns the constant string::npos if searchText is not found. If a match is found, the dot operator is used again to output the contents of the record in lines 28–31.

Listing 9.15 SearchExpenses Function

```
1: /* Name: SearchExpenses
2:  * Parms: allExp    The list of expense records
3:  *           numRecs  The number of expense records in the list
4:  * Description: This function allows the user to search
5:  * for keywords in the contents of any expense records.
6:  */
7:
8: bool SearchExpenses(const ExpenseRec allExp[], int numRecs) {
9:      string searchText;
10:     string aRecord;
11:     int pos = 1;
12:
13:
14:     cout << "Enter a search text: ";
15:     cin.ignore();   // Need to clear the input buffer
16:     getline(cin, searchText); // Read entire line of text
17:
18:
19:     // Examine each record for the search text
20:     for (int i = 0; i < numRecs; i++) {
21:
22:             // Concatenate the fields into one string
23:             aRecord = allExp[i].date + " " + allExp[i].theCategory;
24:
25:             // Search the record for any occurrence of the search text
26:             if (aRecord.find(searchText) != string::npos) {
27:                     // If a match, output the entire record
28:                     cout << pos << ":";
29:                     cout << setw(12) << allExp[i].date;
30:                     cout << setw(15) << allExp[i].theCategory;
31:                     cout << setw(8)  << "$" << allExp[i].value << endl;
32:                     pos++;
33:             }
34:     }
35:
36:     return true;
37: }
```

Listings 9.16 and 9.17 are opposite operations. The function in Listing 9.16 is called RemoveExpense, and the function in Listing 9.17 is called AddExpense. These functions update the array of expenses, which is why they use pass-by-reference for all parameters that can be affected by a change in the size of the array. This includes the array, the number of elements in the array, and the array's maximum capacity.

The RemoveExpense function in Listing 9.16 allows the user to remove as many items as he would like, but only one at a time. The loop starting on line 14 accomplishes this part of the task. The ExpenseReport function is called on line 16 to display the expenses currently stored in the database. This is a nice example of code reuse. The positions of the records in the array also act as menu options. The user selects a position to delete that element from the array in line 20. Deleting an element from an array uses an algorithm known as a shift-left. This means that the elements of the array are shifted to the left to overwrite the deleted element. The loop on lines 32–33 accomplishes this task. After the shifting, the number of elements in the list is decremented by one in line 37.

Listing 9.16 RemoveExpense Function

```
1: /* Name: RemoveExpense
2: * Parms: allExp    The list of expense records
3: *         numRecs   The number of expense records in the list
4: *         size      The maximum size of the list
5: * Description: This function removes an expense report from
6: * list after being presented with a list of records as options.
7: */
8:
9: bool RemoveExpense(ExpenseRec allExp[], int& numRecs, int& size) {
10:      int rowToDelete;
11:      char answer;
12:
13:
14:      do {
15:          // Display list of expenses to select from
16:          ExpenseReport(allExp, numRecs);
17:          cout << "-1: To Return to main menu" << endl;
18:          cout << "\n\n";
```

```
19:            cout << "Enter the number of the row you would like to remove: ";
20:            cin >> rowToDelete;
21:
22:            // Delete row that exists
23:            if (rowToDelete >= 1 && rowToDelete <= numRecs) {
24:
25:                displayRec(allExp[rowToDelete-1]);
26:                cout << "Are you sure you want to delete the above entry? ";
27:                cin >> answer;
28:
29:
30:                if (tolower(answer) == 'y') {
31:                    // Shift cells over the deleted element
32:                    for (int i = (rowToDelete - 1); i < (numRecs - 1); i++) {
33:                        allExp[i] = allExp[i+1];
34:                    }
35:
36:                    // Reduce the number of records
37:                    numRecs-;
38:                }
39:
40:            }
41:
42:     // Exit if user inputs -1
43:     } while (rowToDelete != -1);
44:
45:
46:     return true;
47: }
```

The AddExpenses function in Listing 9.17 allows the user to add expense records to the database. The user is asked to input the information for the new expense record; the inputs for each field using the dot operator are shown on lines 16, 19, and 23. After the number of records is increased, the function checks to see if the array is full. If it is, the array needs to be allocated more memory locations. Adding more memory locations is a four-step process:

1. Create a temporary array of new memory locations that is larger than the current array.

2. Copy the data from the current array of expense records to the temporary array.

3. Deallocate the memory that the current array expense records use.

4. Assign the array of new memory locations to the array of expense records.

These four steps can be expensive for a computer to perform because step 2 requires copying the entire array, which can take time, depending on how large the array is. Also, steps 1 and 2 require that, for a period of time, you need twice as much memory to perform the copy operation. Therefore, in these situations a programmer will decide to minimize the cost over time by significantly increasing the size of the array when it becomes full. This means you can perform many future add operations before you need to perform this costly operation again. The four steps are found in Listing 9.17 on line 41 for step 1, lines 44–45 for step 2, line 49 for step 3, and line 52 for step 4. These lines of code use pointer variables by declaring temp as a pointer to temporarily point to the temporary storage location. In addition, dynamic memory allocation is used on line 41 to make the temporary array twice as large as the current array.

Listing 9.17 AddExpense Function

```
1: /* Name: AddExpense
2:  * Parms: allExp     The list of expense records
3:  *             numRecs   The number of expense records in the list
4:  *             size      The maximum size of the list
5:  * Description: This function allows the user to enter a new
6:  * expense and adds it to the list of expense records.
7:  */
8:
9:
10: bool AddExpense(ExpenseRec allExp[], int& numRecs, int& size) {
11:     char answer;
12:
13:     do {
14:             // First, get the expense record data
15:             cout << "Enter date: ";
16:             cin >> allExp[numRecs].date;
17:
```

```
18:                    cout << "Enter category: ";
19:                    cin >> allExp[numRecs].theCategory;
20:
21:                    cout << "Enter amount: $";
22:                    cin >> allExp[numRecs].value;
23:
24:                    cout << "You entered the following: \n\n";
25:                    displayRec(allExp[numRecs]);
26:
27:                    cout << "Is the data entered correctly (y/n)? ";
28:                    cin >> answer;
29:
30:                    // Only accept the data if the user responds with y/yes
31:            } while (tolower(answer) != 'y');
32:
33:        // Increase the number of records
34:        numRecs++;
35:
36:        // Allocate more memory for the list if it's full
37:        if (numRecs == size) {
38:                ExpenseRec *temp; // Temporary space
39:
40:                // Allocate twice as much space
41:                temp = new ExpenseRec[2*size];
42:
43:                // Copy current data into the newly allocated space
44:                for (int i = 0; i < size; i++) {
45:                        temp[i] = allExp[i];
46:                }
47:
48:                // Deallocate the old space
49:                delete allExp;
50:
51:                // Assign the new space to the list
52:                allExp = temp;
53:        }
54:
55:        return true;
56: }
```

This concludes the explanation for the Expense Report case study program. The full source code is available on the companion website. You are encouraged to compile and learn from the source code. You can modify the algorithms and add your own features.

SUMMARY

This chapter presented two medium-scale programs—Blackjack and Expense Report—which illustrate the use of parallel arrays, pass-by-reference, dynamic memory allocation, and records in C++. In parallel arrays, you coordinate the data in different arrays so it appears they are stored together. This is useful in languages that do not support records. Pass-by-reference is used for performance and flexibility. Pass-by-reference allows you to build functions that update more than one value for the calling function. Pass-by-reference also makes passing records and arrays to functions more efficient by not copying the contents of these structures. The dynamic memory allocation uses pointers to allow your programs to allocate memory when they need it versus having to make all memory allocations up front. This flexibility allows your programs to adapt to the size of the user's data. Finally, you can use records in C++ to colocate related data as an alternative to parallel arrays. In addition, records allow you to create simple database applications. A class was used in this chapter to present records. You will read more about them in Chapters 11 and 12. Finally, this chapter introduced the concept of managing data files using C++. You learned how to open, process, and close the files.

EXERCISES

The following questions test your knowledge of the material from this chapter. You can find the answers to these questions on the book's companion website at www.courseptr.com/downloads.

1. Update the Blackjack program to allow the user to select the number of players to play the game. Your program should dynamically allocate enough memory to support the user's desires.

2. Write a program that reads a list of numbers into an array that is dynamically allocated and then produces the average for those numbers.

3. Write an address book program that allows you to store information for as many friends as you would like. The program should be menu driven and provide the ability to add, remove, display, and search records. Each record should contain the person's first name, last name, phone number, and email address. You should use dynamic memory allocation to allow the program to handle any number of records.

4. Write a program that reads the contents of a file and outputs the file in reverse order using an array of strings. Each array entry should represent a line in the file.

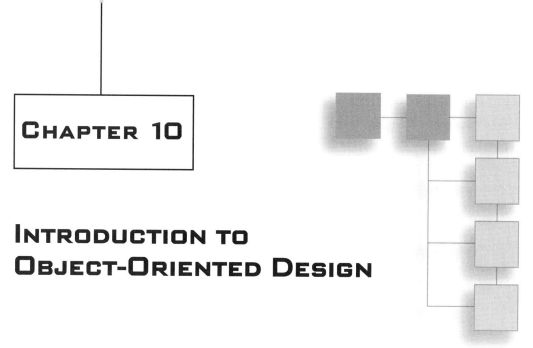

CHAPTER 10

INTRODUCTION TO OBJECT-ORIENTED DESIGN

In This Chapter

- Overview of OOP
- The Principles of OOP
- OOP as Simulation
- Object-Oriented Design Process

> Controlling complexity is the essence of computer programming.
>
> —Brian Kernigan

Object-oriented programming (OOP) is a programming model that is based on writing programs using objects. Object-oriented design (OOD) is the design methodology that you use to develop object-oriented programs. Objects are not a new concept to computing. Artificial intelligence researchers at the Massachusetts Institute of Technology (MIT) were the first to use the idea of objects, in the 1950s. However, the first programming language to introduce the concept of objects was Simula, invented during the 1960s. Simula was invented to be a programming language for writing simulation software. Simulations contain entities that have properties and perform actions. For example, a simulation of a fast food restaurant would need to model the customers, the employees, and the food items. Each customer, employee, or food item is viewed as an object that has properties (characteristics about the object) and methods (the actions/capabilities that the object is able to perform).

The 1980s made OOP popular because there was a "software crisis" occurring. The software crisis involved people thinking of sophisticated applications to create, at the same time the software development methodologies were insufficient to effectively build those systems. In other words, people's imaginations for what software could be and do stretched beyond the capabilities of the programming tools and methods. The reliance on strictly procedural and structured programming was not enough to tackle the more sophisticated and complex ideas. You have been learning procedural and structured programming from the start of this book and may be wondering why you did not just learn OOP first. It's a valid question. The first part of the answer is that OOP is primarily needed with complex solution designs. Previously, the problems you were solving did not require the power of OOD and OOP. The second part of the answer is that great object-oriented programs require you to be proficient in writing great algorithms and use both top-down and bottom-up design.

This chapter begins with an overview of OOP and concludes with an explanation and example of the OOD process.

OVERVIEW OF OOP

OOP has some foundational concepts that you need to understand before you can learn how to accomplish an OOD. These concepts can be illustrated using scenarios from everyday life. In this section, you learn the foundational concepts of OOP in the context of an everyday scenario.

Consider a scenario in which you want to have a special custom suit made as a birthday present for your dad. You are required to have the suit delivered on his birthday because he does not live in your town. The following is a description of the sequence of events that would probably take place:

1. You would look for a tailor in your town who could make custom suits. This search may require you to use your computer, phone, or local business pages.

2. Once you find the tailor, you tell him that you need a custom suit made, and it needs to be delivered on your father's birthday.

3. The tailor decides to accept the order, so you supply the tailor with the date for delivery; your dad's measurements, name, and address; and a swatch of the fabric that you need for the suit.

4. When the suit is complete, the tailor contacts you, and you pay for the work he did. The tailor makes arrangements for shipping the suit.

5. The tailor provides the shipping company with the package, your dad's name and address, and payment for shipping.

6. The shipping company takes the package and determines the best route for delivering the package by the due date.

7. When the package is delivered, you get a phone call thanking you for the great and thoughtful gift.

This scenario involves agents, methods, responsibilities, and messages. These four concepts are also found in OOP. *Agents* are the entities in the scenario that interact and perform actions. Examples of agents are you (the person purchasing the gift), the tailor, the shipping company, and the recipient. The *methods* are the actions that agents perform. For example, taking payments is a method, creating a suit is a method, and shipping a package is a method. *Responsibility* is the mapping of a method to an agent. For example, the taking payments method is mapped to both the shipping company and the tailor because they know how to take a payment for a product or service. The last concept is *messages*, which are the data provided to an agent. A message is usually coupled with a method. For example, you might provide the tailor with a message containing the measurements for your dad and a swatch, which then invokes the tailor to produce a suit.

Looking back at the scenario, you can rewrite it using the previous four concepts of agents, methods, responsibilities, and messages:

1. You (*agent*) send a *message* to the tailor (*agent*) that contains the measurements, cloth style, name and address of your dad, and the delivery date. It is the tailor's *responsibility* to satisfy your request.

2. The tailor (*agent*) uses the information in the *message* to perform *methods* to produce and ship the suit.

3. The tailor (*agent*) sends you a *message* that contains the invoice, and you (*agent*) use your *method* to produce a *message* to the tailor that contains the money to pay the invoice. The tailor (*agent*) uses a *method* to process the payment.

4. The tailor (*agent*) sends a message to the shipping company (*agent*) that contains the delivery date and destination information. It is the shipping company's *responsibility* to ship the package.

5. The shipping company (*agent*) uses the *message* to invoke *methods* for determining the best route for shipping and for performing the shipping.

6. Your dad (*agent*) receives the package as a *message* and then uses his *methods* to call you (*agent*) and thank you.

You can see how the four concepts—agents, methods, responsibilities, and messages—can simulate the scenario. This should give a hint about how the thought process for OOP is different from the structured procedural process you have been doing to this point. In top-down and bottom-up design, the solutions were centered on determining the proper functions and how they would work together to solve the problem. In OOP, the central figures are the agents, and determining a solution is centered on coordinating the agents to solve the problem.

THE PRINCIPLES OF OOP

OOP concepts have been introduced using an everyday scenario. In this section, you continue to use the same scenario to explore the governing principles of OOP. The principles of OOP are the rules that govern the OOP concepts. There are four main OOP principles:

- Messages initiate methods.
- Information hiding is the ability to hide/protect data from improper updates.
- Objects (aka agents) are instances of classes.
- Classes are organized in a hierarchy and utilize inheritance.

The first principle is that messages initiate methods. This principle enforces the connection between messages and methods. The messages are the data that is sent to an object. The method is the algorithm that is executed as a response to the message that was sent. The methods that are associated with an object are the responsibilities or features that the object supports. The tailor object receives the message that contains the measurements and cloth type. The tailor object then uses these components of the message to produce the suit. The suit is produced using an algorithm that the tailor has learned and perfected with experience. In programming, the object might be a bank account. The message might contain an amount of money that is to be withdrawn from the account. The bank account uses its withdrawal method that contains the algorithm for updating the account properly and issuing a receipt and the cash for the withdrawal. In these two examples, you see that methods are executed in response to messages and that methods contain the algorithms that perform the desired action.

The second principle is information hiding, which is where the language provides a way to protect an object's information from being tampered with from the outside. This principle contributes to the improved reliability of object-oriented applications. Objects in OOP contain attributes that define the information that the object is responsible for maintaining. For example, the shipping company agent would have information regarding its delivery routes, flight information, and driver schedules that are maintained to properly deliver packages. It does not allow other shipping companies or customers to directly access this information. Imagine the problems caused if customers could make changes to the delivery routes to get their packages sooner. In software, it is common to have an object that is used by several different applications. The applications that use the object should not be able to deliberately or accidentally change attributes of the object that will alter its behavior. For example, consider the bank account object. The withdrawal method knows how to deduct funds from the account, and it verifies that the balance can support the deducted amount. However, without information hiding, a programmer could access the balance directly and alter it without the safeguards built into the methods. This would cause the object to become unstable, and the balance could not be trusted. In both the real-world example and the software example, it is apparent that without information hiding, objects can become unreliable.

The principles of information hiding and messaging work hand in hand to provide the object abstraction. An *abstraction* is an entity in computer science that provides an interface that defines its functionality while hiding the detailed information that is used to provide that functionality. The messaging provides the functionality of the object (that is, the activities the object is responsible for), and information hiding hides critical properties from direct access.

The third principle of OOP is that classes are used to create objects. The class defines the properties and methods of the objects that it describes. Classes also organize objects into a hierarchy that enables the inheritance principle. An object is considered an *instance* of a class. For example, your tailor is one instance of the class of tailors. The class of tailors describes all the capabilities of all tailors. The bank account class would describe the functionality of a bank account, and your checking account would be an instance of this class. The class concept is one that you have been exposed to indirectly with data types. You can consider the integer data type a class because it describes the type of data and the operations that can be performed on that data. When you create a variable myNum, you are creating an instance of the integer data type class. You should keep this analogy in mind when you learn how C++ handles OOP.

The final principle is inheritance and class hierarchy. This principle also contributes to the reliability of the software, but it is most recognized for promoting code reuse. The *class hierarchy* is the notion that you can arrange classes in a hierarchical fashion, where one class can enclose the other class, as shown in the Venn diagram in Figure 10.1. In this figure, your tailor is an instance of the tailor class. The tailor class describes the properties and methods for all tailors. The tailor class is enclosed within the business owner class, because tailors also have the properties and methods of a business owner. The human class encloses the business owner class, because all business owners have properties and methods from the human class. This hierarchical structure shows the relationships between classes; it also demonstrates the notion of inheritance. *Inheritance* occurs when a class receives the properties and methods from its parent class. Figure 10.2 shows an inheritance tree.

The inheritance tree in Figure 10.2 shows the class hierarchy in a different format. This structure is called a *tree*. Trees have *nodes* (boxes) and *branches* (lines). The *root* of the tree is the node at the top of the figure where the class

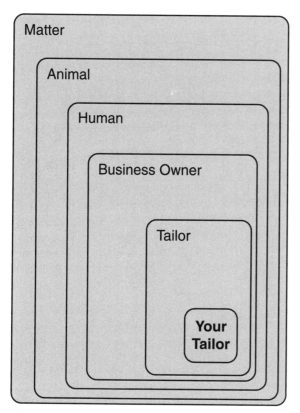

Figure 10.1
Demonstration of a class hierarchy from the custom suit example.

matter is located. The tree branches move downward to the left and right. The bottom nodes of the tree are called the *leaves*. The leaves in a tree diagram are *instances*. The other nodes represent *classes*. Consider the inheritance properties involving the classes named animal, human, and dog. Both human and dog inherit from animal. For example, animals have a heart, and human and dog classes inherit this property from the animal class. Another example is that animals have a way of locomotion; the human and dog classes inherit this ability from the animal class. In this case, locomotion is inherited and has to be specialized because fish swim using their fins, humans can walk/run using their two legs, and dogs can walk/run using four legs. In some cases the inheritance is just the inclusion of a property or method without specialization. In other cases, the methods need to be specialized by the child class that is inheriting it from its parent class.

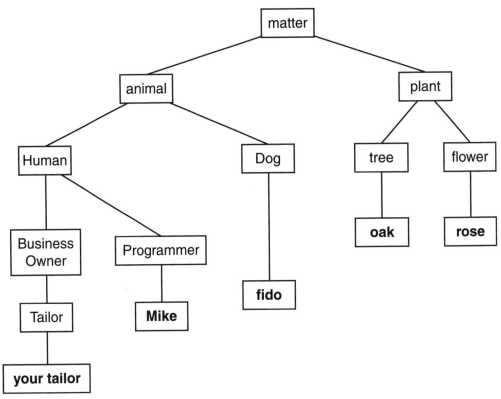

Figure 10.2
An example of an inheritance tree that includes the Your Tailor object.

OOP as Simulation

When you create an object-oriented program, it contains a collection of objects. These objects can send messages to one another just like you and the tailor interact and the tailor and the shipper interact. How does the simulation start? In the tailor scenario, the object must be created. This includes creating you, the tailor, the shipping company, and the recipient. Then an object must send a message. In the tailor example, you send a message to the tailor. Your message to the tailor starts a chain reaction of messages invoking methods that send other messages to invoke methods. For example, your message invokes the tailor's method to create and ship the suit. The tailor's method to ship the suit sends a message to the shipping company to handle the shipping using its method. This method of execution is in contrast to the structured programs with function execution that starts with the `main` function executing lines of code. The `main` function calls functions that may or may not call other functions. Then control is returned to `main`, where other instructions are executed and more functions are called.

The introduction to OOP introduced new concepts and principles, but it also introduced a new way of thinking about the solution to a problem and program execution. Now the issue is how to take a problem statement and develop an OOD. This requires a new design process that is centered on creating objects and assigning responsibilities, which is the topic of the next section.

OBJECT-ORIENTED DESIGN PROCESS

The OOD process differs from the structured function-based design that has been used in this book to this point. In that design, you used top-down and bottom-up design to identify functions. In the top-down design, you broke down the problem into smaller and smaller functions. In the bottom-up design process, you surveyed your libraries to find functions that could help solve the problem. You then composed your solution from these functions. If a function did not exist, you had to create that function to complete the design.

OOD focuses on identifying objects in the problem and assigning responsibilities to the objects. This is sometimes referred to as responsibility-driven design (RDD). The process uses both top-down and bottom-up design concepts. The top-down phase of the process identifies the objects and methods. Then bottom-up thinking assigns responsibilities and assembles a program from the objects.

The RDD process promotes nonoverlapping of methods because a method becomes the responsibility of a particular object. This in turn leads to independence between the objects. For example, the tailor can exist independently of the shipping company. Independence in software design has interesting ramifications. First, independence improves reliability because an object can be thoroughly tested prior to adding it to the program. Second, independent objects can be reused in other programs; therefore, a given object can solve many problems because it is not dependent on a particular problem. Finally, independent objects improve the management of software development for teams of programmers. Each programmer can be assigned an object to design, implement, and test. Once each programmer has done this, he can use all the objects together to implement the program software.

The Blackjack Problem

In this section, you develop an object-oriented solution to the Blackjack game. You use the same description for Blackjack that was expressed in Chapter 7, "Top-Down Design":

> Blackjack is a card game in which each player including the dealer is dealt two cards. Each player looks at his cards and determines if the sum of the values of the cards is equal to 21. If a player has 21, that player wins. If a player has less than 21, he has the option of taking more cards or staying with the cards he has. The game is over when someone has exactly 21 or until everyone either goes over 21 (a bust) or stays. The winner is the player with the highest total that is less than 21. The card values are based on the number on the card for cards 2–10; all face cards are valued at 10, and aces are either 1 or 11. Therefore, you could be dealt an ace and a queen and your total would be 21 (10 points for the queen + 11 for the ace). In addition, if you have a king and a 10 of diamonds in your hand and are dealt an ace, you also have 21 because 10 + 10 + 1 is 21. In this case, the ace is used as 1 instead of 11.

This description was used before to develop structured programming designs using functions, but you can analyze the same problem description differently to develop an OOD. This is the case with any problem description, so you could look at the problems proposed in all the previous chapters and compose OODs.

The OOD Process: Step 1 (Classes)

Locating the objects is about determining classes. The classes form the structure that your object instances will be based upon. During this first step of the process, you should be thinking of identifying classes of objects and not object instances. In addition, you should think of classes as having a well-defined set of responsibilities and having minimal dependence on other classes to promote independence.

Step 1 is to read the problem description and identify all the nouns that are in the description. It is sometimes helpful to write these nouns in a list. After you have written your list of nouns, use the following rules to refine the list:

- There are nouns that have the same meaning and should not be duplicated in the list. Look for synonyms, and remove all duplicates.

- Each noun may or may not contribute to the solution of the problem. You should remove any noun that is not a direct contributor to the solution. Use the context of how the noun is used in the description to evaluate its contribution.

- There will be some nouns that are instances and not classes. If the noun only represents a specific object, it's an instance and not a class. You should remove these because the goal in this step is to identify classes and not instances.

- Some nouns are simple values or pronouns. You should remove these simple values because usually they are properties of classes, but not classes themselves.

- Rename any nouns that may provide a better meaning for the word.

As an example, if you made a list of nouns from the Blackjack description, you would have a list like the following:

card

game

player

dealer

cards

sum

values

21

bust

option

someone

everyone

winner

number

10

1

11

ace

queen

total

king

diamonds

hand

This list contains all the nouns from the problem description from Blackjack. You can remove the numbers 21, 10, 1, and 11 because those are single values and not classes. You can also remove sum, values, ace, queen, king, total, number, someone, everyone, winner, bust, option, and diamonds because they are also single values and pronouns. You can remove game because it's a general term that is not necessary to solve the problem. You may be looking at card and cards and thinking they are synonyms, but in reality they are not. Cards actually refers to a hand in the problem, and card is one card from that hand. Because the list contains both cards and hand, you can select the one you prefer; in this list, hand is preferred over cards. If you cross out these words, you are left with the following:

card

~~game~~

player

dealer

~~cards~~

~~sum~~

~~values~~

~~21~~

~~bust~~

~~option~~

~~someone~~

~~everyone~~

~~winner~~

~~number~~

~~10~~

~~1~~

~~11~~

~~ace~~

~~queen~~

~~total~~

~~king~~

diamonds

hand

This new list is more refined because it contains your best candidates for classes. You should keep in mind that this is really your first cut. You may determine later in the process to add a class or remove a class. This is usually because the problem description/specification may contain some assumptions that it expects the reader to include implicitly. As you continue the design process, these classes will show themselves when you start to assign responsibilities.

The OOD Process: Step 2 (Responsibilities)

This step of the process is where you assign responsibilities to the classes in the refined list from step 1. In this step, you are identifying the following about each class:

- **Properties.** The information that the class is responsible for maintaining. Ask yourself, "What does a class need to know in the solution to this problem?"

- **Methods.** The actions that the class is responsible for performing. Ask yourself, "What does the class need to be able to do in the solution to this problem?"

Asking the question about properties and examining the original list of nouns can identify properties. The nouns that you eliminated because they only represented a single value are usually either properties or instances of the class. As you determine the properties, you can develop Unified Modeling Language (UML) diagrams to represent this information, as shown in Figure 10.3.

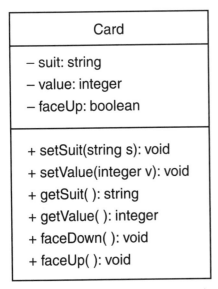

Figure 10.3
An example of a UML class diagram.

UML diagrams organize information related to classes and display the relationship between classes. The UML class diagram shown in Figure 10.3 contains three parts from top to bottom: the class name, the properties, and the methods. Also, you see that the class members have + or − next to them. The + symbol signifies that the class member is public. Public means that it is accessible to other parts of the software. The − symbol indicates the class member is private. Private means that the member is hidden from access by other parts of the software. In general, your data members are private, whereas your methods are public.

The `Card` class UML diagram in Figure 10.3 is one of the classes that you need for the Blackjack design. The `Card` class contains two properties: `suit` and `value`. The `suit` of the card is hearts, diamonds, spades, or clubs, and the `value` is ace, 2–10, jack, queen, or king; `faceUp` is a Boolean value that determines if the card is face up or face down. The `Card` class also contains six methods: `setSuit(s)`, `setValue(v)`, `getSuit()`, `getValue()`, `faceDown()`, and `faceUp()`. These methods are the responsibilities of a card. The methods `setSuit(s)` and `setValue(v)` are also known as *setters*. They are responsible for allowing another part of the software to update the `suit` or `value` of the card. The methods are safer to use than having direct access to the data because a method can ensure that the property is set properly. The methods `getSuit()` and `getValue()` are called *getters*. Getters provide the values of the `suit` and `value` properties of the `Card` class to other parts of the software. Not every property needs to have a getter or a setter; it depends on what you think other software components need access to and how much access they need. The other methods `faceDown()` and `faceUp()` are regular public methods. These two methods manipulate the `faceUp` private property by changing it to `true` when the card is face up and `false` when the card is face down.

During this phase of the OOD process of assigning responsibilities, you also determine if there are relationships between the class structures. There are structural relationships you should identify:

- **Inheritance relationship.** This is based on the inheritance principle and shows class specializations.

- **Composite relationship.** This is where a class has properties that are instances of other classes.

Figure 10.4 shows an example of inheritance in UML using the Player and Dealer classes. There is an arrow from the Dealer class to the Player class to show that the Dealer class inherits from the Player class. These two classes are in an inheritance relationship because in this design, the Dealer class is seen as a specialization of the Player class. The Dealer class is a specialization because the dealer has a card deck property in addition to its hand. The dealer also has some different and specialized responsibilities. The dealer has the responsibility to deal cards, and because the game is computer controlled, it has some artificial intelligence to determine if it should take another card. For these reasons, the Dealer class also has a dealCards() method as a specialized anotherCard().

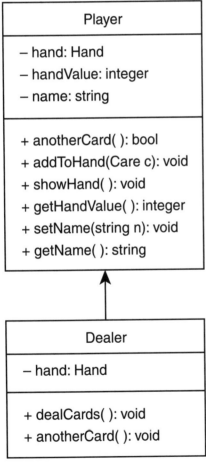

Figure 10.4
An example of a UML inheritance diagram.

The composite relationship is shown in Figure 10.5 using the Dealer class. UML shows a composite relationship by a line with a diamond on one end. The composite relationship in Figure 10.5 shows how the Dealer class is composed with a Deck class object as one of its properties. A class can be composed from more than one class as needed.

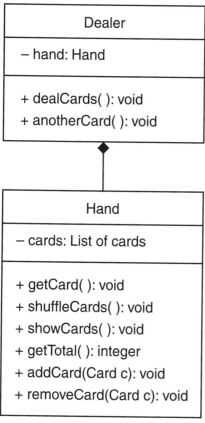

Figure 10.5
An example of a UML composite diagram.

UML provides a structured way of representing object-oriented software design. It enables you to complete the second phase of the OOD by assigning responsibilities using class diagrams and by providing mechanisms that show important structural relationships. The next step is to define the interactions between classes.

The OOD Process: Step 3 (Interactions)

The final step for the OOD process is to define the interactions between classes. In this section, two approaches are presented on how to describe class interactions. The first type of interaction shows the execution sequence of the program; this interaction is shown in sequence diagrams. The second type of interaction is captured in collaboration diagrams that show how objects pass messages to one another.

The first interaction diagram is the sequence diagram, and a sample sequence diagram is shown in Figure 10.6. The diagram has a list of classes and objects along the top. The object name is before the colon, and the class name follows the colon; for example, aObj is the object name, and Class A is the name of the object's class. The timeline moves from the top of the diagram to the bottom. The arrows in the diagram show where a method is invoked. For example, the aObj object first invokes the bObj's method named getName(). This is followed by bObj invoking the display() method that belongs to cObj. It is also common to have comments in a column to the right or left to provide an overview of what a particular sequence is showing.

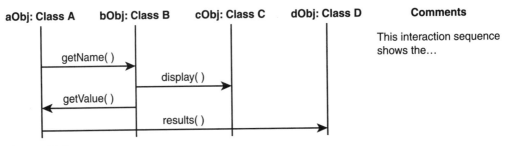

Figure 10.6
An example of a sequence diagram that shows interactions between some generic classes.

Figure 10.7 shows a sequence diagram that you might find as part of a Blackjack game. In this scenario, the theDealer object is requesting from each Player class object whether or not it wants another card. The method AnotherCard() belongs to the Player class, so each object p1, p2, and p3 has the same method of responding to the dealer.

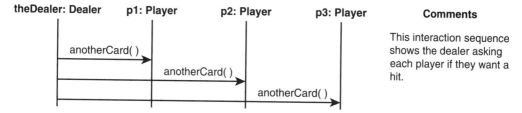

theDealer: Dealer   **p1: Player**   **p2: Player**   **p3: Player**   **Comments**

anotherCard( )

anotherCard( )

anotherCard( )

This interaction sequence shows the dealer asking each player if they want a hit.

Figure 10.7
An example of a sequence diagram that shows interactions between a Dealer object and Player objects in Blackjack.

You can build a sequence diagram from the start to the end of the program execution. However, it is not as useful because the pattern of execution of the program depends on the data values. Therefore, it is customary to have several sequence diagrams in a design document that explain the important sequences of your design. For example, in Blackjack you have individual sequence diagrams to show the game being initialized, the cards being dealt, the players taking hits, and a player winning. The idea is that you capture the essence of how the design would work in several key scenarios.

The second type of interaction diagram is the collaboration diagram. An example collaboration diagram from Blackjack is shown in Figure 10.8. The collaboration diagram does not have time associated with it. It does allow you to show more of the structure of your design by including the messages along with the methods. The lines connecting the objects showing that they have some direct interaction with one another illustrate the structure.

The methods in Figure 10.8 show the messages that are being sent to the objects and values that are being returned to objects. For example, the message being sent to the deck object is getCard( ), and it returns a Card object that contains the ace of spades. Also, notice that the p2 object accepts a card and returns a true value to the theDealer object that then sends another message that contains a Card object representing the ace of spades. Another example of the structure being revealed is where notation theDealer.deck is used. This notation demonstrates that the deck object is actually a part of the theDealer object, which reinforces the composition of the Dealer class.

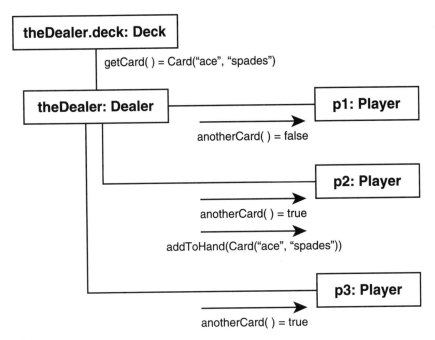

Figure 10.8
An example of a collaboration diagram that shows interactions between a Dealer object and Player objects in Blackjack.

Two interaction diagram types have been presented to you. When you are designing an object-oriented program, you can use either diagram or both types of diagrams for your design documents.

SUMMARY

This chapter has provided an introduction to OOP and OOD. The first part of this chapter presented the key concepts that are the foundation for OOP: agents, responsibilities, messages, and methods. It also presented the four principles of OOP: messages initiate methods, information hiding protects instance data, objects are instances of classes, and classes are organized in hierarchies. These are the foundation for understanding OOP.

Next, the chapter presented a process for performing OOD within the context of the Blackjack game. This process showed how examining the problem description for nouns and verbs allows you to identify classes and responsibilities. In addition, UML class diagrams were introduced along with interaction diagrams.

EXERCISES

The following questions test your knowledge of the material from this chapter. You can find the answers to these questions on the book's companion website at www.courseptr.com/downloads.

1. Visit a fast food restaurant, and write a scenario of what happens in the restaurant when you place an order. Your scenario should identify the agents, messages, responsibilities, and methods used.

2. Pretend you have to write a class to represent your cell phone. What attributes/properties would this class have? What methods would you need to provide?

3. Search the Internet for a description of the Battleship board game and read the description to identify the names of potential classes.

4. Write an OOD for the Battleship board game. Your OOD should show the classes along with their attributes and methods. In addition, you should include inheritance diagrams and interaction diagrams as needed.

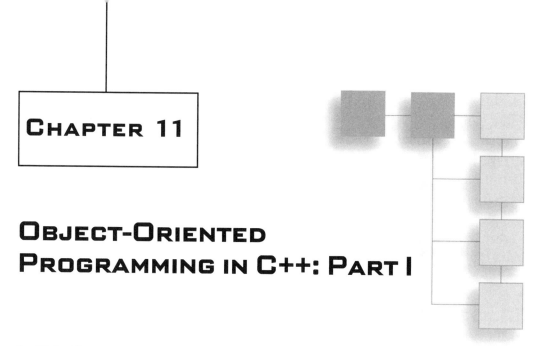

CHAPTER 11

OBJECT-ORIENTED PROGRAMMING IN C++: PART I

In This Chapter

- Classes as Types
- Case Study: Cyber Bank Application
- Case Study: The Fraction Data Type

> In C++ it's harder to shoot yourself in the foot, but when you do,
> you blow off your whole leg.
>
> —Bjarne Stroustrup

Object-oriented programming (OOP) in C++ is centered on the class construct. You saw the class construct in Chapter 9, "Medium-Scale Problems," where it was used to create data records for a database. However, the class has a much more important role in C++: creating abstract data types. An *abstract data type* (ADT) is a user-defined data type. These ADTs behave like the classes discussed in Chapter 10, "Introduction to Object-Oriented Design." ADTs describe the structure (attributes and properties) and operations (responsibilities) for a collection of objects. Classes in C++ can define messages and methods, provide information hiding, create object instances, and form hierarchies with inheritance abilities.

In this chapter, you learn the basics of C++ classes for OOP. Classes in C++ allow you to define the data members of an object and the methods of the object. This chapter also shows how to use objects individually and within an array. In addition, some implementation details are addressed, including construction and destruction of objects, pointers used as data members, operator overloading, and handling of multiple files in an application. This chapter ends with the presentation of a full object-oriented application for the Cyber Bank and Fraction class that shows how to create an additional numeric data type.

CLASSES AS TYPES

In C++, the class structure creates abstract data types. These abstract data types are then used as the blueprint for creating objects. You have come in contact with objects in C++, but they were not identified as objects earlier in the book. For example, cin is an object from the istream class, and cout is an object of the ostream class. These objects were created as part of the standard C++ library. You also created objects in previous chapters. For example, the string data type is really a C++ class. When you declared strings like this:

```
string firstName;
```

you declared a string object called firstName. In all these examples, the common thread is that classes create types: string, istream, and ostream. Is OOP really about creating types? In reality, that is exactly what it is about. In Chapter 10, you learned that objects belong to a class, and the class describes the properties and methods that each object in the class has. The tailor who made the custom suit was an object or instance of the class of tailors. All tailors can sew and cut cloth. A type performs the same function as a class. A data type such as int describes what an integer is as a sequence of bits that can be evaluated as a decimal number, and it defines the types of operations that can be performed, such as addition and subtraction. Therefore, classes allow you as a programmer to create your own types so that you can have objects in your program that better match the problem description.

Declaring a Class

In OOP, the first task is to specify all your classes. You will use your UML diagrams as a guide for the declaration. The class declaration has the following format:

```
class <className> {
    <declarations>;
    <access specifications>;
};
```

Classes have names, and inside are declarations for data members and member functions. The data members are the properties of the class, and the member functions are the actions that the class can perform. The access specifications determine the level of information hiding. Consider the UML diagram for the Card class from Chapter 10 in Figure 11.1.

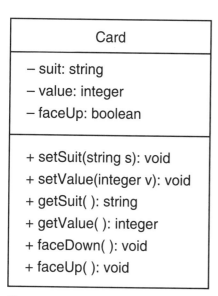

Figure 11.1
A UML diagram for the Card class.

The UML diagram in Figure 11.1 contains data members at the top of the diagram. These are the properties of a playing card: suit, value, and faceup. Listing 11.1 shows how this part of the UML diagram is constructed in C++.

Listing 11.1 A Partial Card Class Declaration

```
class Card {
private:
   string suit;
   int value;
   bool faceup;
public:
   // To be determined
};
```

Listing 11.1 demonstrates the use of access specifiers. The summary of the access specifiers is shown in Table 11.1.

Table 11.1 Summary of Access Specifiers

Specifier Name	Description
private	There is no access granted to other software components.
public	There is full access granted to other software components.
protected	There is full access granted to subclasses in the inheritance hierarchy, but no access is granted to other software components.

These access specifiers control the level of information hiding. The two most common specifiers are public and private. They are directly taken from the UML diagram, where + and − are used, respectively. Listing 11.1 also shows data members that have been declared as part of the class. These data member declarations belong to the private section of the class because they represent the properties that only member functions should access. Please make a note to yourself that you can have more than one private, public, or protected section and that you can arrange the sections in any order. However, it is better to have only one of each section and to remain consistent in a program that has multiple classes. Listing 11.2 shows member functions for the Card class.

Listing 11.2 A Complete Card Class Declaration

```
class Card {
private:
    string suit;
    int value;
    bool faceup;
public:
    void setSuit(string s);
    void setValue(integer v);
    string getSuit() const;
    int getValue() const;
    void faceDown();
    void faceUp();
};
```

Listing 11.2 adds the member function declarations to the class declaration. Notice that there are still setters and getters. These are the member functions that allow other software components to set values of the data members or get values of the data members. Not all data members require this type of exposure. The value of the `faceup` data member cannot be directly set. It is indirectly set by turning the card faceup or facedown with the respective member functions. In some cases, a `private` data member does not allow setting or getting.

Note

The technical names for getters and setters are accessors and mutators. Accessors provide access to a `private` data member but should not change the data member. On the other hand, mutators change data members.

Listing 11.2 also shows how to use `const` on a member function. In this case, the `const` modifier denotes that the member function does not change the value of a `private` or `protected` data member of the object.

Defining Member Functions

The member functions are declared as part of the class declaration. The declarations resemble function prototypes because they serve a similar purpose by declaring what member functions or methods are part of the class. In this section, you learn how to define methods.

The `Card` class has six methods declared: `setSuit`, `setValue`, `getSuit`, `getValue`, `faceDown`, and `faceUp`. Member function definitions have the following format:

```
<return-type> <className>::<Function Name>(<parameters>) <modifier> {
    <statements>
}
```

Most of these components are the same as functions you have been writing throughout the book. The difference is the `<className>::<Function Name>` part of the header. The `::` is called the *scope resolution operator*. The scope resolution operator says that `<Function Name>` belongs to the class named `<className>`. This is needed because member function definitions are not done within the scope of the class declaration, and they may not even be in the same file, as you will see later. The other difference is the `<modifier>` that is employed for the const that was used on the getters. The code in Listing 11.3 shows examples of member function definitions.

Listing 11.3 Member Function Definitions

```
void Card::setSuit(string s) {
    suit = s;
}
string Card::getSuit() const {
    return suit;
}
void Card::faceUp() {
    faceup = true;
}
```

The examples in Listing 11.3 show how the different types of member functions can be defined. Notice how short the member functions are; this is usually going to be the case with setters and getters. The `setSuit` member function takes the parameter `s` and assigns it to the data member `suit`. The `getSuit` member function returns the value of the `private` data member `suit`. These are examples of setters and getters.

Note

Member functions and methods are typically used as shown here, but some professional programmers add more to their setters to protect the data member from being set with incorrect values. For example, you should not set the suit to anything other than clubs, spades, diamonds, or hearts. Consider the following changes:

```
void Card::setSuit(string s) {
    if (s == "clubs" || s == "spades" ||
        s == "diamonds" || s == "hearts")
        suit = s;
    else
        suit = "undefined";
}
```

This version of the setSuit member function only sets the suit member to a valid suit or to "undefined". This ensures that the suit data member has consistent values for all Card objects.

Member function definitions can also be inlined. An inlined member function improves the performance of the object; furthermore, it is more convenient for the programmer. Inlining a member function means that the definition is made a part of the class declaration instead of having a separate definition like those shown in Listing 11.3. You should only use inlining for small member functions, such as setters and getters. Listing 11.4 shows an example of the Card class with inlined member functions.

Listing 11.4 Example of Inlined Member Functions

```
class Card {
private:
    string suit;
    int value;
    bool faceup;
public:
    void setSuit(string s) {
        suit = s;
    }

    void setValue(integer v) {
        value = v;
    }
```

```
        string getSuit() const {
            return suit;
        }

        int getValue() const {
            return value;
        }

        void faceDown() {
            faceup = false;
        }

        void faceUp()() {
            faceup = true;
        }

};
```

The class declaration in Listing 11.4 includes the inlined member functions. As you can see, inlined member functions have a syntax that is just like the format used for free functions. You do not have to include the membership using the scope resolution operator, because the inlined member functions are defined within the scope declaration of the class.

This section described how to create a class in C++. Classes are type descriptions that are commonly known as ADTs. The class defines the data members and the member functions of the class. In the next section, you learn how to use classes to create instances or objects and how to work with objects.

Creating and Using Instances of a Class

At this point, you know how to create a class, and you know that a class is the way you define a new type. Defining an instance or object of the class is just like defining a new variable of a particular data type:

```
<className> <objectIdentifier>;
```

This format should look familiar. To declare a playing card, you use the following code:

```
Card playingCard;
```

This declares an object named `playingCard` that you can now use in a program. This is sometimes called the *instantiation* of a class because you are creating an instance of the class. Figure 11.2 shows a visualization of the `playingCard` object. The data members are represented as being inside the object to represent the `private` visibility.

playingCard

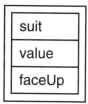

Figure 11.2
A visualization for an object from the Card class.

You can also create an entire array of objects, just like you can create an array of integers and floats:

`Card deck[52];`

This declaration declares an array name `deck`. It creates an array of 52 `Card` objects. Figure 11.3 provides visualization for an array of objects.

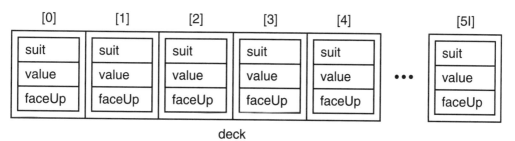

Figure 11.3
A visualization for an array of objects from the Card class.

An array of objects is a concept that Chapter 9 used to create an array of records. Each element in the array contains its own set of data members. The next section shows how to access data members and member functions of an object.

Accessing Members of the Class

In Chapter 9, you learned how to use classes to represent records. When you need to access a field, you use the dot operator (.) to access each field. You use the same notation to access data members and member functions. Suppose you have the same playingCard object. You might access its members this way:

```
playingCard.setSuit("spades");
playingCard.setValue(7);
```

The dot operator separates the object name from the member. If the object is an element in an array, you still use the dot operator:

```
deck[25].setSuit("spades");
deck[25].setValue(7);
```

Using the subscript accesses each object in an array. Therefore, you use the dot operator after the object to identify the member of that object. Figure 11.4 shows what would happen to the object after either pair of instructions executes. Whether your object is standalone or within an array, this is what happens after the setSuit and setValue methods are executed. The current class does not have default initialization, so the initial value of faceUp is unknown. Initializing of objects is discussed later in this chapter.

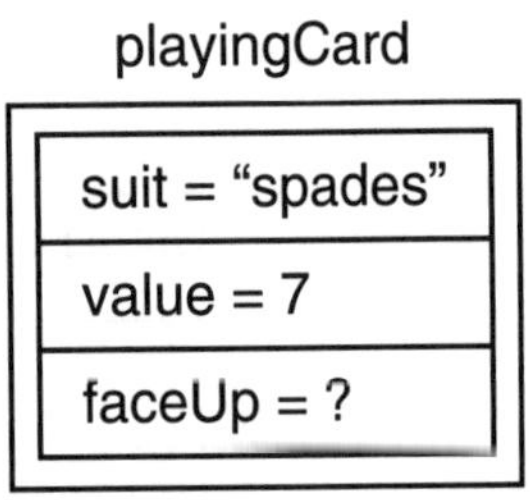

playingCard

| suit = "spades" |
| value = 7 |
| faceUp = ? |

Figure 11.4
A visualization for the object after a few setters have been executed.

Recall that some members of the class were in the `public` section, whereas others were in the `private` section. This is where the difference shows. Each of the examples is of `public` members that are accessible by other parts of the software not considered part of the class. However, consider these examples:

```
playingCard.faceup = false;
playingCard.value = 100;
```

In both cases, `private` data members are being directly accessed. Both of these lines of code cause a compiler error that says you cannot access `private` members outside the scope of the class. This means these lines of code exist in a function that is not a part of the class; therefore, they do not have direct access to the `private` members.

Initializing Data Members of the Class

You are probably wondering if you have to write several lines of code just to initialize an object. For example, you could initialize the `playingCard` object to some set values by doing the following:

```
Card playingCard;
playingCard.setSuit("spades");
playingCard.setValue(1);
playingCard.faceDown();
```

These four lines of code instantiate the object and initialize the object to be an ace of spades that is facedown. You can imagine that it would be tedious to execute a sequence of setters to initialize an object. Therefore, C++ offers another way to initialize objects through the use of a constructor. Every class has a *default constructor* that is the default function implicitly called when an object is instantiated. Constructors perform the following types of tasks:

- Initialize the `private` data members of the object at instantiation.
- Allocate memory for `private` data members that are pointers.

The class declaration in Listing 11.5 shows the `Card` class declaration with a constructor added.

Listing 11.5 A Complete Card Class Declaration

```
class Card {
private:
   string suit;
   int value;
   bool faceup;
public:
   Card();
   void setSuit(string s);
   void setValue(integer v);
   string getSuit() const;
   int getValue() const;
   void faceDown();
   void faceUp();
};
```

Every constructor has the same name as the class. In this case, the class is named Card, so the constructor is also named Card. The default constructor has no parameters. You can write other constructors that have parameters. Although the definition of the constructor can be inlined, it is usually not inlined. Therefore, a definition for the Card default constructor might look like this:

```
Card::Card() {
    suit = "unknown";
    value = 0;
    faceup = false;
}
```

This constructor initializes cards to have an unknown suit, a zero value, and a facedown position. You could choose any initial value you want. There are other ways to write constructors that allow you to customize the defaults at instantiation time. For a moment, consider initializing an integer variable at the time of declaration:

```
int maximumLoad = 1000;
```

This line of code creates the integer variable named maximumLoad. It also initializes this variable to 1000. Suppose you want to initialize the playerCard in a special way other than its default; you might use the following code:

```
Card playerCard(1, "spades", true);
```

This code initializes `playerCard` as the ace of spades, and it is faceup. The problem here is that the default constructor is not equipped to handle this. Therefore, you must use another constructor. The class declaration resembles the code in Listing 11.6.

Listing 11.6 Card Class with Parameterized Constructor

```
class Card {
private:
   string suit;
   int value;
   bool faceup;
public:
   Card();
   Card(int v, string s, bool face);
   void setSuit(string s);
   void setValue(integer v);
   string getSuit() const;
   int getValue() const;
   void faceDown();
   void faceUp();
};
```

Listing 11.6 shows the new constructor in addition to the default constructor, which provides flexibility. The new constructor is called a *parameterized constructor*, and it allows the programmer to pass arguments during the instantiation time. You can have as many parameters as needed to support the goals of the class. This constructor is written as follows:

```
Card::Card(int v, string s, bool face){
   suit = s;
   value = v;
   faceup = face;
}
```

This constructor has the parameters for each of the `private` data members, so all of them can be set at instantiation. Now there are two constructors, but you can reduce to one constructor by using default arguments. *Default arguments* are those that have a default value assigned if the programmer does not specify a value. The constructor's declaration is changed to this:

```
Card(int v = 0, string s = "unknown", bool face = true);
```

This is the declaration showing the default values for each of the parameters. The definition of the constructor looks like the following:

```
Card::Card(int v = 0, string s = "unknown", bool face = true){
    suit = s;
    value = v;
    faceup = face;
}
```

You can use this parameterized constructor with default arguments in several ways. You can instantiate an object with or without parameters, and there are other options in between:

1. `Card playerCard(1, "spades", true);`

2. `Card playerCard;`

3. `Card playerCard(1);`

4. `Card playerCard(1, "spades");`

In the first option in the list, the arguments override all the defaults. In the second option, only the default arguments are used. In the third option, the first default argument is overridden, but the last two arguments are filled with default values. In the fourth option, the first two default arguments are overridden, and the last argument is based on the default value. When you use default arguments, no argument can be skipped. Therefore, the following is not an option because it skips the middle argument:

```
Card playerCard(1, ,true);
```

Deallocating Data Members of the Class

The inverse function for the constructor is the destructor. You can use the constructor to allocate memory when there are pointer data members. In this case, the allocated memory needs to be returned to the system when the program no longer needs the object. Sometimes the memory is returned at the end of the program, but other times the memory is returned during the program execution. In either case, the class's destructor is called on to deallocate the memory.

The destructor must be declared within the class declaration. It has the same name as the constructor, with a prepended tilde (˜). For example, consider the Card class with a destructor declaration, as shown in Listing 11.7. The method named ˜Card() is the destructor.

Listing 11.7 Card Class with Destructor

```
class Card {
private:
    string suit;
    int value;
    bool faceup;
public:
    Card(int v = 0, string s = "unknown", bool face = true);
    ~Card();
    void setSuit(string s);
    void setValue(integer v);
    string getSuit() const;
    int getValue() const;
    void faceDown();
    void faceUp();
};
```

The destructor is executed automatically when the function it instantiated has terminated or when the delete command is used on the object. In general, destructors are empty, because if you are using C++ core types and the string type, your constructor did not allocate dynamic memory using the new operation. Therefore, the definition of the destructor for the Card class is this:

```
Card::~Card() {}
```

However, if you have a class in which your constructor is allocating dynamic memory using the new operator, you have a pointer as a private data member, and you need to use the destructor to deallocate that memory. An example of a card deck class is shown in Listing 11.8. The Deck class has a constructor and a destructor to allocate and deallocate the deck of cards.

Listing 11.8 A Deck Class Using Dynamic Memory

```
1: class Deck {
2: private:
3:     Card* theDeck;
4:     int numOfCards;
5: public:
6:     Deck(int n = 52);
7:     ~Deck();
8:     void setSize(int s);
9:     int getSize();
10:    Card getNextCard() const;
11:    void shuffle();
12: };
13:
14: Deck::Deck(int n = 52) {
15:     numOfCards = n;
16:     theDeck = new Card[numOfCards];
17:     shuffle();
18: }
19:
20: Deck::~Deck() {
21:    Delete [] theDeck;
22: }
```

The constructor on lines 14–18 allows you to create a deck with 52 cards or any other number of cards you want. It dynamically allocates the array of Card objects and then uses the shuffle() method to fill the deck with actual card values after the memory has been allocated. The destructor on lines 20–21 is not empty because there was memory dynamically allocated by the class's constructor. It uses the delete operation to deallocate the theDeck array. The [] operator is used because theDeck is an array and not a single value.

As a programmer, when you dynamically allocate memory in an object, it is your responsibility to build the destructor to properly deallocate the memory. If you do not build this method, your program creates a memory leak in your system and leads to system instability over time.

CASE STUDY: CYBER BANK APPLICATION

The Cyber Bank is an application that manages bank accounts through a menu-driven interface. The software allows the user to deposit, withdraw, balance checks, and create transaction ledger reports. Each withdrawal and deposit transaction is logged into a transaction ledger that can be viewed at any time.

This application is designed with two classes: Account and Transaction. The UML class diagrams for the Account and Transaction classes are shown in Figure 11.5.

The UML class diagrams in Figure 11.5 show the private data members for both classes. You also see that the Account class is a composite class. The Account class uses the Transaction class to create a list of transactions. This is why there is an aggregate relationship between the two classes. There is also an example of a private method. resizeTransLedger() is a private method that the deposit() and withdraw() methods use to increase the size of the ledger when its maximum size has been reached.

Handling Multiple Source Code Files

In large software projects, the applications are created using more than one source code file. In an OOP program, the source code files are divided according to the classes. Two files are dedicated to each class: a header file and an implementation file. The name of the header file ends with the file extension .h, and the name of the implementation file ends with .cpp. For example, there are two classes in this program. That means four files are created, and they are shown in Table 11.2.

Table 11.2 Source Code Files for Cyber Bank

Name of File	Description
Account.h	Contains the Account class declaration
Account.cpp	Contains definitions for noninlined member functions for the Account class
Transaction.h	Contains the Transaction class declaration
Transaction.cpp	Contains the definitions of noninlined member functions for the Transaction class

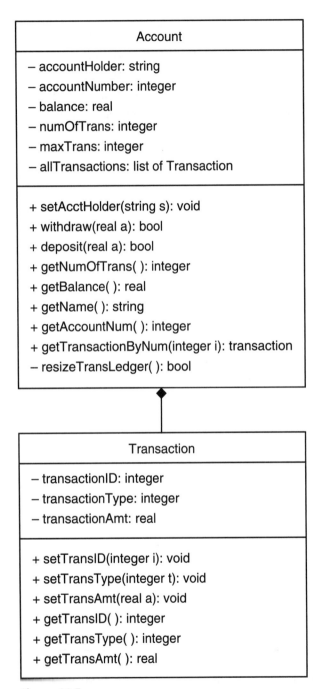

Figure 11.5
UML class diagrams for Cyber Bank application.

The header file is called the interface file because it contains the class declaration that defines everything a programmer needs to use the class. The class declaration contains the name of the class that instantiates objects and the member function prototypes that define the methods that can be used on the object. The implementation file contains the definitions of free functions and member functions that support the class.

The header files are included in your program using the #include directive. This is the same #include directive that you have been using to include iostream, string, and others. Figure 11.6 shows a map of how the #includes are set up for the Cyber Bank application.

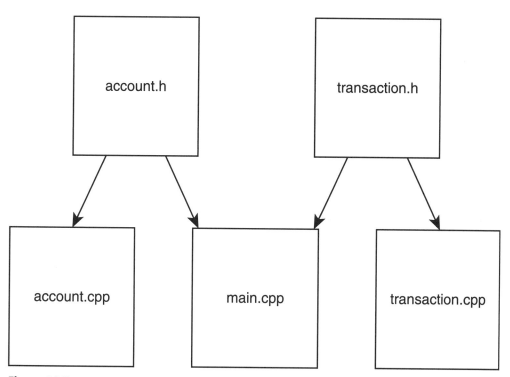

Figure 11.6
A diagram of how Cyber Bank is divided into separate files as header files and implementation files.

The map in Figure 11.6 shows that five files make up the Cyber Bank application. The account.h file is included in both the account.cpp file and the main.cpp file. It is included in the account.cpp file because these two files work together to provide the Account class, and it's included in the main.cpp because this is where Account objects are instantiated and used. The account.h file contains all the information regarding which methods are available to the Account objects and how to use them. The transaction.h file is included in the transaction.cpp, main.cpp, and account.h files. The account.h file needs the transaction.h file because the Account class uses the Transaction class. The transaction.cpp file needs the transaction.h file to provide the Transaction class for the application, and the main.cpp file needs to instantiate objects of the Transaction class.

Compiling each of the .cpp files individually and then joining them to create a single binary executable file builds the program.

Cyber Bank Application Sample Output

The Cyber Bank application is a menu-driven application, and its sample output is shown in Listing 11.9. It shows the account processing withdrawals and deposits as well as balance queries and transaction log generation.

Listing 11.9 Cyber Bank Sample Output

```
                Cyber Bank Menu
- - - - - - - - - - - - - - - - - - - - - - - - - - - - -
A) Show account balance
B) Make a deposit
C) Make a withdrawal
D) Show all transactions
E) Exit and Logout
Please make your choice: a
Account: 470001
Your current balance is: $500.00
                Cyber Bank Menu
- - - - - - - - - - - - - - - - - - - - - - - - - - - - -
A) Show account balance
B) Make a deposit
C) Make a withdrawal
```

D) Show all transactions
E) Exit and Logout
Please make your choice: b
Please enter the amount for deposit: $200.00
deposit made successfully
                    Cyber Bank Menu
- -
A) Show account balance
B) Make a deposit
C) Make a withdrawal
D) Show all transactions
E) Exit and Logout
Please make your choice: c
Please enter the amount to withdraw: $50.00
withdrawal made successfully
                    Cyber Bank Menu
- -
A) Show account balance
B) Make a deposit
C) Make a withdrawal
D) Show all transactions
E) Exit and Logout
Please make your choice: d
Transaction Ledger
Account Name: Mikposit 200.00
2 Withdrawal 50.00
                    Cyber Bank Menu
- -
A) Show account balance
B) Make a deposit
C) Make a withdrawal
D) Show all transactions
E) Exit and Logout
Please make your choice: a
Account: 470001
Your current balance is: $650.00
                    Cyber Bank Menu
- -
A) Show account balance
B) Make a deposit

C) Make a withdrawal
D) Show all transactions
E) Exit and Logout
Please make your choice: e
Thank you for visiting First Cyber Bank

Cyber Bank Application Source Code

In this section, you see each of the source code files in the Cyber Bank application. You get to examine the contents of the files and learn how the application works. The first file is the `account.h` file that is shown in Listing 11.10. At the beginning of the file on lines 1 and 2, you see some new preprocessor directives using the # symbol. These two lines prevent the .h file from being included more than once and causing duplicate declarations of the class.

Line 14 is where the parameterized constructor is located. It has all default arguments, which allows it to be used as a default constructor as well as a parameterized constructor. Line 23 is where the destructor is located. The destructor is needed in this application because the class contains a `private` data member that is a pointer to a dynamic array of `Transaction` objects. This class also demonstrates the use of inline methods for the setters, getters, constructor, and destructor. The other methods are defined in the `account` `.cpp` file.

Listing 11.10 Cyber Bank (account.h)

```
1: #ifndef ACCOUNT_H
2: #define ACCOUNT_H
3:
4: #include "Transaction.h"
5: #include <string>
6: #include <iostream>
7:
8: using namespace std;
9:
10:
11: class Account {
```

```
12: public:
13:
14:     Account(const std::string& name="", int acct=0, double bal=0) {
15:             accountHolder = name;
16:             accountNumber = acct;
17:             balance = bal;
18:             numOfTrans = 0;
19:             maxTrans = 10;
20:             allTransactions = new Transaction[maxTrans];
21:     }
22:
23:     ~Account() {
24:             delete [] allTransactions;
25:     }
26:
27:     // Getters
28:     double getNumOfTrans() const {
29:             return numOfTrans;
30:     }
31:
32:     double getBalance() const {
33:             return balance;
34:     }
35:
36:     string getName() const {
37:             return accountHolder;
38:     }
39:
40:     int getAccountNum() const {
41:             return accountNumber;
42:     }
43:
44:
45:
46:     // Setters
47:     void setAcctHolder(const string& name) {
48:             accountHolder = name;
49:     }
50:
```

```
51:        // Account interface
52:        bool withdraw(double amount);
53:
54:        bool deposit(double amount);
55:
56:        // Transactions interface
57:        Transaction getTransactionByNum(int i) const;
58:
59:        // Security
60:        bool validateLogin(int acctNum, const string& pass) const;
61:
62:
63: private:
64:        string accountHolder;     // Name on the account
65:        int accountNumber;        // Account number
66:        string accountPassword;   // Account password
67:        double balance;           // Account balance
68:        int numOfTrans;           // Number of transactions
69:        int maxTrans;             // Maximum number of transactions for the array
70:        Transaction* allTransactions;    // Array of all transactions
71:
72:        // Increases the size of the ledger when needed
73:        bool resizeTransLedger();
74:
75: };
76:
77: #endif // ACCOUNT_H
```

The next file to examine is account.cpp, which is shown in Listing 11.11. This file contains the definitions of the methods from the Account class that were not inlined. The withdrawal() method is defined on lines 10–36. It starts by making sure the withdrawal request is less than the current balance to prevent overdrafts. Then it checks to see if the transaction ledger is already full. If the ledger is not full, the transaction is added to the ledger using lines 29–31. If the ledger is full, the resizeTransLedger() method is called to resize the ledger by allocating more memory. The resizeTransLedger() method is defined on lines 98–120. This code allocates a new array for a new list and copies the old data to the new array.

Listing 11.11 Cyber Bank (account.cpp)

```
1: // Public methods
2:
3: /* Name; withdrawal
4:  * Description: process a withdrawal request on the account
5:  * Parms:
6:  *            amt              The amount of the withdrawal
7:  * Return: true for successful withdrawal, and false if not successful
8:  */
9:
10: bool Account::withdraw(double amt) {
11:
12:     // Ensure there is enough money in the account to make the withdrawal
13:     if (balance < amt) {
14:            return false;
15:     } else { // Process the withdrawal
16:
17:            balance -= amt;
18:            numOfTrans++;
19:
20:            if (numOfTrans == maxTrans) { // Ledger is full
21:                    if (!resizeTransLedger()) {
22:                            cerr << "Out of Memory" << endl;
23:                            exit(-1);
24:                    }
25:
26:            }
27:
28:            // Add withdrawal to the transaction log
29:            allTransactions[numOfTrans-1].setTransID(numOfTrans);
30:            allTransactions[numOfTrans-1].setTransType(0);
31:            allTransactions[numOfTrans-1].setTransAmt(amt);
32:
33:            return true;
34:     }
35:
36: }
37:
38:
```

```
39: /* Name; deposit
40: * Description: process a deposit request on the account
41: * Parms:
42: *             amt            The amount of the deposit
43: * Return: true for a successful deposit and false for unsuccessful deposit
44: */
45:
46: bool Account::deposit(double amt) {
47:
48:     // Process the transaction
49:     balance += amt;
50:     numOfTrans++;
51:
52:     if (numOfTrans == maxTrans) { // Ledger is full
53:             if (!resizeTransLedger()) {
54:                     cerr << "Out of Memory" << endl;
55:                     exit(-1);
56:             }
57:
58:     }
59:
60:     // Add deposit to the transaction log
61:     allTransactions[numOfTrans-1].setTransID(numOfTrans);
62:     allTransactions[numOfTrans-1].setTransType(1);
63:     allTransactions[numOfTrans-1].setTransAmt(amt);
64:
65:     return true;
66:
67: }
68:
69:
70: /* Name; getTransactionByNum
71: * Description: Obtain a transaction by the number of the transaction
72: * Parms:
73: *             i                position of the transaction in the list
74: * Return: Transaction at position i
75: */
76:
77: Transaction Account::getTransactionByNum(int i) const {
78:     Transaction empty;
```

```
79:
80:     if (i >= 1 && i <= numOfTrans)
81:             return allTransactions[i-1];
82:     else
83:             return empty;
84:
85:
86: }
87:
88: // Private methods
89:
90:  /* Name; resizeTransLedger
91:   * Description: increase the size of array to accommodate
92:   * new transactions by doubling the current size.
93:   * Parms:
94:   *           none
95:   * Return: true if successful, false if out of memory
96:   */
97:
98: bool Account::resizeTransLedger() {
99:      Transaction* temp;
100:
101:     // Create temporary array twice current size
102:     temp = new Transaction[2 * maxTrans];
103:
104:     // If out of memory, stop
105:     if (temp == NULL) return false;
106:
107:     // Copy old transactions to new list
108:     for (int i = 0; i < numOfTrans; i++) {
109:             temp[i] = allTransactions[i];
110:     }
111:
112:     // Deallocate memory for old list
113:     delete [] allTransactions;
114:
115:     // Assign newly allocated memory to list pointer
116:     allTransactions = temp;
117:
118:     return true;
```

```
119:
120: }
```

Listing 11.12 shows the transaction.h file that contains the Transaction class. This class is responsible for creating a single Transaction object. A transaction has three data members: the ID, the transaction type, and the amount. The transaction is an integer data type, where 0 means a withdrawal and 1 means a deposit. There are setters and getters to access each of the data members.

Listing 11.12 Cyber Bank (transaction.h)

```
1: #ifndef TRANSACTION_H
2: #define TRANSACTION_H
3:
4: using namespace std;
5:
6: class Transaction {
7: public:
8:      // Constructor
9:      Transaction() {
10:
11:     }
12:
13:     // Getters
14:     int getTransID() {
15:             return transactionID;
16:     }
17:
18:     int getTransType() {
19:             return transactionType;
20:     }
21:
22:     double getTransAmt() {
23:             return transactionAmt;
24:     }
25:
26:     // Setters
27:     void setTransID(int id) {
28:             transactionID = id;
29:     }
```

```
30:
31:     void setTransType(int type) {
32:             transactionType = type;
33:     }
34:
35:     void setTransAmt(double amt) {
36:             transactionAmt = amt;
37:     }
38:
39:
40: private:
41:     int transactionID;          // Transaction ID
42:     int transactionType;        // Transaction type
43:                                 // 0 - withdrawal
44:                                 // 1 - deposits
45:     double transactionAmt;      // Amount in the transaction
46: };
47:
48: #endif // TRANSACTION_H
```

The transaction.cpp is currently empty because all the methods for this class are setters and getters, so they were inlined. This file is included in the companion site for completeness and to allow for adding other methods to enhance this class that cannot be inlined.

The final file that makes up the Cyber Bank application is the main.cpp that is listed in Listing 11.13. This listing has the main() function that is responsible for instantiating an Account object. It initializes the object with the name "Mike Johnson", the account number 470001, and the balance of $500.00. Then this function is responsible for displaying the menu and processing the user's choice. The user's choice determines which function is called to process the selection. There is one function per menu selection. The makeWithdrawal() and make-Deposit() functions process withdrawals and deposits. Both of these functions have if-else statements that use the result of the withdrawal() and deposit() member functions to determine if the transaction was processed successfully.

The showAllTrans() function is on lines 148–181 and displays the transaction ledger. This function instantiates a Transaction object that is the current transaction for the loop to process. The for loop iterates over all the transactions in the list, and for each one it shows the information about the transaction, including whether the transaction is a withdrawal or deposit. The program encodes withdrawal as 0 and deposit as 1. This function makes the translation so the strings Withdrawal and Deposit are in the output instead of 0 or 1.

Listing 11.13 Cyber Bank (main.cpp)

```
1: // System header files
2: #include <iostream>
3: #include <string>
4: #include <iomanip>
5:
6:
7: // Cyber Bank header files
8: #include "Account.h"
9: #include "Transaction.h"
10:
11: using namespace std;
12:
13: // Constants
14: const int MAX_ACCTS = 10;
15:
16: // Function prototypes
17: void showAllTrans(const Account&);
18: void showMenu();
19: void makeDeposit(Account&);
20: void makeWithdrawal(Account&);
21: void showBalance(const Account&);
22: void openAccount(Account[], int&);
23: int login(Account[], int);
24:
25:
26: int main()
27: {
28:     Account Checking("Mike Johnson", 470001, 500);   // Account object
29:     char selection;                                  // Menu selection
30:
31:     // Set for all output to have two decimal places
32:     cout << fixed << showpoint <<  setprecision(2);
33:
34:
```

```
35:     // Controls the menu and processing selections
36:     do {
37:         showMenu();   // Display menu
38:
39:         // Process the selection from the user
40:         cin >> selection;
41:         cin.ignore(80, '\n');    // Ignores extraneous input
42:
43:         switch (selection) {
44:             case 'a':
45:             case 'A':
46:                 showBalance(Checking);
47:                 break;
48:             case 'b':
49:             case 'B':
50:                 makeDeposit(Checking);
51:                 break;
52:             case 'c':
53:             case 'C':
54:                 makeWithdrawal(Checking);
55:                 break;
56:             case 'd':
57:                 showAllTrans(Checking);
58:                 break;
59:             case 'e':
60:             case 'E':
61:                 cout << "Thank you for visiting First Cyber Bank" << endl;
62:                 return 0;
63:             default:
64:                 cout << "Invalid selection. Please try again" << endl;
65:                 break;
66:         };
67:
68:     } while (true);
69:
70:     return 0;
71: }
72:
73:
74: /* Name: showMenu
```

```
75:    * Description: Displays the menu
76:    * Parms: none
77:    */
78:
79: void showMenu() {
80:      cout << "\t\tCyber Bank Menu\n";
81:      cout << "-------------------------------------------\n";
82:      cout << "A) Show account balance\n";
83:      cout << "B) Make a deposit\n";
84:      cout << "C) Make a withdrawal\n";
85:      cout << "D) Show all transactions\n";
86:      cout << "E) Exit and Logout\n";
87:      cout << "Please make your choice: ";
88: }
89:
90:
91: /* Name: makeDeposit
92:    * Description: Process deposit menu selection
93:    * Parms:
94:    *       acct          Bank account to process
95:    */
96:
97: void makeDeposit(Account& acct) {
98:      double amount;
99:
100:     cout << "Please enter the amount for deposit: $";
101:     cin >> amount;
102:
103:     if (acct.deposit(amount))
104:             cout << "deposit made successfully" << endl;
105:     else
106:             cout << "deposit error: contact your branch" << endl;
107: }
108:
109: /* Name: makeWithdrawal
110:    * Description: Process withdrawal menu selection
111:    * Parms:
112:    *       acct          Bank account to process
113.    */
114:
```

```
115: void makeWithdrawal(Account& acct) {
116:     double amount;
117:
118:     cout << "Please enter the amount to withdraw: $";
119:     cin >> amount;
120:
121:
122:     if (acct.withdraw(amount))
123:             cout << "withdrawal made successfully" << endl;
124:     else
125:             cout << "withdrawal error: contact your branch" << endl;
126: }
127:
128:
129: /* Name: showBalance
130:  * Description: Shows account number and balance for the account
131:  * Parms:
132:  *       acct        Bank account to process
133:  */
134:
135: void showBalance(const Account& acct) {
136:     cout << "Account: " << acct.getAccountNum() << endl;
137:     cout << "Your current balance is: $";
138:     cout << acct.getBalance() << endl;
139: }
140:
141:
142: /* Name: showAllTrans
143:  * Description: Display full transaction ledger
144:  * Parms:
145:  *       acct        Bank account to process
146:  */
147:
148: void showAllTrans(const Account& acct) {
149:     string transType;   // Type after decoding
150:     Transaction currentTrans; // Transaction being processed
151:
152:
153:     cout << "Transaction Ledger" << endl;
154:     cout << "Account Name: " << acct.getName() << endl;
```

```
155:        cout << "Account Number: " << acct.getAccountNum() << endl;
156:
157:        // Process each transaction one at a time
158:        for (int i = 1; i <= acct.getNumOfTrans(); i++) {
159:
160:                // Obtain next transaction
161:                currentTrans = acct.getTransactionByNum(i);
162:
163:                cout << currentTrans.getTransID() << " ";
164:
165:                // Transaction type code is decoded
166:                switch (currentTrans.getTransType()) {
167:                        case 0:
168:                                transType = "Withdrawal";
169:                                break;
170:                        case 1:
171:                                transType = "Deposit";
172:                                break;
173:                        default:
174:                                transType = "Unknown";
175:                                break;
176:                };
177:
178:                cout << transType << " ";
179:
180:                cout << currentTrans.getTransAmt() << endl;
181:        }
182: }
```

The Cyber Bank application shows how you can use OOP in C++ to control the complexity of an application. However, there is more that you can do with this application.

CASE STUDY: THE FRACTION DATA TYPE

This section presents a new data type that handles fractions. Most programming languages treat fractions as real numbers, so when you want to represent 1/2 or 1/3, you are expected to use 0.5 and 0.3, respectively. If you attempt to enter something like X = 1/2 + 1/3, the / is treated as a division symbol, and in this case you get 0 for X because of the integer division. So there may be applications when you want to actually work with fractions and all their arithmetic operations. The Fraction class is a good starting point. While learning about the Fraction class, you will also learn about a feature found in C++ that is called operator overloading. *Operator overloading* occurs when the standard operators used for arithmetic, input/output, comparison, and assignment operators are defined to work with your user-defined type. This is so that you can have code that has a natural look and feel with your new type.

Example of Using the Fraction Data Type

To better understand what needs to be done, it's important to see some examples of how you might use a fraction data type. Listing 11.14 shows some C++ code that demonstrates how you would use a Fraction class if it existed. This program instantiates a few fraction objects and then prompts the user to input two fractions in the natural format. The program then reads the fractions from the input stream. This requires the program to get the numerator and denominator from the input and store those in the Fraction objects fract1 and fract2. The program then computes a sum of the two fractions. If you think about this for a while, that requires the addition operation to determine a common denominator and then add the fractions together and reduce the output. Then the program outputs the result. The comparison operations in the if statement must change the fractions to have common denominators again to properly compare them. As you can see, there are some steps behind the scenes that need to be performed to make these operations work. This is the essence of operator overloading.

Listing 11.14 Using the Fraction Class

```
Fraction fract1;
Fraction fract2;
Fraction fract3;

cout << "Please enter two fractions with as a/b: ";
cin >> fract1;
cin >> fract2;
fract3 = fract1 + fract2;
```

```
cout << fract3 << endl;
if (fract3 >= fract2)
    cout << "That's good to know" << endl;
else
    cout << "That can't be. something must be wrong" << endl;
```

Now that you have an idea of how to use the Fraction class, you should start learning how this would be done in C++. The next section discusses operator overloading, which is at the core of understanding how to create types that use operators in a natural way.

Operator Overloading in C++

C++ enables programmers to define common operators to work with their class. This ability is called *operator overloading*. It requires programmers to define functions that are used as substitutes for the behavior of the operation. For example, the string class allows you to use the + operator to perform string concatenation. In a typical setting, this operator is used only for numeric values to add them together. However, it is a convenient notation to use for combining strings. Therefore, the + operator is overloaded to support the string class.

You can overload a whole host of operators in C++, including all arithmetic and logic operations, assignment operators, and type-casting operators. You cannot overload the parentheses, square brackets, dot operator, pointer deference, or pointer address-of operators. You also cannot change a binary operator into a unary operator and vice versa. For example, if you overload the * operator, you have to set it up to always expect two operands: A * B.

Overloading Using friend Functions

Operator overloading functions can be defined as member functions in most cases. (The exception is with the extraction and insertion operators for input/output.) Those operators that cannot be overloaded as member functions or do not look natural as member functions can be overloaded using free functions.

Free functions are not considered part of the class, so they do not have direct access to the private data members of the class. However, operators frequently need access to the private data members. Therefore, the functions need this access to the `private` data members, and C++ provides a mechanism to achieve this by classifying the free functions as `friend` functions.

Note

In your own life, you trust your friends with secret or private information that you would not give to a stranger. Likewise, in C++ when you create a class, you can designate other parts of the software to have special access to your private data members because they are trusted.

Any class or function can be designated in the class declaration as a `friend` function. Later in this chapter, you see examples of `friend` functions for the `Fraction` class that is implemented here.

Overloading Binary Arithmetic and Logic Operators

Binary arithmetic and logic operators are overloaded using similar concepts because they have two operands. When you are overloading an arithmetic operator, you use the following format:

```
<className>  operator<symbol>(<className> const& left,
                             <className> const& right) {
<statements>
}
```

The `operator<symbol>` is the name of the function. The `<symbol>` is replaced by the arithmetic/logic symbol that is being defined. For example, if you are defining the + operator, you would have the name `operator+`, and if it were for the * operator, it would have the name `operator*`.

The operands of the function are named `left` and `right` because the operation has a value on its left and on its right. You can name these parameters anything that you like, but it's easier to remember them if you name them `left` and `right` because the order matters in operator overloading. The operands are `const` because the operator does not alter the values of the operands.

The body of the function is where the algorithm for performing the operation exists. When the function is complete, it returns an object of type `<className>`. This allows the operator to be chained together, as illustrated in Figure 11.7. *Chaining* means that the output of one operation becomes the input of the next

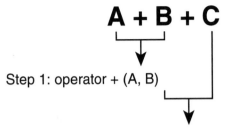

Step 1: operator + (A, B)

Step 2: operator + (<result of 1 >, C)

Figure 11.7
Operator functions are applied this way in an expression.

operation. This figure shows an `operator+` function for a class named `Foo`. The function adds the two `Foo` objects together and puts the answer in `result`, which is also a `Foo` object. It then returns a `Foo` object.

Figure 11.7 also shows how the expression `A + B + C` is solved by finding the result of `A + B` first; this is expanded into `operator+(A, B)`. The result of that function call is then used to call `operator+` again, with the result of `operator+(A, B)` and `C`. The result of the second function call is the result of the expression. This does not work if your arithmetic overload fails to return a resulting object.

Logic operations are similar to arithmetic operations, except they return Boolean values:

```
bool operator<symbol>(<className> const& left,
                      <className> const& right) {
<statements>
}
```

There are examples of arithmetic and logic overloads in the `Fraction` class that are discussed later in this chapter.

Overloading Assignment Operators

Assignment operators are typically implemented as member functions because they are more naturally expressed this way. However, you can also implement them as free functions. The names of these functions are similar to the names of the arithmetic and logic operations in that they use the keyword operator as the prefix of their names. The following is a format for overloading assignment operators:

```
<className> <className>::operator<symbol>(<type> const& source) {
  <statements>
}
```

In this format, the <symbol> can be any assignment operator, such as =, +=, -=, *=, or /=. The <type> is the data type that you would like to be involved in the assignment. This is because the parameter is the value being used as the source of the assignment, which is on the right side of the assignment. The destination of the assignment is the object that invokes this function. For example, consider the following line of code:

```
myObject = AnotherObject;
```

In this example, myObject is the destination, and AnotherObject is the source. The value of AnotherObject is copied into myObject. The copying takes place in the definition of the function. Another way to execute this operator-overloaded function is to use it like a member function:

```
myObject.operator=(AnotherObject);
```

This example is equivalent to the previous statement. This version also shows why there is only one parameter and why this function alters myObject but not AnotherObject.

You'll see examples of assignment operators in the Fraction class later in this chapter.

Overloading Input and Output Operators

The input and output operators are known as the insertion operator (>>) for input and the extraction operator (<<) for output. You must define these operators as free functions. The input and output operators use the istream and ostream classes; therefore, the header file must include the iostream header. The formats for the extraction and insertion operators follow:

```
<istream type>& operator>>(<istream type>& input,
                           <className> const& right) {
```

```
<statements>
return input;
}
<ostream type>& operator>>(<ostream type>& output,
                           <className> const& right) {
<statements>
return output;
}
```

The `operator>>` and `operator<<` functions are attached to specific types of input/output streams. The `<istream type>` could be `istream` for standard input or `ifstream` for file input. The `<ostream type>` could be `ostream` for standard output or `ofstream` for file output. The streams are returned from the functions to allow chaining together input and output streams in the same manner as the arithmetic operations. An example of how this works is illustrated in Figure 11.8.

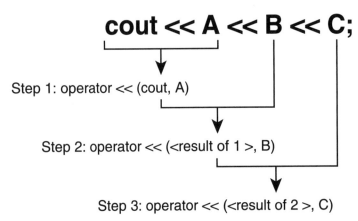

Figure 11.8
How a chain of extraction operators is evaluated.

Each function returns a reference to the original `ostream` object, which in Figure 11.8 is `cout`. The reference from evaluating the first extraction operator to output operand A in step 1 becomes the first parameter in step 2 to output operand B, and that returns the reference to be used in step 3 to output operand C.

The Fraction Class Source Code

This section shows the details of the Fraction class source code and highlights the use of operator overloading. The first file is the fraction.h file that is shown in Listing 11.15. The Fraction class implements a denominator and numerator as integers on lines 11–12. These data members are private; the value of a fraction cannot be altered without using one of its methods.

Listing 11.15 shows three constructors on lines 17–19. These constructors allow the numerator and denominator to be specified, only the numerator, or the default. A default destructor is shown on line 20.

The friend functions on lines 22–42 are free functions, so they are not considered members of the class. However, they need access to the denominator and numerator that are private data members of the Fraction class. Therefore, these functions are declared with the friend modifier to denote that they are friends of the Fraction class instead of members of the class. The first collection of friend functions is the input/output functions:

```
friend ostream& operator<<(ostream&, const Fraction&);
friend istream& operator>>(istream&, Fraction&);
```

These functions follow the templates presented in the previous section. They are both handling the Fraction class objects as their second parameters. The next set of functions is for arithmetic operations:

```
friend Fraction operator*(Fraction const&, Fraction const&);
friend Fraction operator+(Fraction const&, Fraction const&);
friend Fraction operator/(Fraction const&, Fraction const&);
friend Fraction operator-(Fraction const&, Fraction const&);
```

Each of these functions requires two Fraction object parameters to add, multiply, subtract, or divide with. The return type for each function is also a Fraction object. After these overloads, there are functions to overload the logical operations:

```
friend bool operator!=(Fraction const&, Fraction const&);
friend bool operator<(Fraction const&, Fraction const&);
friend bool operator>(Fraction const&, Fraction const&);
friend bool operator<=(Fraction const&, Fraction const&);
friend bool operator>=(Fraction const&, Fraction const&);
```

These functions follow a similar format to the arithmetic operations, with the exception of the return type. Each function returns a bool type because these operators are used within Boolean expressions. The final collection of functions is for the assignment functions:

```
Fraction operator=(Fraction const&);
Fraction operator++();
Fraction operator--();
Fraction operator++(int);
Fraction operator--(int);
Fraction operator+=(Fraction const&);
Fraction operator-=(Fraction const&);
Fraction operator*=(Fraction const&);
```

The assignment functions handle the standard assignment operation and the shortcut accumulation and assignment operations. Two look interesting: operator++() and operator++(int). The issue here is how to represent the difference between i++ and ++i. The prefix version is represented by operator++(), and postfix is represented by operator++(int).

Listing 11.15 Fraction Class (fraction.h)

```
1: #ifndef FRACTION_H
2: #define FRACTION_H
3:
4: #include <iostream> // Access to istream and ostream
5:
6: using namespace std;
7:
8:
9: class Fraction {
10: private:
11:     int numerator;
12:     int denominator;
13:
14: public:
15:
16:     // Fraction constructors and destructors
17:     Fraction(int, int);
18:     Fraction(int);
19:     Fraction();
```

```
20:        ~Fraction();
21:
22:        // Fraction I/O operations
23:        friend ostream& operator<<(ostream&, const Fraction&);
24:        friend istream& operator>>(istream&, Fraction&);
25:
26:        // Fraction reduction
27:        Fraction reduce() const;
28:
29:        // Fraction arithmetic operators
30:        friend Fraction operator*(Fraction const&, Fraction const&);
31:        friend Fraction operator+(Fraction const&, Fraction const&);
32:        friend Fraction operator/(Fraction const&, Fraction const&);
33:        friend Fraction operator-(Fraction const&, Fraction const&);
34:
35:
36:        // Fraction comparison operators
37:        friend bool operator==(Fraction const&, Fraction const&);
38:        friend bool operator!=(Fraction const&, Fraction const&);
39:        friend bool operator<(Fraction const&, Fraction const&);
40:        friend bool operator>(Fraction const&, Fraction const&);
41:        friend bool operator<=(Fraction const&, Fraction const&);
42:        friend bool operator>=(Fraction const&, Fraction const&);
43:
44:        // Fraction assignment operators
45:        Fraction operator=(Fraction const&);
46:        Fraction operator++();
47:        Fraction operator-();
48:        Fraction operator++(int);
49:        Fraction operator-(int);
50:        Fraction operator+=(Fraction const&);
51:        Fraction operator-=(Fraction const&);
52:        Fraction operator*=(Fraction const&);
53:
54:
55:        // Fraction conversion operators
56:        operator float ();
57:
58:
59: };
```

```
60:
61: #endif // FRACTION_H
```

The code shown in Listing 11.16 is for the `fraction.cpp` file. This file contains all the definitions of the functions. The entire file is displayed here so that you can examine it. There are similarities throughout the file because the operations in the same groupings are not very different from one another. The key functions and methods are explained here.

Listing 11.16 Fraction Class (fraction.cpp)

```
1: #include "fraction.h"
2: #include <cmath>
3:
4: Fraction::Fraction() {
5:      numerator = 0;
6:      denominator = 1;
7: }
8:
9: Fraction::Fraction(int n, int d) {
10:      numerator = n;
11:      denominator = d;
12: }
13:
14: Fraction::Fraction(int opnd) {
15:      numerator = opnd;
16:      denominator = 1;
17: }
18:
19:
20:
21: Fraction::s ~Fraction() {
22:
23: }
24:
25:
26: Fraction Fraction::reduce() const {
27:      Fraction temp(numerator, denominator);
28:      bool found = false;
30:      int target = (temp.numerator > temp.denominator) ? temp.denominator :
            temp.numerator;
```

```
31:
32:        for (int factor = target; (factor > 1) && (!found); factor--) {
33:            if ( ((temp.numerator % factor) == 0) &&
34:                 ((temp.denominator % factor) == 0) ) {
35:                        temp.numerator = temp.numerator / factor;
36:                        temp.denominator = temp.denominator / factor;
37:                        found = true;
38:                }
39:        }
40:
41:        return temp;
42: }
43:
44:
45:
46: // Friend functions
47: Fraction operator*(Fraction const& f1, Fraction const& f2) {
48:        Fraction result;
49:
50:
51:        result.numerator = f1.numerator*f2.numerator;
52:        result.denominator = f1.denominator*f2.denominator;
53:        return result;
54:
55: }
56:
57: Fraction operator+(Fraction const& f1, Fraction const& f2) {
58:        Fraction result;
59:
60:        result.numerator = f1.numerator*f2.denominator + f2.numerator*f1.
           denominator;
61:        result.denominator = f1.denominator*f2.denominator;
62:
63:        return result;
64: }
65:
66: Fraction operator/(Fraction const& f1, Fraction const& f2) {
67:        Fraction result;
68:
69:        result.numerator = f1.numerator*f2.denominator;
```

```
70:        result.denominator = f1.denominator*f2.numerator;
71:     return result;
72:
73: }
74:
75: Fraction operator-(Fraction const& f1, Fraction const& f2) {
76:     Fraction result;
77:
78:        result.numerator = f1.numerator*f2.denominator - f2.numerator*f1.
           denominator;
79:        result.denominator = f1.denominator*f2.denominator;
80:
81:     return result;
82: }
83:
84: ostream& operator<<(ostream& os, const Fraction& f) {
85:
86:        os << f.numerator << "/" << f.denominator;
87:     return os;
88: }
89:
90:
91: istream& operator>>(istream& is, Fraction& f) {
92:     char slash;
93:     is >> f.numerator;
94:     is >> slash;
95:     if (slash != '/') {
96:                is.setstate(ios::badbit|ios::failbit);
97:                f.numerator = 0;
98:                f.denominator = 1;
99:     } else {
100:               is >> f.denominator;
101:     }
102:
103:    return is;
104: }
105:
106:
107: bool operator!=(Fraction const& f1, Fraction const&f2) {
```

```
108:      return !(f1 == f1);
109: }
110:
111:
112: bool operator==(Fraction const& f1, Fraction const&f2) {
113:      Fraction fleft = f1;
114:      Fraction fright = f2;
115:
116:      fleft.reduce();
117:      fright.reduce();
118:
119:      return (fleft.numerator == fright.numerator) &&
120:      (fleft.denominator == fright.denominator);
121: }
122:
123:
124: bool operator<(Fraction const& f1, Fraction const& f2) {
125:      int lNumerator = f1.numerator*f2.denominator;
126:      int rNumerator = f2.numerator*f1.denominator;
127:
128:      return lNumerator < rNumerator;
129: }
130:
131:
132: bool operator>(Fraction const& f1, Fraction const& f2) {
133:      int lNumerator = f1.numerator*f2.denominator;
134:      int rNumerator = f2.numerator*f1.denominator;
135:
136:      return lNumerator > rNumerator;
137: }
138:
139:
140: bool operator<=(Fraction const& f1, Fraction const& f2) {
141:      return (f1 == f2) || (f1 < f2);
142: }
143:
144:
145: bool operator>=(Fraction const& f1, Fraction const& f2) {
146:      return (f1 == f2) || (f1 > f2);
147: }
```

```
148:
149:
150:
151: Fraction Fraction::operator=(Fraction const& opnd) {
152:
153:     numerator = opnd.numerator;
154:     denominator = opnd.denominator;
155:
156:     return *this;
157: }
158:
159: Fraction Fraction::operator++() {
160:     numerator += denominator;
161:
162:     return *this;
163: }
164:
165:
166:
167: Fraction Fraction::operator--() {
168:     numerator -= denominator;
169:
170:     return *this;
171: }
172:
173: Fraction Fraction::operator++(int) {
174:     Fraction old = *this;
175:     numerator += denominator;
176:     return old;
177: }
178:
179: Fraction Fraction::operator--(int) {
180:     Fraction old = *this;
181:     numerator -= denominator;
182:     return old;
183: }
184:
185: Fraction Fraction::operator+=(Fraction const& opnd) {
186:     *this = *this + opnd;
187:
```

```
188:     return *this;
189: }
190:
191:
192:
193: Fraction Fraction::operator-=(Fraction const& opnd) {
194:     *this = *this - opnd;
195:
196:     return *this;
197:
198: }
199:
200:
201: Fraction Fraction::operator*=(Fraction const& opnd) {
202:     *this = *this * opnd;
203:
204:     return *this;
205: }
206:
207: Fraction::operator float () {
208:             return (float)numerator/(float)denominator;
209:     }
```

The first function to discuss is the member function named Fraction::reduce() on lines 26–39. This method must find the greatest common factor (GCF) between the denominator and numerator to fully reduce the fraction. For example, consider having the fraction 16/24. The greatest common factor is 8, so the reduced fraction is 2/3. To find the GCF, the algorithm decides to search for factors of the smallest value between the numerator and denominator. In this example, 16 is the smallest value, so the numerator is selected. The for loop on lines 32–39 examines each number starting at 16 down to 1 in order: 16, 15, 14, 13, 12, and so on. When it finds a number that divides both the numerator and denominator evenly, it divides them each, and the loop stops. The algorithm uses the % operator to determine even divisibility.

The second function is the free function named operator*(Fraction const&, Fraction const&), which performs multiplication between two fractions. Two fractions are multiplied by multiplying the numerators and the denominators. For example, 4/5 * 7/8 is equal to 28/40. This function does not reduce the result.

This design decision reflects the fact that the arithmetic operation is separate from reduction operation. The definition for this function is on lines 47–55. The function creates a local temporary `fraction` object to be the result. The next two lines multiply the numerators and denominators and store the result in the temporary `fraction` object. The final step is to return a copy of the result as the result of the multiplication operation.

The third function is a free one for input named `operator>>(istream&, Fraction&)`. It reads a fraction as input in the format of `n/d`, where the `/` is included. This function recognizes that this means two integers are read and one character. Lines 93–94 read an integer and a character from the input stream. The `if-else` statement on lines 95–101 tests to make sure the second input value is a `/` character. If it's a `/` character, the denominator is read on line 100. If it's not a `/` character, the stream is set to a fail state, which means it will not accept more input unless it is cleared first.

The fourth function is a free one for comparing equality, and it is named `operator==(Fraction const&, Fraction const&)`. This function determines whether two fractions are equal. To determine equality, the fractions need to have the same denominator and numerator in their reduced state; or if they have the same denominator, you can just test the numerators for equality. The former method is used in this function. Both the fractions are reduced on lines 116–117. Then the numerators and denominators can be tested for equality, and result of that comparison is returned as the result of the function.

At this point, you have examined the contents of the `Fraction` class and should have an understanding of how it works. Listing 11.17 shows a testing program that is in the `main` function. The purpose of this function is to show some ways to use the operators that were implemented in the `Fraction` class. If it seems that the tests are contrived, this is true. Often a programmer uses a test file such as this to determine the correctness of the class that he has built. The output from this test program is shown in Listing 11.18.

Listing 11.17 Fraction Class Testing (main.cpp)

```
1: // System headers
2: #include <iostream>
```

```
3:
4: // Fraction header
5: #include "fraction.h"
6:
7: using namespace std;
8:
9: int main() {
10:
11:       // Instantiate fraction objects
12:       Fraction myNum;
13:       Fraction myNum2(5, 6);
14:       Fraction myNum3(15, 6);
15:       Fraction newVal;
16:
17:       // Echo fraction objects to test extraction operator
18:       cout << "First number: " << myNum << "(defalut)" << endl;
19:       cout << "Second number: " << myNum2 << "(initializer)" << endl;
20:       cout << "Third number: " << myNum3 << "(initializer)" << endl;
21:
22:       // Reduce the third fraction: test reduction and assignment overload
23:       myNum3 = myNum3.reduce();
24:       cout << "Reduced Third number: " << myNum3 << endl;
25:
26:       // Test fraction multiplication and assignment
27:       newVal = myNum3 * myNum3;
28:       cout << "result of assign and mult: " << newVal << endl;
29:
30:       // Test fraction division
31:       newVal = myNum3 / myNum3;
32:       cout << "result of assign and divide: " << newVal << endl;
33:
34:       // Reduce and then perform more operations
35:       newVal = newVal.reduce();
36:
37:       cout << "Reduce the result: " << newVal << endl;
38:       cout << "result after addition: " << newVal + myNum3 << endl;
39:       cout << "result after subtraction: " << myNum3 - newVal << endl;
40:
41:       // Test the equality operator
42:       cout << "equals: " << (myNum3 == myNum3) << endl;
```

```
43:        cout << "not equals: " << (myNum3 != myNum3) << endl;
44:
45:        // Instantiate new objects for more comparison tests
46:        Fraction oneThird = Fraction(1, 3);
47:        Fraction oneHalf = Fraction(1, 2);
48:
49:        // Test the less-than operator
50:        cout << "Less than: " << (oneThird < oneHalf) << endl;
51:
52:        // Test the greater-than operator
53:        cout << "Greater than: " << (oneThird > oneHalf) << endl;
54:
55:        // Test the less-than and equal operator
56:        cout << "less than and equals: " << (oneThird <= oneHalf) << endl;
57:
58:        // Test the greater-than and equal operator
59:        cout << "greater than and equals: " << (oneThird >= oneHalf) << endl;
60:
61:        // Test the conversion of an integer to a fraction
62:        cout << "conversion to from int: " << (Fraction)5 << endl;
63:
64:        // Test the conversion of a floating point to a fraction
65:        cout << "conversion to float: " << (float)oneThird << endl;
66:
67:        // Testing the input of a fraction
68:        cout << "Enter a fraction: ";
69:        cin >> myNum;
70:
71:        if (cin)
72:                cout << "input okay, you entered " << myNum << endl;
73:        else
74:                cout << "input failed" << endl;
75:
76:        return 0;
77: }
```

Listing 11.18 Output from Fraction Class Testing

```
First number: 0/1(default)
Second number: 5/6(initializer)
```

```
Third number: 15/6(initializer)
Reduced Third number: 5/2
result of assign and mult: 25/4
result of assign and divide: 10/10
Reduce the result: 1/1
result after addition: 7/2
result after subtraction: 3/2
equals: 1
not equals: 0
Less than: 1
Greater than: 0
less than and equals: 1
greater than and equals: 0
conversion to from int: 5/1
conversion to float: 0.333333
Enter a fraction: 5/6
input okay, you entered 5/6
```

This section has presented another extensive use of operator overloading to create other data types that work seamlessly with well-known operations. You can use these techniques to create classes for vectors, money, and polynomials.

SUMMARY

This chapter presented an introduction to OOP in C++ and explored various features from C++ that support OOP:

- Class declaration
- Member function/method definition
- Visibility declarations
- Constructors/destructors
- Access to object members
- Creating instances of classes
- Operator overloading

These features are the introductory features that show the way to implement the methods/messages, information hiding, and objects as instances of class principles of OOP.

This chapter also presented two significant case studies to demonstrate the power of C++ classes: Cyber Bank and Fractions. The first showed how you can use classes together to solve complex problems using the OOP methodology. The second showed how you can use classes in C++ to create a fully integrated user-defined type.

EXERCISES

1. Add the capability for check withdrawals at the Cyber Bank. You can do this by adding the capability to withdraw money by check, which requires a check number. The current withdrawal method is assumed to be a cash withdrawal, which should remain as a feature. You also need to update the transaction list to include check numbers when the transaction is a check.

2. Write a class that represents a television remote control. The remote control has an LCD display to show the current channel and volume levels. The remote control has buttons for Channel Up, Channel Down, Volume Up, Volume Down, and Power On/Off. The volume should have a maximum setting of 10 and a minimum setting of 0. There should be 50 channels: 1–50. Write a main program that instantiates a remote control object and shows how each of the member functions will work.

3. Write a class that represents a tic-tac-toe board. There should be two methods that allow you to set Xs and to set Os in places on the board using row and column coordinates and display the board in its current state. Write a main program that tests your class by instantiating a tic-tac-toe board and testing your member functions. Note: This problem does not require writing a whole tic-tac-toe game because you are not writing the logic for determining a winner or for taking turns. You may consider extending your class and main program to be a tic-tac-toe game.

4. Write a class that represents an alarm clock. The clock class should have the following capabilities:

   - Set mode to 24-hour or 12-hour mode
   - Set the time
   - Set the alarm time
   - Display the time
   - Display the settings: time mode and alarm time
   - Advance time by seconds

5. Write a class to represent money that uses a `double` as the value attribute. The money class must use overloaded operators for input, output, addition, subtraction, multiplication, and division. Write a main program that instantiates money objects and shows how to use the overloaded operations with these objects.

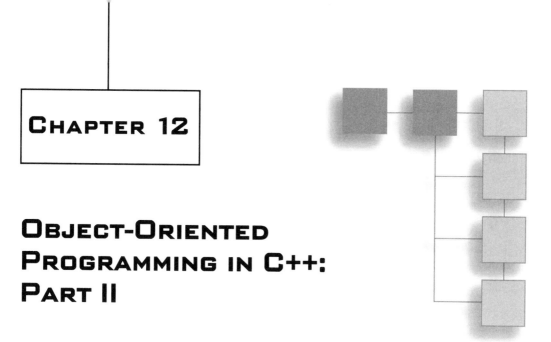

CHAPTER 12

OBJECT-ORIENTED PROGRAMMING IN C++: PART II

In This Chapter

- Pointers to Objects
- Accessing Class Members from an Array of Pointers
- Case Study: Cyber Bank with Multiuser
- Inheritance in C++

> Computer Science is the first engineering discipline in which the
> complexity of the objects created is limited solely by the skill
> of the creator, and not by the strength of raw materials.
>
> —B. Reid

This is the last chapter for this book, but it is not the last chapter in learning about programming or C++. You have built up a nice firm foundation to learn more advanced programming techniques in C++ or perhaps another language. Congratulations on your journey.

This chapter discusses how pointers and objects can be used together for more efficient memory usage. This is important in object-oriented programming (OOP) because objects tend to require large amounts of memory, so the more efficient you are at managing that memory, the better. You also learn how the fourth principal of OOP, inheritance, is applied to the C++ I/O library and a database example. Finally, you learn the fundamental rules and syntax regarding inheritance in C++.

POINTERS TO OBJECTS

You have learned about pointers and how they can be used to manage dynamic memory. In C++, objects are typically large and require significantly more memory to store than variables of core data types. Consider the following declarations:

```
Account myAccount;
int number;
```

The first declaration is an instantiation of an object of the Account class discussed in Chapter 11, "Object-Oriented Programming in C++: Part I." The private data members for an object in this class are two strings, three ints, one double, and an array of transactions. (There are two ints and one double per transaction.) It would be easy for the myAccount object to be 100 times the size of the integer number, depending on the size of the transaction's array. This means that you want to avoid making copies of these objects whenever possible. Consider the following code:

```
Account allAccounts[1000];
Account* listOfAccounts = new Account[1000];
```

These lines of code declare arrays using static and dynamic memory allocation. Both would occupy a large amount of memory because of the size of each Account object even when the objects are empty or have only a few transactions. This is where pointers can be handy. Consider the following declarations:

```
Account* allAccounts[1000];
Account** listOfAccounts = new Account*[1000];
```

These declarations declare arrays of pointers to Account objects. The difference is shown in Figure 12.1. The array of Account objects allocates memory for N Account objects. On the other hand, the array of Account pointers only allocates enough memory for N pointers, which are much smaller. Then it allocates Account objects as needed, and they are maintained in a pool of Account objects. The result is a more efficient use of memory.

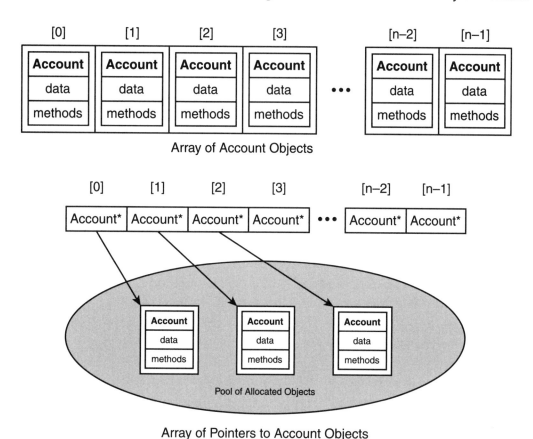

Figure 12.1
Array of Account objects versus an array of Account object pointers.

ACCESSING CLASS MEMBERS
FROM AN ARRAY OF POINTERS

When you have an array of objects, the dot operator is used to access the members of the objects in the arrays. For example, in Chapter 11, the Account class has an array of Transaction objects. The following code sets the members of a Transaction object in the array:

```
allTransactions[numOfTrans-1].setTransID(numOfTrans);
allTransactions[numOfTrans-1].setTransType(0);
allTransactions[numOfTrans-1].setTransAmt(amt);
```

The dot operator is used in each to access the member functions of the Transaction object at location numOfTrans-1 in the array named allTransactions. There is another operator for accessing the members on an object through a pointer. The operator is called an *arrow operator*. The arrow operator is made by using the dash and the greater-than symbol, and it looks like this: ->. You can use the arrow operator to access members of an object via the pointer:

```
Account* savings;
savings = new Account("David", "1234", 254567, 500.00)
cout << "Name: " << Savings->getName() << endl;
cout << "Account: " << Savings->getAccountNum() << endl;
```

The savings pointer is declared and then assigned to point to the location for David's account. The cout statements display David and 254567 as the values returned by the getName() and getAccountNum() methods. You can use the arrow operator the same way as the dot operator in arrays:

```
Account* accountsList[10];
accountsList[0] = new Account("David", "1234", 254567, 500.00)
cout << "Name: " << accountsList[0]->getName() << endl;
cout << "Account: " << accountsList[0]->getAccountNum() << endl;
```

The array is allocated 10 Account pointers, and then the first Account pointer in the array is assigned to allocated memory of a new Account object. Therefore, each element in the array is a pointer to an Account object, but not an actual Account object. The lines that follow show how the arrow operator accesses the members through the pointer in the array.

CASE STUDY: CYBER BANK WITH MULTIUSER

Version 2 of Cyber Bank needs to be released. It will contain all the features of version 1, shown in Chapter 11. It also will have multiuser capability with password protection. The UML diagram in Figure 12.2 shows the UML class diagrams and how they are related by an aggregation. The Account is an aggregate of the Transaction class as it was in version 1. The newly added features to the classes are shown in bold.

The Account class has a new data member to manage the password for the account and a new method that validates the password with the account number. The Transaction class is unchanged.

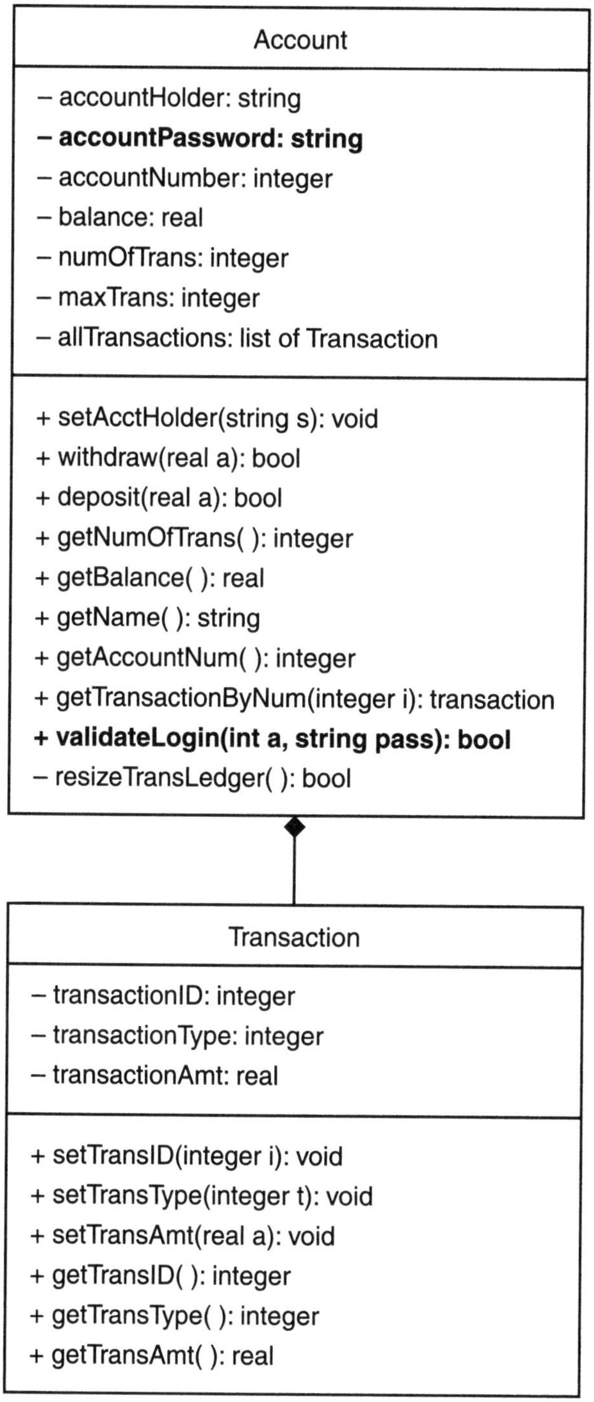

Account
– accountHolder: string
– **accountPassword: string**
– accountNumber: integer
– balance: real
– numOfTrans: integer
– maxTrans: integer
– allTransactions: list of Transaction
+ setAcctHolder(string s): void
+ withdraw(real a): bool
+ deposit(real a): bool
+ getNumOfTrans( ): integer
+ getBalance( ): real
+ getName( ): string
+ getAccountNum( ): integer
+ getTransactionByNum(integer i): transaction
+ **validateLogin(int a, string pass): bool**
– resizeTransLedger( ): bool

Transaction
– transactionID: integer
– transactionType: integer
– transactionAmt: real
+ setTransID(integer i): void
+ setTransType(integer t): void
+ setTransAmt(real a): void
+ getTransID( ): integer
+ getTransType( ): integer
+ getTransAmt( ): real

Figure 12.2
UML diagram containing an Account class and a Transaction class.

Cyber Bank Version 2 in Action

The new version of Cyber Bank adds two more menu options. One of the options is for creating new accounts, and the other option allows you to log into an account. Listing 12.1 shows an example of the interaction with Cyber Bank version 2. The demonstration starts by opening two new accounts. Then it logs in to each account, performing transactions on each. The software keeps the transactions separate.

Listing 12.1 Output from Cyber Bank Version 2

```
            Cyber Bank Menu
------------------------------------
A) Show account balance
B) Make a deposit
C) Make a withdrawal
D) Show all transactions
E) Log into an account
F) Open a new account
G) Exit and Logout
Please make your choice: A
                Cyber Bank Menu
------------------------------------
A) Show account balance
B) Make a deposit
C) Make a withdrawal
D) Show all transactions
E) Log into an account
F) Open a new account
G) Exit and Logout
Please make your choice: F
Enter name: Mickey Mouse
Enter password: 54321
Enter starting balance: 1000
Your account number is: 40001
                Cyber Bank Menu
------------------------------------
A) Show account balance
B) Make a deposit
C) Make a withdrawal
```

D) Show all transactions
E) Log into an account
F) Open a new account
G) Exit and Logout
Please make your choice: F
Enter name: Donald Duck
Enter password: 12345
Enter starting balance: 500
Your account number is: 40002
                    Cyber Bank Menu

A) Show account balance
B) Make a deposit
C) Make a withdrawal
D) Show all transactions
E) Log into an account
F) Open a new account
G) Exit and Logout
Please make your choice: E
Account Number: 40001
Password: 54321
Login Successful
                    Cyber Bank Menu

A) Show account balance
B) Make a deposit
C) Make a withdrawal
D) Show all transactions
E) Log into an account
F) Open a new account
G) Exit and Logout
Please make your choice: A
Your current balance is: $1000.00
                    Cyber Bank Menu

A) Show account balance
B) Make a deposit
C) Make a withdrawal
D) Show all transactions
E) Log into an account

F) Open a new account
G) Exit and Logout
Please make your choice: B
Please enter the amount for deposit: $500
Deposit made successfully
                    Cyber Bank Menu

A) Show account balance
B) Make a deposit
C) Make a withdrawal
D) Show all transactions
E) Log into an account
F) Open a new account
G) Exit and Logout
Please make your choice: C
Please enter the amount to withdraw: $100
withdrawal made successfully
                    Cyber Bank Menu

A) Show account balance
B) Make a deposit
C) Make a withdrawal
D) Show all transactions
E) Log into an account
F) Open a new account
G) Exit and Logout
Please make your choice: D
Transaction Ledger
Account Name: Mickey Mouse
Account Number: 40001
1 Deposit 500.00
2 Withdrawal 100.00
                    Cyber Bank Menu

A) Show account balance
B) Make a deposit
C) Make a withdrawal
D) Show all transactions
E) Log into an account
F) Open a new account

```
G) Exit and Logout
Please make your choice: A
Your current balance is: $1400.00
                    Cyber Bank Menu
-------------------------------------
A) Show account balance
B) Make a deposit
C) Make a withdrawal
D) Show all transactions
E) Log into an account
F) Open a new account
G) Exit and Logout
Please make your choice: E
Account Number: 40002
Password: 12345
Login Successful
                    Cyber Bank Menu
-------------------------------------
A) Show account balance
B) Make a deposit
C) Make a withdrawal
D) Show all transactions
E) Log into an account
F) Open a new account
G) Exit and Logout
Please make your choice: A
Your current balance is: $500.00
                    Cyber Bank Menu
-------------------------------------
A) Show account balance
B) Make a deposit
C) Make a withdrawal
D) Show all transactions
E) Log into an account
F) Open a new account
G) Exit and Logout
Please make your choice: B
Please enter the amount for deposit: $300
deposit made successfully
```

```
                        Cyber Bank Menu
         ------------------------------------
         A) Show account balance
         B) Make a deposit
         C) Make a withdrawal
         D) Show all transactions
         E) Log into an account
         F) Open a new account
         G) Exit and Logout
         Please make your choice: D
         Transaction Ledger
         Account Name: Donald Duck
         Account Number: 40002
         1 Deposit 300.00
```

The transcript of the session with Cyber Bank reveals the new features; however, you are encouraged to build the program yourself to explore its features more deeply.

Cyber Bank Version 2 Source Code

This version of Cyber Bank uses the same code files as the version in Chapter 11. The only files that have changed are Account.h, Account.cpp, and main.cpp. Therefore, this section only showcases the new files and discusses how the additional features were implemented, taking advantage of arrays of pointers. The majority of the changes occur in main.cpp, so Listing 12.2 shows the new main.cpp file.

The first change happens on lines 20 and 21, where two new functions have been created. The openAccount() function is there to create new accounts, and the login() function enables the multiuser ability by validating logins.

The second change is subtle; it is on all the function prototypes. The function that in version 1 accepted Account objects now accepts Account* because the application relies on accessing Account objects via pointers. This is also the reason for the Account*[] in the prototypes that need access to the entire array of Account object pointers.

The third change is on lines 26–28, where the array of Account pointers is declared to enable support for multiple accounts, and there are two integer variables declared to help manage the array of accounts. The first integer represents how many accounts have been created and are in the array, and the second integer holds the index of the array that is pointing to the currently logged-in account. If currentAccount is –1, there is no account currently logged in. This is important to the fourth change. The array of Account pointers also requires changes globally within the file to all functions that access class member functions. Each of these member functions is now accessed using the arrow operator.

The fourth change is to recognize that when an account has not been logged into or if there are no accounts in the system, the majority of the menu options should not be available. You will see in the switch statement starting on line 48 that each case has an if statement that guards the corresponding function call. It does not allow the function to be called unless there are accounts created and one of them is currently logged in.

The fifth change is the addition of the login() function that validates user logins. This function is located on lines 203–232. This function asks the user for the account number and password. No sophisticated encryption scheme is used. The function uses a linear search of the allAccounts array to find an account where the account number and password match. If one is found, the index of the array for that account is returned; otherwise a –1 is returned. The sixth and final change is the addition of the openAccount function that creates new accounts for the system. This function determines if the number of accounts has exceeded the size of the storage reserved for accounts. If it has not exceeded this value, the new account is opened by asking for the user's name, password, and starting balance. The next step is on line 262, where the new account object is allocated dynamically and assigned to the pointer in the next available account location in the allAccounts array.

Listing 12.2 Cyber Bank Version 2 (main.cpp)

```
1: #include <iostream>
2: #include <string>
3: #include <iomanip>
4:
5: // Banking header files
6: #include "Account.h"
7: #include "Transaction.h"
8:
```

```
 9: using namespace std;
10:
11: // Constants
12: const int MAX_ACCTS = 10;
13:
14: // Function prototypes
15: void showAllTrans(const Account*);
16: void showMenu();
17: void makeDeposit(Account*);
18: void makeWithdrawal(Account*);
19: void showBalance(const Account*);
20: void openAccount(Account*[], int&);
21: int login(Account*[], int);
22:
23:
24: int main()
25: {
26:     Account* allAccounts[MAX_ACCTS]; // Array of accounts
27:     int numberOfAccounts = 0;        // Number of open accounts
28:     int currentAccount = -1;         // Currently logged-in account
29:     char selection;                  // Menu selection
30:
31:     // Set for all output to have two decimal places
32:     cout << fixed << showpoint <<   setprecision(2);
33:
34:     // Controls the menu and processing selections
35:     do {
36:             showMenu(); // Displays the menu
37:
38:             // Processes the selection from the user
39:             cin >> selection;
40:             cin.ignore(80, '\n');   // Ignores the extraneous input
41:
42:             switch (selection) {
43:                     case 'a':
44:                     case 'A':
45:                         if (numberOfAccounts > 0 && currentAccount != -1)
46:                             showBalance(allAccounts[currentAccount]);
47:                         break;
48:                     case 'b':
```

```
49:                        case 'B':
50:                          if (numberOfAccounts > 0 && currentAccount != -1)
51:                            makeDeposit(allAccounts[currentAccount]);
52:                          break;
53:                        case 'c':
54:                        case 'C':
55:                          if (numberOfAccounts > 0 && currentAccount != -1)
56:                            makeWithdrawal(allAccounts[currentAccount]);
57:                          break;
58:                        case 'd':
59:                        case 'D':
60:                          if (numberOfAccounts > 0 && currentAccount != -1)
61:                             showAllTrans(allAccounts[currentAccount]);
62:                          break;
63:                        case 'e':
64:                        case 'E':
65:                          if (numberOfAccounts > 0) {
66:                             currentAccount = login(allAccounts,
                                                      numberOfAccounts);
67:                             if (currentAccount == -1)
68:                               cout << "Sorry: Login failed" << endl;
69:                             else
70:                               cout << "Login Successful" << endl;
71:                          }
72:                             break;
73:                        case 'f':
74:                        case 'F':
75:                          openAccount(allAccounts, numberOfAccounts);
76:                          break;
77:                        case 'g':
78:                        case 'G':
79:                          cout << "Thank you for visiting First Cyber Bank"
                                  << endl;
80:                          return 0;
81:                        default:
82:                          cout << "You entered an invalid selection.";
                                  << "Please try again" << endl;
83:                          break;
84:               };
85:
```

```
86:      } while (true);
87:
88:      return 0;
89: }
90:
91:
92:
93: /* Name: showMenu
94:  * Description: Displays the menu
95:  * Parms: none
96:  */
97:
98: void showMenu() {
99:      cout << "\t\tCyber Bank Menu\n";
100:     cout << "----------------------------------------\n";
101:     cout << "A) Show account balance\n";
102:     cout << "B) Make a deposit\n";
103:     cout << "C) Make a withdrawal\n";
104:     cout << "D) Show all transactions\n";
105:     cout << "E) Log into an account\n";
106:     cout << "F) Open a new account\n";
107:     cout << "G) Exit and Logout\n";
108:     cout << "Please make your choice: ";
109: }
110:
111:
112: /* Name: makeDeposit
113:  * Description: Process deposit menu selection
114:  * Parms:
115:  *        acct          ptr to Bank account to process
116:  */
117:
118: void makeDeposit(Account* acct) {
119:     double amount;
120:
121:     cout << "Please enter the amount for deposit: $";
122:     cin >> amount;
123:
124:     if (acct->deposit(amount))
125:             cout << "deposit made successfully" << endl;
```

```
126:     else
127:             cout << "deposit error: contact your branch" << endl;
128:
129: }
130:
131: /* Name: makeWithdrawal
132:  * Description: Process withdrawal menu selection
133:  * Parms:
134:  *      acct        ptr to Bank account to process
135:  */
136:
137: void makeWithdrawal(Account* acct) {
138:     double amount;
139:
140:     cout << "Please enter the amount to withdraw: $";
141:     cin >> amount;
142:
143:     if (acct->withdraw(amount))
144:             cout << "withdrawal made successfully" << endl;
145:     else
146:             cout << "withdrawal error: contact your branch" << endl;
147:
148:
149: }
150:
151: /* Name: showBalance
152:  * Description: Shows account number and balance for the account
153:  * Parms:
154:  *      acct        ptr to Bank account to process
155:  */
156:
157: void showBalance(const Account* acct) {
158:     cout << "Your current balance is: $";
159:     cout << acct->getBalance() << endl;
160: }
161:
162:
163: /* Name: showAllTrans
164:  * Description: Display full transaction ledger
165:  * Parms:
```

```
166:  *     acct       Bank account to process
167:  */
168:
169: void showAllTrans(const Account* acct) {
170:     string transType;
171:     Transaction currentTrans;
172:
173:
174:     cout << "Transaction Ledger" << endl;
175:     cout << "Account Name: " << acct->getName() << endl;
176:     cout << "Account Number: " << acct->getAccountNum() << endl;
177:
178:     for (int i = 1; i <= acct->getNumOfTrans(); i++) {
179:
180:             currentTrans = acct->getTransactionByNum(i);
181:
182:             cout << currentTrans.getTransID() << " ";
183:
184:             switch (currentTrans.getTransType()) {
185:                     case 0:
186:                             transType = "Withdrawal";
187:                             break;
188:                     case 1:
189:                             transType = "Deposit";
190:                             break;
191:                     default:
192:                             transType = "Unknown";
193:                             break;
194:             };
195:
196:             cout << transType << " ";
197:
198:             cout << currentTrans.getTransAmt() << endl;
199:
200:     }
201: }
202:
203: /* Name: login
204:  * Description: Processes an account login by checking account number
205:  * and password before allowing access.
```

```
206:   * Parms:
207:   *      Accts[]              an array of ptrs to Account objects
208:   *      numAccts    the number of accounts in the array
209:   */
210:
211: int login(Account* Accts[], int numAccts) {
212:     int acctNum;
213:     string password;
214:
215:     cout << "Account Number: ";
216:     cin >> acctNum;
217:
218:     cout << "Password: ";
219:     cin >> password;
220:
221:
222:     // Searches accounts for the entered account number
223:     for (int i = 0; i < numAccts; i++) {
224:             // If account is found, validates password
225:             if (Accts[i]->getAccountNum() == acctNum)
226:                     if (Accts[i]->validateLogin(acctNum, password))
227:                             return i;
228:     }
229:
230:     return -1; // Access denied
231:
232: }
233:
234:
235: /* Name: openAccount
236:  * Description: Allow a new account to be opened with name, password, and
237:  * initial balance. The account number is sequentially assigned.
238:  * Parms:
239:  *      Accts[]              an array of ptrs to Account objects
240:  *      numAccts    the number of accounts in the array
241:  */
242:
243: void openAccount(Account* Accts[], int& numAccts) {
244:     string name;
245:     string passwd;
```

```
246:      double startBal;
247:      int accountNum;
248:
249:      if (numAccts < MAX_ACCTS) {
250:              cout << "Enter name: ";
251:              getline (cin,name);
252:
253:              cout << "Enter password: ";
254:              cin >> passwd;
255:
256:              cout << "Enter starting balance: ";
257:              cin >> startBal;
258:
259:              numAccts++;
260:              accountNum = 40000 + numAccts;
261:
262:              Accts[numAccts-1] = new Account(name, passwd,
                                                  accountNum, startBal);
263:
264:              cout << "Your account number is: ";
265:                  << Accts[numAccts-1]->getAccountNum() << endl;
266:      }
267:
268: }
```

The next file that was updated is the header file for the Account class. The
account.h file is shown in Listing 12.3. This file has changes to support the
password and password validation. The constructor is updated on line 14 to
have a parameter that is used to set a password at instantiation time. On lines 60
and 61, the validateLogin() method is declared. This function is responsible for
testing to see if the account number and password match the values stored in the
Account object. The body of this function is shown in Listing 12.4.

Listing 12.3 Cyber Bank Version 2 (account.h)

```
1: #ifndef ACCOUNT_H
2: #define ACCOUNT_H
3:
4: #include "Transaction.h"
5: #include <string>
6: #include <iostream>
```

```
7:
8: using namespace std;
9:
10:
11: class Account {
12: public:
13:
14:      Account(const string& name="", const string& pass="",
                int acct=0, double bal=0) {
15:              accountHolder = name;
16:              accountPassword = pass;
17:              accountNumber = acct;
18:              balance = bal;
19:              numOfTrans = 0;
20:              maxTrans = 10;
21:              allTransactions = new Transaction[maxTrans];
22:      }
23:
24:      ~Account() {
25:              delete [] allTransactions;
26:      }
27:
28:      // Getters
29:      double getNumOfTrans() const {
30:              return numOfTrans;
31:      }
32:
33:      double getBalance() const {
34:              return balance;
35:      }
36:
37:      string getName() const {
38:              return accountHolder;
39:      }
40:
41:      int getAccountNum() const {
42:              return accountNumber;
43:      }
44:
45:
46:
```

```
47:        // Setters
48:        void setAcctHolder(const string& name) {
49:                accountHolder = name;
50:        }
51:
52:        // Account interface
53:        bool withdraw(double amount);
54:
55:        bool deposit(double amount);
56:
57:        // Transactions interface
58:        Transaction getTransactionByNum(int i) const;
59:
60:        // Authenticate logins
61:        bool validateLogin(int acctNum, const string& pass) const;
62:
63:
64: private:
65:        string accountHolder;    // Name on the account
66:        int accountNumber;       // Account number
67:        string accountPassword; // Account password
68:        double balance;          // Account balance
69:        int numOfTrans;          // Number of transactions
70:        int maxTrans;            // Maximum number of transactions for the array
71:        Transaction* allTransactions;    // Array of all transactions
72:
73:        // Increases the size of the ledger when needed
74:        bool resizeTransLedger();
75:
76: };
77:
78: #endif // ACCOUNT_H
```

The only other change is the definition of the new method used for validating logins. This function is located in the account.cpp file and is shown in Listing 12.4.

Listing 12.4 validateLogin Method Definition

```
/* Name: validateLogin
 * Description: compares account number and password parameters
 * to the values stored in the object for equality.
```

```
 * Parms:
 *                     acctNum                       account number for account
to be validated
 *       pass         password for the account to be validated
 * Return: true if the parameters match the object, otherwise false.
 */
bool Account::validateLogin(int acctNum, const string& pass) const {
         return (acctNum == accountNumber && accountPassword == pass);
}
```

This concludes the source code changes for Cyber Bank version 2. You can find all the source code for this case study on the companion website. You should see if you can add more features to Cyber Bank. In the next section, you learn about inheritance in C++.

INHERITANCE IN C++

Inheritance is the fourth principal of OOP. It allows a programmer to create a new class by specializing an existing class. This means that the newly created class can add or remove features from the existing class. The existing class is called the *base class* in C++, and the newly created specialized class is called the *derived class* in C++. In this section, you are introduced to the basics regarding inheritance in C++.

Inheritance Examples

The C++ standard I/O library is a perfect example of the power of inheritance. Figure 12.3 shows a portion of the I/O library classes and instances. The base class for the C++ I/O standard library is ios_base. The ios class is derived from the ios_base class. This is an example of inheritance. The ios class is the base class for istream and ostream. The istream class is designed to handle input, and the ostream class handles output. This is an example of specialization by taking away features. The ios class can support keyboard input, screen output, file input, and file output, as examples. The istream class only supports file input and keyboard input, and the ostream class handles only file and screen output. There are three standard ostream instances that are created: cout, cerr, and clog, and there is one istream instance created: cin. The iostream class uses multiple inheritance to provide a union of the istream and ostream classes.

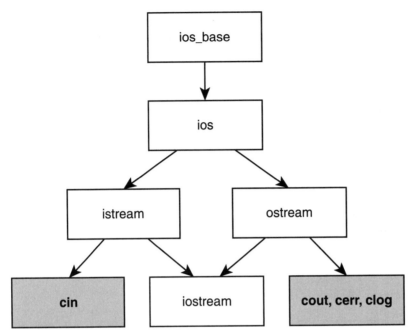

Figure 12.3
Inheritance between classes in the C++ I/O library.

The structure of the I/O library allows the library to reuse code from upper levels of the hierarchy. The structure also allows for specialization. For example, if you have a program that only needs data input support, you can just use the istream library instead of iostream, which includes a lot of waste. This is possible because inheritance provides the vehicle for creating specialized classes.

A university database provides another example; the database for a university needs to track information for various types of people on campus. For example, you have students, graduate students, hourly employees, and salaried employees. You want to build a typing system that allows you to reuse as much code as possible. An example inheritance hierarchy is shown in Figure 12.4. This hierarchy starts with a base class named Person. Each derived class that is derived from Person adds attributes that are more specific to the derived class. However, at the same time, each derived class is able to access the attributes and methods of the base class. There is an example of multiple inheritance in which the WorkStudyStudent derives from the EmpHourly and Student classes.

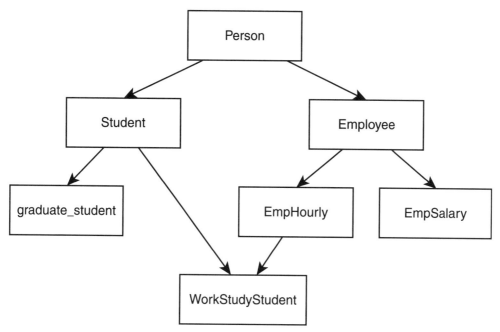

Figure 12.4
Inheritance in the C++ I/O library.

The C++ I/O library classes and the university database provide examples of single inheritance and multiple inheritance. To have a better understanding of how your code could benefit, you need to see how these hierarchies would be implemented in C++.

Implementing Inheritance in C++

Implementing inheritance in C++ requires little syntax and lots of benefits. Inheritance in C++ takes place at the class declaration. The general format for inheritance is the following:

```
class <className> : public <base className> {
< declarations>
};
```

The derived class inherits all the `public` and `protected` members of the base class and can directly access them. However, `private` members of the base class can only be accessed through the base class's getters and setters. In other words, `private` really means private—even family.

Listing 12.5 shows the base class for the university database named Person. It also shows the Employee- and Student-derived classes. These are not meant to be the entire class. Assume that all private properties have getters and setters in their respective public sections. The Student and Employee classes have all the attributes of the Person class through its getters and setters. This means that you do not have to repeatedly write code in each of the derived classes of Person to handle name, Social Security number, gender, and age. Another way to look at this is that both students and employees are people and share those common attributes.

In Listing 12.5, notice that only line 13, the display() method, has the keyword virtual in front of it. This means that C++ expects the derived classes to specialize this method. Not all methods need to be denoted as virtual methods. For example, your getters and setters are not likely to be virtual functions because they are specific to the class, so those that are created for the base class would not be redefined in derived classes. In the case of display(), each class would want to have its own specific version of display(), and you would not want to have to change the name. Also, the keyword virtual allows you to implement polymorphism in C++. This will be discussed later in this section.

Listing 12.5 Base Class and Derived Classes in University Database

```
1: // Class person that is used to create objects for any person
2: class Person {
3: private:
4:          string fname;              // Person's first name
5:          string mname;              // Person's middle name
6:          string lname;              // Person's last name
7:
8:          string socSecNumer;        // Person's SSN
9:          char gender;               // Person's gender
10:          int age;                   // Person's age
11: public:
12:          Person();                  // Constructor for Person class
13:          virtual void display();    // Display virtual function
14: };
15:
16:
17: // Class student that specializes from person
18: class Student : public Person {
```

```
19: private:
20:          float gpa;                    // Student's GPA
21:          string major;                 // Student's major
22:          string minor;                 // Student's minor
23:          int classification;           // Student's classification
24: public:
25:          Student();                    // Constructor for Student class
26:          void display();               // Display function (polymorphic)
27:
28: };
29:
30: // Class employee inherits specializes from person
31: class Employee : public Person {
32: private:
33:          string department;            // Employee's department
34:          string position;              // Employee's position
35: public:
36:          Employee();                   // Employee constructor
37:          void display();               // Display function (polymorphic)
38: };
```

The hierarchy continues to the next level in Listing 12.6. The GraduateStudent, EmpHourly, and EmpSalary classes are using inheritance. You can create as many levels of inheritance as you would like in your programs. It can take some time to develop a good hierarchy, but you will be rewarded by doing so.

Listing 12.6 Next Level of Derived Classes in University Database

```
1: // Class graduate student specializes from student
2: class GraduateStudent : public Student {
3: private:
4:      string fundingAgency;    // Grad student's funding support
5:      double stipend;          // Grad student's stipend
6: public:
7:      GraduateStudent();       // Grad student constructor
8:      void display();          // Display function (polymorphic)
9: };
10:
11:
12: // Class hourly employee specializes from employee
13: class EmpHourly : public Employee {
```

```
14: private:
15:      int hoursWorked;        // Hourly employee's work hours
16:      double hourlyRate;      // Hourly employee's pay rate
17:      double overtimeRate;    // Hourly employee's overtime rate
18: public:
19:      EmpHourly();            // Hourly employee constructor
20:      void display();         // Display function (polymorphic)
21: };
22:
23:
24: // Class salaried employee specializes from employee
25: class EmpSalary : public Employee {
26: private:
27:      double salary;              // Salaried employee's salary
28:      double bonus;               // Salaried employee's bonus
29:      bool vested;                // Salaried employee's vesting status
30: public:
31:      EmpSalary();                // Salaried employee constructor
32:      void display();             // Display function (polymorphic)
33: };
```

Inheritance can be a handy mechanism for code reuse. It allows you to create a framework for the data types in your application, which helps to organize your code and to develop more efficiently by taking advantage of the hierarchical structure.

Inheritance also provides a mechanism that allows you to store different data types in the same array, which can add a tremendous amount of flexibility. For example, suppose you want to create a database of the people in a college or university using the class hierarchy shown in Listings 12.5 and 12.6. You could have the following arrays declared:

```
Student* arrayOfStudents;
GraduateStudent* arrayOfGradStudents;
EmpHourly* arrayOfHourlyEmployees;
EmpSalary* arrayOfSalariedEmployees;
```

These four arrays could work extremely well in a program. However, in a database you will want to have the ability to add, remove, update, and view the database. Using four arrays causes you to have to write these functions for each array because they all have different types. For example, your addEntry function headers could look like this for the Student class:

```
void addEntry(Student list[] , int& size, const Student& newEntry)
void addEntry (GraduateStudent list[], int& size,
               const GraduateStudent& newEntry)
void addEntry (EmpHourly list[], int& size, const EmpHourly& newEntry);
void addEntry (Student list[], int& size, const Student& newEntry);
```

As you can imagine, this is time consuming, and each of these functions will be defined in a similar fashion because the algorithms would be the same in each function; the types would be the only difference. Another approach would be to have one array that holds all the students, graduate students, hourly employees, and salaried employees. Then you could have one version of each function for adding, removing, updating, and viewing the database. Inheritance allows you to do this by creating an array of object pointers using the base class of the inheritance hierarchy. C++ allows you to assign object pointers of derived classes to object pointers of base classes. Consider the following listing:

```
Person* aPerson;
Student* aStudent;
aPerson = new Person;
aStudent = new Student;
aStudent = aPerson;     // Not allowed in C++
aPerson = aStudent;     // Allowed in C++
```

In this code, two pointers to objects are created: aPerson and aStudent. Both are allocated memory. Because Person is the base class, you can assign Student pointers to Person pointers, but not vice versa. Using this rule, you can create an array of Person pointers that you can assign to any of its derived classes:

```
Person* arrayOfUniversityMembers[20000];    // Static array of Person pointers
Person** arrayOfUniversityMembers;          // Dynamic array of Person pointers
```

These two versions produce arrays of Person pointers. The difference is that one has a static size and the other has a dynamic size. For the purposes of this discussion, it does not matter which one you choose because the objective is to have all the different types of objects referred to by the same array.

One of the problems that has to be solved is how C++ determines which method to call when the same method is redefined in each class:

```
arrayOfUniversityMembers[i]->display();
```

In the preceding question, it is not clear from that statement which display() method is called because the pointer could be a pointer to an object of any class in the hierarchy, such as a `Person`, `Student`, or `EmpSalary`. You must resolve this during the execution time of your program because that is the only time the program will know what type of object is being pointed to. This dynamic resolution of method membership is called *polymorphism*.

To better understand polymorphism, consider the full program in Listing 12.7. This program is designed to be a demonstration of how an array of base class pointers can be built. It also provides understanding of how the constructors of the classes interact and how polymorphism is used.

Each class in Listing 12.7 has some `private` data members and two member functions in the `public` section. The constructor is the first member function, and `display()` is the second. The definitions of these member functions are shown on lines 139–207. Notice that each constructor outputs text that shows that you have entered the constructor and exited the constructor:

```
Entering: Person Constructor
Exiting: Person Constructor
```

The preceding lines would be the output from the `Person` class constructor. These outputs will show you that the construction of a particular object is determined by its place in the inheritance tree. For example, a `Student` object is constructed by using the `Person` and `Student` constructors because a `Student` object is composed of data and methods from both classes.

The `main` function starting on line 83 creates an array of `Person` pointers on line 85. The program then proceeds to line 95, which is the start of the `for` loop. The loop is designed to randomly select a class to use for creating an object to be pointed to by the `Person` pointers in the array. Because `Person` is the base class, its pointers can be assigned pointers for any of the derived classes. The `switch` statement makes a decision based on the random number where new objects are created and their pointers assigned to the current element of the array. When the objects are created using the `new` operation, the constructors for those objects are executed.

Line 124 is where the polymorphism occurs. The `display()` method is executed based on what type of pointer was assigned to the position in the `switch` statement. Polymorphism is enabled by the `virtual` modifier used on line 17 in the `Student` base class.

Listing 12.7 C++ Program of Inheritance and Polymorphism Demonstration

```
1: #include <iostream>
2:
3: using namespace std;
4:
5: // Class person that is used to create objects for any person
6: class Person {
7: private:
8:      string fname;                    // Person's first name
9:      string mname;                    // Person's middle name
10:     string lname;                    // Person's last name
11:
12:     string socSecNumer;              // Person's SSN
13:     char gender;                     // Person's gender
14:     int age;                         // Person's age
15: public:
16:     Person();                        // Constructor for Person class
17:     virtual void display();          // Display virtual function
18: };
19:
20:
21: // Class student that specializes from person
22: class Student : public Person {
23: private:
24:     float gpa;                       // Student's GPA
25:     string major;                    // Student's major
26:     string minor;                    // Student's minor
27:     int classification;              // Student's classification
28: public:
29:     Student();                       // Constructor for Student class
30:     void display();                  // Display function (polymorphic)
31:
32: };
33:
34:
35: // Class graduate student specializes from student
36: class GraduateStudent : public Student {
37: private:
38:     string fundingAgency;            // Grad student's funding support
```

```
39:        double stipend;                    // Grad student's stipend
40: public:
41:        GraduateStudent();                 // Grad student constructor
42:        void display();                    // Display function (polymorphic)
43: };
44:
45:
46: // Class employee inherits specializes from person
47: class Employee : public Person {
48: private:
49:        string department;                 // Employee's department
50:        string position;                   // Employee's position
51: public:
52:        Employee();                        // Employee constructor
53:        void display();                    // Display function (polymorphic)
54: };
55:
56:
57: // Class hourly employee specializes from employee
58: class EmpHourly : public Employee {
59: private:
60:        int hoursWorked;                   // Hourly employee's work hours
61:        double hourlyRate;                 // Hourly employee's pay rate
62:        double overtimeRate;               // Hourly employee's overtime rate
63: public:
64:        EmpHourly();                       // Hourly employee constructor
65:        void display();                    // Display function (polymorphic)
66: };
67:
68:
69: // Class salaried employee specializes from employee
70: class EmpSalary : public Employee {
71: private:
72:        double salary;                     // Salaried employee's salary
73:        double bonus;                      // Salaried employee's bonus
74:        bool vested;                       // Salaried employee's vesting status
75: public:
76:        EmpSalary();                       // Salaried employee constructor
77:        void display();                    // Display function (polymorphic)
78: };
79:
80:
```

```
81:
82:
83: int main () {
84:
85:      Person* allPeople[10];   // An array of 10 Person object pointers
86:
87:      // Initialize random number generator
88:      srand(time(NULL));
89:
90:
91:      // This loop randomly selects an object to create in each position
92:      // of the array. Demonstrates how an array using the base class can be
93:      // used to hold derived typed pointers. This loop will produce 10
94:      // randomly selected object pointer types.
95:      for (int i = 0; i < 10; i++) {
96:
97:              cout << i << ": ";
98:
99:              // Choose one of the six classes to create an object pointer
100:             switch (rand() % 6) {
101:                     case 0:
102:                             allPeople[i] = new Person;
103:                             break;
104:                     case 1:
105:                             allPeople[i] = new Student;
106:                             break;
107:                     case 2:
108:                             allPeople[i] = new Employee;
109:                             break;
110:                     case 3:
111:                             allPeople[i] = new GraduateStudent;
112:                             break;
113:                     case 4:
114:                             allPeople[i] = new EmpHourly;
115:                             break;
116:                     case 5:
117:                             allPeople[i] = new EmpSalary;
118:                             break;
119:                     default:
120:                             break;
121:             }
122:
```

```
123:              // Determines appropriate display method by using polymorphism
124:              allPeople[i]->display();
125:
126:    }
127:
128:    return 0;
129: }
130:
131:
132: // The following are constructor and display pairs.
133: // Constructors: Have an output statement to show that the
134: // constructor is entered and exited.
135: // Display: The method that displays a message corresponding
136: // to the class that the function is connected to.
137:
138:
139: // Constructor for Person class
140: Person::Person() {
141:    cout << "\tEntering: Person Constructor" << endl;
142:    cout << "\tExiting: Person Constructor" << endl;
143: }
144:
145:
146: // Display for Person class (base class)
147: void Person::display() {
148:    cout << "person" << endl;
149: }
150:
151: // Constructor for Student class
152: Student::Student() {
153:    cout << "\tEntering: Student Constructor" << endl;
154:    cout << "\tExiting: Student Constructor" << endl;
155: }
156:
157:
158: // Display for Student class
159: void Student::display() {
160:    cout << "Student" << endl;
161. }
162:
```

```
163: // Constructor for GraduateStudent class
164: GraduateStudent::GraduateStudent() {
165:     cout << "\tEntering: GraduateStudent Constructor" << endl;
166:     cout << "\tExiting: GraduateStudent Constructor" << endl;
167: }
168:
169:
170: // Display for GraduateStudent class
171: void GraduateStudent::display() {
172:     cout << "Grad Student" << endl;
173: }
174:
175:
176: // Constructor for Employee class
177: Employee::Employee() {
178:     cout << "\tEntering: Employee Constructor" << endl;
179:     cout << "\tExiting: Employee Constructor" << endl;
180: }
181:
182: // Display for Employee class
183: void Employee::display() {
184:     cout << "Employee" << endl;
185: }
186:
187: // Constructor for EmpHourly class
188: EmpHourly::EmpHourly() {
189:     cout << "\tEntering: EmpHourly Constructor" << endl;
190:     cout << "\tExiting: EmpHourly Constructor" << endl;
191: }
192:
193: // Display for EmpHourly class
194: void EmpHourly::display() {
195:     cout << "Hourly Employee" << endl;
196: }
197:
198: // Constructor for EmpSalary class
199: EmpSalary::EmpSalary() {
200:     cout << "\tEntering: EmpSalary Constructor" << endl;
201:     cout << "\tExiting: EmpSalary Constructor" << endl;
202: }
```

```
203:
204: // Display for EmpSalary class
205: void EmpSalary::display() {
206:     cout << "Salaried Employee" << endl;
207: }
```

A result of this demonstration program is shown in Listing 12.8. If you run this program yourself, your results will vary because of the randomness of the program. The output of the program is formatted to make it easier to understand. The number followed by a colon is the position of the pointer in the array. The indented text is generated from the constructors that create the object of the randomly selected class. The nonindented text is the output from the call to display(). Consider the following excerpt:

```
  2:      Entering: Person Constructor
          Exiting: Person Constructor
          Entering: Employee Constructor
          Exiting: Employee Constructor
          Entering: EmpSalary Constructor
          Exiting: EmpSalary Constructor
Salaried Employee
```

This item is in position 2 of the array. It has randomly chosen the EmpSalary class. The EmpSalary class creates salaried employees. These objects are formed by creating their Person and Employee parts. Therefore, you see that the Person and Employee constructors are executed in addition to the EmpSalary constructor. If you look at the inheritance tree for these classes, you see that the constructors that are called correlate with the classes in the path from the base class to the desired derived class. Finally, the output Salaried Employee comes from the display() method of the EmpSalary class. C++ knows that even though the array contains Person pointers, it must determine the type of the object that it is pointing to and then execute the proper display() method. This is the polymorphism in action.

Listing 12.8 Output of Inheritance and Polymorphism Demonstration Program

```
  0:      Entering: Person Constructor
          Fxiting: Person Constructor
          Entering: Employee Constructor
          Exiting: Employee Constructor
```

```
Employee
1:       Entering: Person Constructor
         Exiting: Person Constructor
         Entering: Employee Constructor
         Exiting: Employee Constructor
Employee
2:       Entering: Person Constructor
         Exiting: Person Constructor
         Entering: Employee Constructor
         Exiting: Employee Constructor
         Entering: EmpSalary Constructor
         Exiting: EmpSalary Constructor
Salaried Employee
3:       Entering: Person Constructor
         Exiting: Person Constructor
         Entering: Employee Constructor
         Exiting: Employee Constructor
         Entering: EmpSalary Constructor
         Exiting: EmpSalary Constructor
Salaried Employee
4:       Entering: Person Constructor
         Exiting: Person Constructor
         Entering: Student Constructor
         Exiting: Student Constructor
Student
5:       Entering: Person Constructor
         Exiting: Person Constructor
         Entering: Student Constructor
         Exiting: Student Constructor
Student
6:       Entering: Person Constructor
         Exiting: Person Constructor
         Entering: Student Constructor
         Exiting: Student Constructor
         Entering: GraduateStudent Constructor
         Exiting: GraduateStudent Constructor
Grad Student
7:       Entering: Person Constructor
         Exiting: Person Constructor
         Entering: Employee Constructor
         Exiting: Employee Constructor
```

```
        Entering: EmpHourly Constructor
        Exiting: EmpHourly Constructor
Hourly Employee
8:      Entering: Person Constructor
        Exiting: Person Constructor
Person
9:      Entering: Person Constructor
        Exiting: Person Constructor
        Entering: Employee Constructor
        Exiting: Employee Constructor
        Entering: EmpHourly Constructor
        Exiting: EmpHourly Constructor
Hourly Employee
```

This program demonstrates that you can create an array using pointers to the base class and then assign pointers to derived class objects. It also shows how polymorphism works to allow C++ to dynamically invoke the correct method when that method is being specialized by the derived classes.

SUMMARY

This chapter showed how to use pointers to make working with objects more efficient in your programs. You saw how creating an array of pointers to objects is similar to creating an array of objects, but you use the arrow operator instead of the dot operator. You also learned to use memory more efficiently. In addition, you explored the fourth principal of OOP: inheritance. You saw examples of inheritance from the C++ I/O library and from a database example. Finally, you learned how to use C++ syntax for inheritance and polymorphism. C++ is a vast language, and there is still more to learn that is beyond the scope of this book. You should be encouraged that you have been exposed to a range of programming techniques and you have learned a professional programming language. Take this knowledge and build upon it to learn even more.

EXERCISES

The following questions test your knowledge of the material from this chapter. You can find the answers to these questions on the book's companion website at www.courseptr.com/downloads.

1. Use the Cyber Bank as your basis and add the ability to process checks. There should be a menu item for issuing a check. This operation should ask the user to enter the name of the payee and the amount. Your software should maintain the check numbers, so you need to add support to keep up with what the next check number should be. Your transaction view should include your checks: check number, payee, and amount.

2. Write a program that acts as a grade book. It should have a `Student` class that contains students' names, student ID, an array of grades, a numeric average, and a letter grade. The program should have a menu that allows the user to add students, remove students by student ID, and display grades. The software should compute the numeric grade and letter grade when the user adds a student.

3. Create a class hierarchy for shapes. Each shape will have an area and circumference method that returns its area and circumference. You should start with the base class name `Polygon` and then have derived classes: square, rectangle, circle, and triangle. There are different ways to create the hierarchy, but try to maximize code reuse. Each of your classes will need setters and getters as well. Then write a `main` function that tests your classes.

4. Use the set of classes for university members, and write a menu-driven program that maintains a list of university members. The program should allow the user to add a new member and display current members.

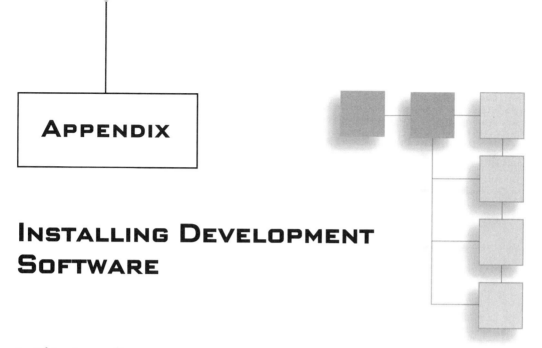

APPENDIX

INSTALLING DEVELOPMENT SOFTWARE

In This Appendix

- Windows: Visual Studio Express 2010
- Max OS X: Xcode

> "The city's central computer told you? R2D2, you know better than
> to trust a strange computer!"
>
> —C3PO

You may be using a Windows machine, a Mac OS X machine, or some other type of operating system. In all cases, you need to install the development software that will help you type, build, debug, and execute your C++ programs.

This appendix shows you how to install software for Windows and Mac OS X platforms. If you have another platform, you need to do a search online for a C++ compiler that will work for your system. It is not difficult to find software for other systems, such as Linux.

If you have Windows, you will install Visual Studio Express 2010. This software is free of charge, but it does require a registration process that is also shown here. If you are using Mac OS X, you will be installing the Xcode software.

This appendix shows you step by step how to install the software for your system, and it shows you some of the basic functions of the software.

WINDOWS: VISUAL STUDIO EXPRESS 2010

In this section, you learn how to install, register, and use the Visual Studio Express system. To make sure you know where this is heading, here is the overview of the activities:

1. Visit the Microsoft website.

2. Download the installation package.

3. Install the software.

4. Open and test the software.

5. Configure and register the software. (You must do this to use Visual Studio Express 2010 past 30 days.)

Visit the Website

Step 1. Use your web browser and visit the following site:

www.microsoft.com/express/Downloads

This site is shown in Figure A.1. You can download several Express versions of Microsoft software.

Figure A.1
Visual Studio Express home page.

Step 2. Select the Visual C++ Express link, and choose the language that is appropriate for you.

Download the Installation Package

Step 3. Figure A.2 shows the next dialog box, which asks you to run or save the file that is being downloaded. You should choose Save, which saves the file to the folder called `Downloads` or `Documents`. Why choose Save? Choosing Save allows you to select a location to place the install file. This allows you to save a copy of the download file as a backup, and if you have to reinstall, you don't have to hunt through the website to download the file again.

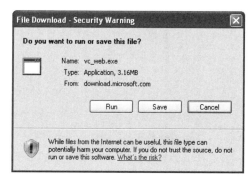

Figure A.2
Download pop-up window in Windows.

Step 4. The Download Complete dialog box shows, as in Figure A.3. You should then select Run. This starts the installation process.

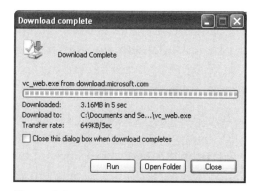

Figure A.3
Download Complete dialog box.

Install the Software

Step 5. Figure A.4 shows the Welcome to Setup dialog box. A note about privacy appears. The check box sends information about your setup and computer configuration. If you do not want this type of information to be sent, you should deselect this box.

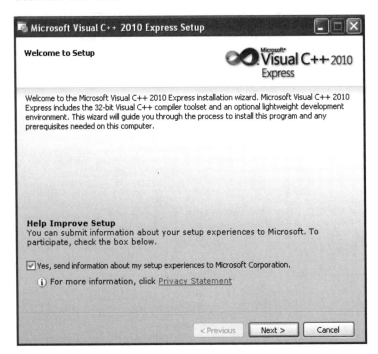

Figure A.4
Welcome to Setup dialog box.

Step 6. You should read the license agreement shown in Figure A.5 and accept it. Primarily this agreement says that you can only develop noncommercial software with Visual C++ Express. If you want to write software to earn money, you need to purchase a license for the professional version of Visual Studio.

Step 7. You should accept all the settings for the next few dialog boxes by selecting Next. Then select Install. You should then see an installation progress bar, as shown in Figure A.6. The installation will probably take about 30 minutes to complete. It must download the software and then perform the installation. If you have a slow Internet connection, the download will take more time. Go get a snack and check on the progress.

Figure A.5
Installation license agreement and configuration.

Figure A.6
The installation progress window.

Open and Test Software

Step 8. To open the software, go to the Start menu and to Programs. You should see Visual C++ Express 2010 on the menu of programs. Start the software.

Step 9. Figure A.7 shows the opening window for Visual C++ Express. It looks like many other applications and contains a familiar menu starting with File and Edit from left to right.

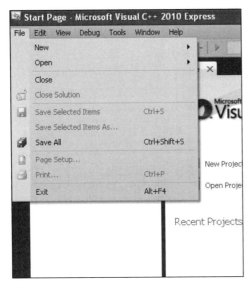

Figure A.7
The Visual C++ Express welcoming window.

Step 10. You are going to test the software by creating your first Visual C++ project.

Projects are becoming more and more common in development software. Typically, development projects that you work on require several files to contain the content that you create and configuration information. The project entity is the package of all these files that allows the development software to more efficiently manage your work.

Whenever you want to write a C++ program using Visual C++, you must begin by creating a project.

Select the File menu, as shown in Figure A.7.

Step 11. Select New from the File menu and then select Project, as shown in Figure A.8.

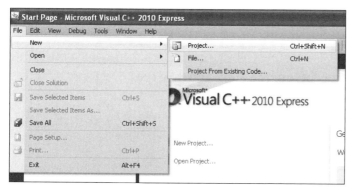

Figure A.8
Selecting a new project from the File menu.

The window shown in Figure A.9 presents a collection of C++ template projects. These templates help you create particular types of C++ programs more rapidly by providing good starting points. For most of the exercises in this book, you will use the CLR Empty Project template.

Step 12. Select the CLR Empty Project template, as shown in Figure A.9.

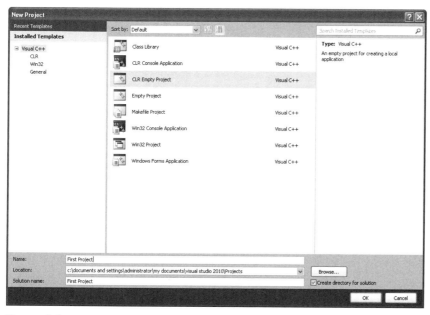

Figure A.9
The New Project window contains several project templates.

The bottom of the window contains a place to enter the project name and location. The name of the project is the name of the program you are creating. For example, if you were developing Firefox, you would use the name Firefox here.

The location is where Visual C++ stores your project. Each project you create has its own folder. All project folders are stored in a Visual C++ Express folder found in your Documents folder.

Step 13. Name your project First Project, as shown in Figure A.9; the location is updated automatically.

Step 14. Select OK to accept the project name.

The empty project template opens with a solution that contains empty folders, as shown in Figure A.10. The other project templates would have files inside these folders. Now you have to create a C++ file for your project. The C++ file is a text file that contains the C++ program instructions that you will be learning to write. As a convention, C++ files have the extension .cpp for C Plus-Plus.

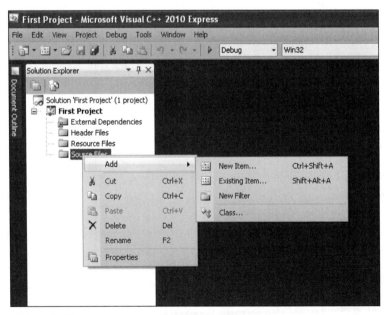

Figure A.10
The newly created project and empty solution.

Step 15. Select the folder called Sources by right-clicking. This shows a pop-up menu like the one in Figure A.10.

Step 16. Choose Add from the menu and then choose New Item, as shown in Figure A.10.

This leads to a window that allows you to select new items to add to a project. The most common items to add are C++ files. In this case, you are adding a .cpp C++ file.

Step 17. Select the C++ File (.cpp) option, as shown in Figure A.11.

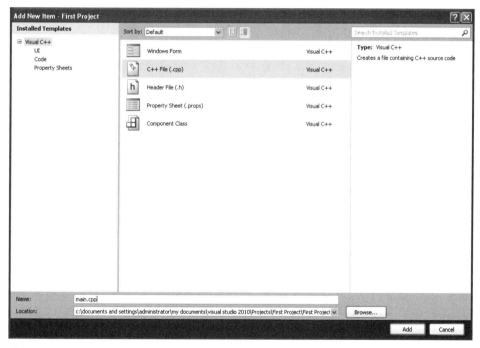

Figure A.11
The New Item selection window.

Step 18. Name the file main.cpp. You can use this name as the first file for all your projects. However, if you want to give each a unique name, that is okay as well.

Step 19. Select OK.

Now you are ready to compose a simple C++ program to test the installation. The main.cpp file should be open in the large part of the project window. Type the following lines of code, as shown in Figure A.12.

Play button

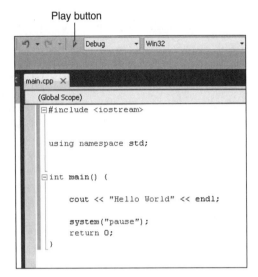

Figure A.12
The new project ready to accept C++ code for testing.

Listing A.1 A Simple Hello World Program

```cpp
#include <iostream>
using namespace std;

int main() {
    cout << "Hello World" << endl;

    system("pause");
    return 0;
}
```

Once you have typed in the lines, check them to make sure you have typed them in properly. The number of blank lines does not affect the result. If you are comfortable with what you have typed, you are ready to build and execute the program.

Step 20. Click the green Play button (green triangle) at the top of the window shown in Figure A.12. This produces a dialog box like the one shown in Figure A.13.

This dialog box alerts you to the fact that you have changed some files, and that if you accept the changes, a new version of the program will be built. Otherwise, you can execute the previous version.

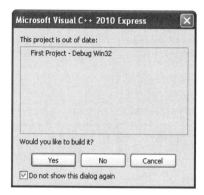

Figure A.13
Building the C++ program.

Step 21. Click in the check box Do Not Show This Dialog Again, and then select Yes.

If your build is successful, you will see a DOS window like the one in Figure A.14, which displays `Hello World`.

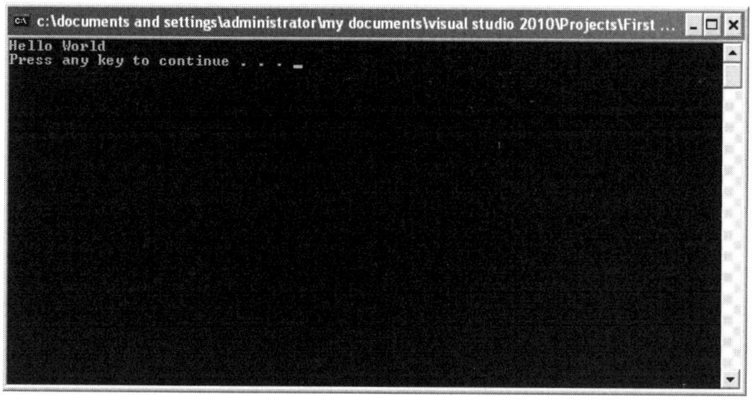

Figure A.14
Executing the test program.

The `Press any key to continue` message comes from where you have the following:

```
system("pause");
```

If you do not have this line, the window closes before you are able to read the output. In this book, you do not see this in the code listings because the code in this book is written to work for any C++ platform. If you are using Windows, remember to put this line of code in your programs before the `return 0` line.

Step 22. Press any key, and the DOS window closes.

The final subsection is for registering the software and cool configuration option.

Configure and Register

Visual C++ is free software; however, Microsoft requires you to register your installation. If you do not register the software, you cannot obtain a license key, and without the key, the software stops working in 30 days.

Step 23. Select the Help menu and then Register Product from the Help menu, as shown in Figure A.15.

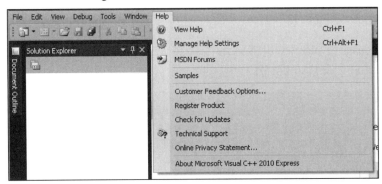

Figure A.15
Registration for the product is located under the Help menu.

The registration dialog box has a button for obtaining your license key and a field for entering the key you obtain. This is shown in Figure A.16.

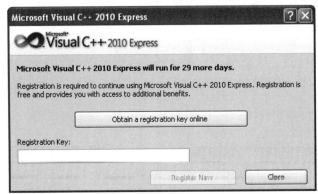

Figure A.16
The registration dialog box.

Step 24. Click the Obtain a Registration Key Online button to launch your web browser.

When the browser window opens, it goes to the Windows Live login and registration page, as shown in Figure A.17. If you have a Windows Live login account already, you may type in the login information to reveal your key. You can then copy and paste the key to the dialog box shown in Figure A.16.

Figure A.17
The Windows Live login/registration page.

However, if you do not have a Windows Live ID and password, you need to obtain permission from your parents to create an account or use an account they can or have created. Then you are given a key that you can copy and paste into the text area in Figure A.16.

Your registration is now complete!

Remember that if you decide to install this software on several machines, you need to register each machine.

Every developer needs to know the line numbers associated with each line of code. The following steps put line numbers next to your lines of code, as shown in Figure A.18. (Compare to Figure A.12.)

Step 25. Select the Tools menu, and then select Options to show the dialog window in Figure A.19.

Step 26. Scroll down the options to Text Editor.

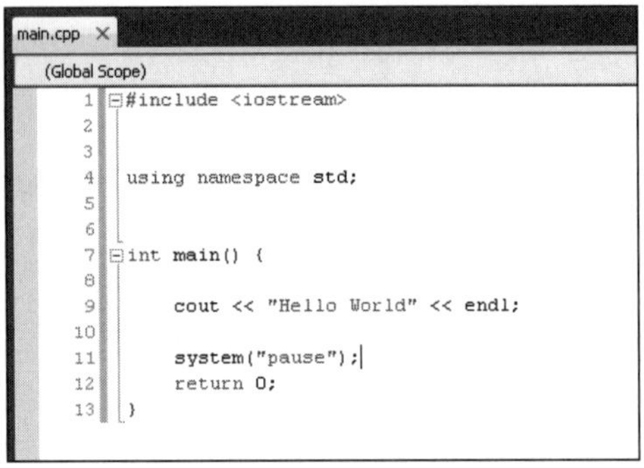

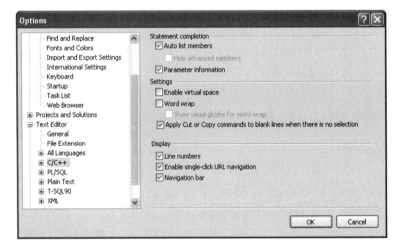

Figure A.18
The Visual C++ window showing the line numbers next to your lines of code.

Figure A.19
The Visual C++ Options dialog box.

Step 27. Click on the + symbol next to Text Editor.

Step 28. Select C/C++ from the unfolded list of options.

Step 29. Select the check box next to Line Numbers.

Step 30. Click Apply and OK.

You now have line numbers! This option should remain intact for every project you create.

Use Other Tutorial Resources

To learn more about using the Visual Studio Development environment, you can check out some of these nice resources online:

- **http://msdn.microsoft.com/en-us/library/bb384842.aspx.** Walkthrough: Working with Projects and Solutions (C++)

- **http://msdn.microsoft.com/en-us/library/bb384834.aspx.** Creating Command-Line Applications (C++)

I encourage you to look for other resources that may give you cool tips to use the software. All you need to do is go to Google and search for Visual C++ 2010 Tutorials or Visual C++ 2010 Tips (or something along those lines) and see what you find.

Mac OS X: Xcode

In this section, you will find the instructions for installing the Xcode development software for Mac OS X. The Xcode development software comes as an optional installation on the DVD that came with your computer. If you don't have the DVD, you can download the software and then follow these instructions. If you need to do this, jump to the section titled "Downloading Xcode Tools," later in this chapter, and then return to these steps.

The following is an overview of the activities performed for the installation:

1. Install the software from the DVD.

2. Open and test software the installation.

3. Configure the software for easier usage.

Install the Software from the DVD

The DVD that comes with your Mac computer contains the initial installation that you found on your computer when you turned it on. In addition, there is optional software.

Step 1. Insert the DVD into the DVD drive and wait for a Finder window to show something like Figure A.20.

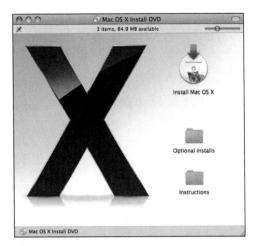

Figure A.20
The DVD contents.

Step 2. Double-click on the folder called Optional Installs, and another finder window opens that looks like Figure A.21. There are two packages. The Optional Installs package contains more than just Xcode.

Figure A.21
The Optional Installs packages.

Step 3. Double-click on the Optional Installs package to reveal the screen shown in Figure A.22. This is the beginning of the actual installation process.

Step 4. Click Continue until you reach the screen shown in Figure A.23. This screen is where you want to make sure that the green arrow is selecting your main hard drive, which is usually known as Macintosh HD. (If you have more than one drive in your computer, you see more than one icon.)

Step 5. Click Continue until the installation starts. The installation may take 30–45 minutes. So have a snack and relax until it is complete. When it's complete, a window like the one in Figure A.24 appears.

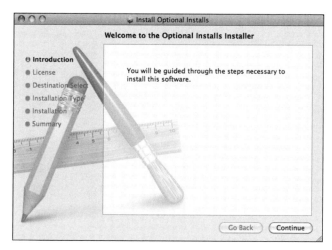

Figure A.22
The start of the installation program.

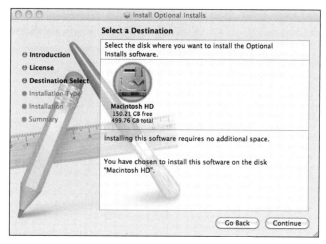

Figure A.23
The destination of the software installation.

Congratulations! The installation is complete! Now it's time to do some simple configuration and testing.

Open and Test Software

The developer software for Macintosh machines is installed inside a developer folder. This folder is located on `Macintosh HD:Developer` and is shown in Figure A.25.

Figure A.24
A successful installation.

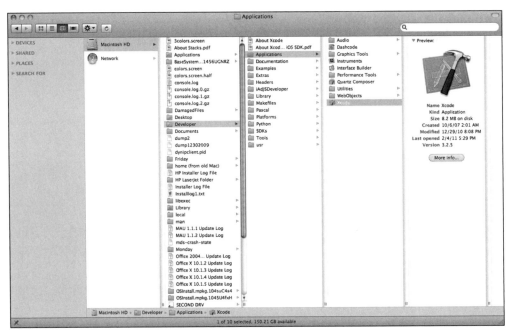

Figure A.25
The location of the Xcode application on your computer.

To start the software, you have to go to `Macintosh HD:Developer/Applications`, as shown in Figure A.25.

Step 6. Double-click on the Xcode icon, and wait for the software to load.

Step 7. Right-click on the Xcode icon in your dock, as shown in Figure A.26, select the Options menu, and then Keep in Dock. This keeps the icon on your dock for easy access in the future.

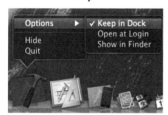

Figure A.26
The location of the Xcode application on your computer.

Step 8. Select the File menu, and then New Project. You see a window like the one in Figure A.27.

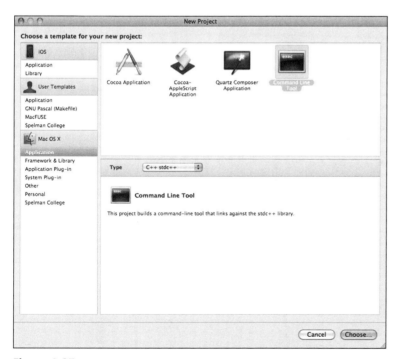

Figure A.27
The Xcode project template organizer.

Projects are becoming more and more common in development software. Typically, development projects that you work on require several files to contain created content and configuration information. The project entity is the package of all these files that allows the development software to more efficiently manage your work.

The templates shown here are meant to be starting points for different types of applications and languages. You will be creating a C++ application following these steps:

Step 9. Click on Application under the Mac OS X section (shown in Figure A.27).

Step 10. Click on the Command Line Tool icon.

Step 11. Select C++ std c++ for Type.

Step 12. Click OK to continue to the screen to name the project.

Step 13. Find where you want to place project folders for your C++ work, name your project Test Project, and save it. See Figure A.28.

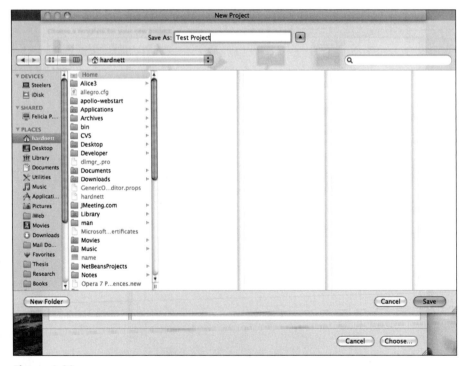

Figure A.28
The location of the Xcode application on your computer.

You now have a project window similar to the one in Figure A.29. This window is where you have access to every aspect of your project. At this time, you need to open the `main.cpp` file that is located in the middle pane of the window.

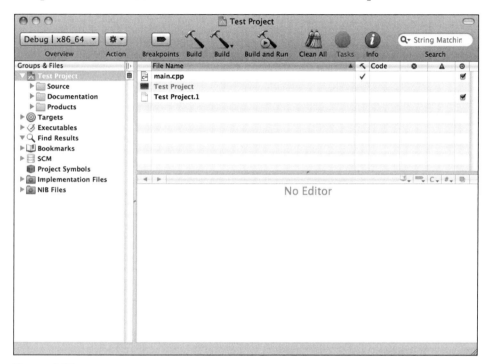

Figure A.29
The Xcode project main window.

Step 14. Double-click on the `main.cpp` file, and it opens to display C++ code that looks like Listing A.2.

Listing A.2 A Simple C++ Program

```cpp
#include <iostream>

int main (int argc, char * const argv[]) {
    // Insert code here...
    std::cout << "Hello, World!\n";
    return 0;
}
```

This is the default program that Xcode places in every C++ project at the start.

Step 15. Click on the Build and Run icon at the top of the project window shown in Figure A.29.

The window in Figure A.30 is the console output window, which displays the result of building and executing the program in your test project. If all is well, you should see the phrase Hello, World! printed on the screen.

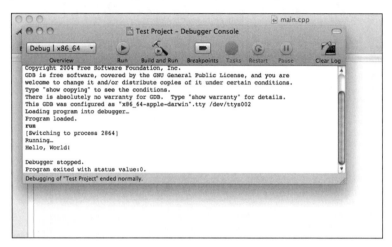

Figure A.30
The result of the Hello World program.

Configure Xcode

You should set some basic configuration preferences on your Xcode to make it more enjoyable to use. Lots of preferences are available to you in Xcode. The preferences in this section are for text editing and indentation.

The preferences shown in Figure A.31 are for text editing features. Make your selected items match those in the figure. The *gutter* is the area to the left of the text that contains information such as line number and other status symbols. The code folding ribbon lets you hide parts of your program from viewing, which is helpful when you have large programs with lots of components and you want to focus on a particular area of the program.

Indentation is an important part of the programming format. It makes parts of the program clearer and groups statements in a visual fashion. It's similar to the indentation you use in your writing. These preferences allow Xcode to help you format your programs in a nice and clean fashion. The number of spaces for indentation levels is usually 3 or 4. The right side of the window is where Xcode

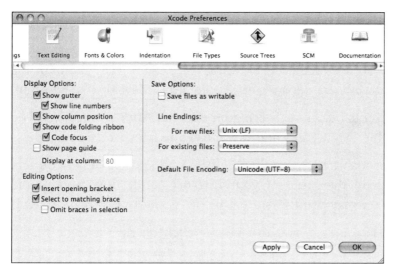

Figure A.31
The Xcode preferences for text editing.

knows that when certain symbols are typed, it needs to automatically indent your code. Make sure your preferences are set the same as those in Figure A.32.

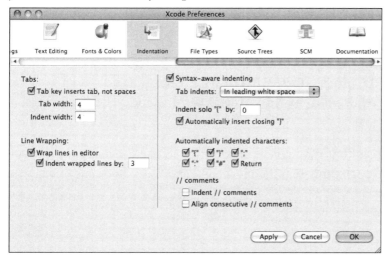

Figure A.32
The Xcode preferences for indentation.

Step 16. After you have completed all the preferences settings, click on OK, and your preferences are saved.

You have completely installed and configured Xcode. Congratulations!

Download Xcode Tools (Optional)

You need to read this section only if you cannot locate the DVD for your Macintosh computer. To download the software, you need to visit the following website and join the developers network for Apple: http://developer.apple.com/.

Consult with your parents before registering on the site. After you register, you can proceed to the Mac Dev Center and download the latest copy of Xcode.

This download will probably be more than 2GB in size and may take hours to download, depending on the speed of your Internet connection. You should allow for this time. You may want to start it before going to bed or to school.

After the download is complete, you can double-click on the `.dmg` file that is downloaded and then continue with step 2 of the Xcode installation.

Use Other Tutorial Resources

To learn more about using the Xcode environment, check out these online resources:

- **http://developer.apple.com/library/mac/navigation/.** Mac OS X Developer Library

- **http://developer.apple.com/library/ios/#documentation/IDEs/ Conceptual/xcode_quick_start/010-Tutorial_Using_Xcode_to_ Write_Hello_World/hello_world_tutorial.html.** Xcode Hello World Tutorial

Look for other resources that may give you cool tips to use the software. All you need to do is go to Google and search for `Xcode Tutorials` or `Xcode Tips`.

INDEX

Symbols and Numerics

+ (addition) operator, 72
* (asterisk), 62
[ ] (brackets), 58
{} (curly brackets), 86
/ (division) operator, 4, 71–73
. (dot) operator, 249, 300
// (double slash), 61
== (equal-to) operator, 82
<< (extraction) operator, 329
> (greater than) operator, 82
>= (greater-than or equal-to) operator, 82
>> (insertion) operator, 329
< (less-than) operator, 82
<= (less-than or equal-to) operator, 82
% (modulus) operator, 71–74
* (multiplication) operator, 72
!= (not equal-to) operator, 82
! (not) operator, 82
/* (slash star), 61
(*/) star slash, 61
- (subtraction) operator, 72
~ (tilde), 305
2D array, 221–222
3D array, 221–222

A

abstract data type (ADT), 291
abstract problem, 29–30
abstraction, 182, 274
access specifier, 294
acronyms, 4
addition (+) operator, 72
ADT (abstract data type), 291
agents, 271–272
algorithm
  abstraction for an, 111
  average computation, 54
  compound interest, 99–100
  defined, 30
  demographic data analysis, 165–168
  flowcharts, 42–48
  hardware based on, 31
  how to develop an, 50–56
  origins of, 30
  partitioning, 140–143
  problem analysis, 50–53
  pseudocode, 31–42
  Quicksort function, 139
  square root computation, 107–108
  translating to C++ language, 86–91
  verifying the, 55–56
  writing the, 53–54
ALU (arithmetic logic unit), 5, 31
analog *versus* digital signal, 9–10

analysis. *See also* problem analysis
argument, 111, 115, 303–304
arithmetic assignment statement, 33–34
arithmetic logic unit (ALU), 5, 31
arithmetic set operations, 70–71
array
  image of, 91
  multidimensional, 219, 221–224
  parallel, 219–221
  single-dimensional, 219
arrow operator, 350
assemble step (program execution), 64
assignment operator, 329
assignment statements
  precedence of operators, 74–75
  translating arithmetic set operations, 70–75
  translating nonarithmetic set operations, 75–77
asterisk (*), 62
average computation, 54

B

backward substitution, 131–132
base class, 367–368, 373

409

statements (*Continued*)
    if-then-else, 35–37, 81–82
    input, 32
    looping, 38, 45, 84–86
    output, 33
    pseudocode, 32–40
    repeat-while, 38–39
    repetitive, 38, 45
    sequential, 32, 70
    set, 70–71
    switch, 170–172, 174
    while-do, 38–39
stepwise refinement
    abstraction, 182
    Blackjack card game
        example, 185–197
    example of, 184–185
    modules, 182
    pictorial example of, 183
    problem/solution, 184
storage devices, 8–9
store result instruction, 5
string class, 325
string data type, 68, 70
string literal, 33
strings
    concatenation, 75
    removing parts of, 79
    replacing portion of, 79
subproblem, 185–197
substr method, 75–76
subtraction (-) operator, 72
SumRange() function, 115
Swap abstraction, 146
switch statement,
    170–172, 174
symbols
    flowchart, 42–46
    punctuation, 65
syntax, 15

T
table tracing, 55–56, 127
task hierarchy diagram, 187
tasks
    functions as, 112
    listing the, 151
template structure, C++
    language, 58–60
testing, 24
tilde (~), 305
top-down design
    basic description of, 181
    versus bottom-up design,
        212–214
    stepwise refinement
        abstraction, 182
        Blackjack card game
            example, 185–198
        example of, 184–185
        modules, 182
        pictorial example of, 183
        problem/solution, 184

U
UML (Unified Modeling
    Language), 282–284
unsigned data type, 68
UserMove() function, 162–163
user's move algorithm,
    154–155
using directives, 59

V
variables
    declaring, 67–70
    finding, 66–67
verifying the algorithm,
    55–56

virtual keyword, 370
virtual object, 4
Visual Basic programming
    language, 12
Visual Studio Express 2010
    configure and register,
        396–398
    download and installation
        package, 387
    open and test software,
        390–396
    software installation,
        388–389
    tutorial resources, 399
    Website, 386–387

W
while forever loop, 141
while loop, 84–85, 119–120
while-do statement, 38–39
white space, 102
Wirth, Nicklaus (stepwise
    refinement), 182
word problems, 28–29
writing data, 3
writing the algorithm, 53–54

X–Z
Xcode software
    configuration, 406–407
    installation, 399–401
    open and test software,
        401–406
    tools, downloading, 408
    tutorial resources, 408